INSIGHT GUIDES

OXFORD

APA PUBLICATIONS L

Part of the Langenscheidt Publishing Group

HOW TO USE THIS BOOK

This book is carefully structured both to convey an understanding of the city and its culture and to guide readers through its attractions and activities:

◆ The Best Of section at the front of the book helps you to prioritize. The first spread contains all the Top Sights, while the Editor's Choice details unique experiences, the best buys or other recommendations.

◆ To understand Oxford, you need to know something of its past. The city's history and culture are described in authoritative essays written by

specialists in their fields who have lived in and documented the city for many years.

◆ The Places section details all the attractions worth seeing. The main places of interest are coordinated by number with the maps.

◆ Each chapter includes lists of recommended restaurants, cafés, pubs and bars.

◆ Photographs throughout the book are chosen not only to illustrate geography and buildings, but also to convey the moods of the city and the life of its people.

◆ The Travel Tips section includes all the practical information you will need, divided into four key sections: transport, accommodation, activities (including nightlife, festivals, the arts, events, tours and sports), and an A–Z of practical tips. Information may be located quickly by using the index on the back cover flap of the book.

◆ A detailed street atlas is included at the back of the book, with all restaurants, cafés, bars, pubs and hotels plotted for your convenience.

PLACES AND SIGHTS

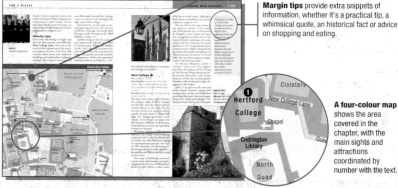

Chapters are **colour-coded** for ease of use. Each neighbourhood has a designated colour corresponding to the orientation map on the inside front cover.

A locator map pinpoints the specific area covered in each chapter.

Margin tips provide extra snippets of information, whether it's a practical tip, a whimsical quote, an historical fact or advice on shopping and eating.

A four-colour map shows the area covered in the chapter, with the main sights and attractions coordinated by number with the text.

PHOTO FEATURES

Photo features offer visual coverage of major sights or unusual attractions. Where relevant, there is a map showing the location and essential information on opening times, entrance charges, transport and contact details.

RESTAURANT LISTINGS

Restaurant listings give the establishment's contact details, opening times and price category, followed by a useful review. Bars and cafés are also covered here. The coloured dot and grid reference refers to the atlas section at the back of the book.

Pubs and Bars

Many of Oxford's finest pubs are close to water. The **Angel & Greyhound** (30 St Clement's Street) is a busy and friendly place, serving good Young's beer and specialising in traditional

TRAVEL TIPS

CYCLING

Cycling is popular in Oxford and, as well as many cycleways, there are clear signs to enable cyclists to avoid the main thoroughfares. You can hire bicycles from several outlets. All kinds of bikes are available, and they supplied with a lock.

Travel Tips provide all the practical knowledge you'll need before and during your trip: how to get there, getting around, where to stay and what to do. The A–Z section is a handy summary of practical information, arranged alphabetically.

Contents

LEFT: Radcliffe Camera flanked by Brasenose College to the left and All Souls College to the right.

Maps

THE BEST OF OXFORD: TOP SIGHTS

From the dreaming spires of Oxford and the beautifully intact interiors of its colleges, churches and chapels, to shopping, dodos and dinosaurs, and the pleasures of a meadow walk

△ From the Alfred Jewel to Egyptian mummies, the **Ashmolean Museum** has collections of extraordinary variety and richness. *See page 165.*

◁ The stately **High Street** is lined with grand colleges interspersed with shops, restaurants and cafés. Walking its length is now also, mercifully, a relatively traffic-free experience, thanks to the city's park-and-ride scheme. *See page 101.*

▷ All shopping appetites can be satisfied in the **Covered Market**. Here are high-class butchers, cheesemongers and delicatessens alongside the city's gift shops, fashion boutiques and cafés. *See page 129.*

▽ The grandest of Oxford's colleges, **Christ Church College** contains the city's cathedral as well as an art gallery, and has featured as a location in the Harry Potter films, Brideshead Revisited and Inspector Morse. *See page 158.*

▽ The **Bodleian Library** complex includes the Divinity School, complete with an ornate vaulted ceiling, and the 15th-century interior of Duke Humfrey's Library. *See page 90.*

△ The **views from Christ Church Meadow** capture Oxford at its most picturesque: walk down to the river and then gaze back at the honey-coloured stone and dreaming spires of the university. *See page 202.*

▷ **University Museum** – this Gothic pile contains an eye-catching collection, from dinosaur skeletons to Savery's famous Dodo painting. *See page 182.*

△ One of England's most extravagant stately homes, **Blenheim Palace** is also notable as the birthplace of wartime leader, Sir Winston Churchill. *See page 222.*

▽ Take a walk around the well stocked **Magdalen Grove Deer Park**, hidden away between the white-stone grandeur of Magdalen College and the Cherwell River. *See page 110.*

△ Sandwiched between the Oxford Canal and the Thames, the green expanse of **Port Meadow** has been used for grazing since the Middle Ages; a stroll here offers respite from the tourist crowds. *See page 210.*

THE BEST OF OXFORD: EDITOR'S CHOICE

Setting priorities, saving money, unique attractions...
here, at a glance, are our recommendations, plus some
tips and tricks even locals won't always know

ONLY IN OXFORD

- **May Morning** true Oxford tradition when choristers sing from the top of Magdalen College Tower and revellers celebrate the advent of summer. *See page 108.*
- **Punting on the Thames** Hire a punt for an ideal way to see the city's riverside scenery and learn to steer in a straight line. *See page 206.*
- **The View from the Tower** The 188ft (55-metre) tower of the University Church of

St Mary the Virgin is a great place for surveying spires and quadrangles. *See page 96.*
- **Book Lover's Paradise** Blackwell's bookshop is a venerable Oxford institution and welcomes brows-

ers and buyers. *See page 145.*
- **Hogwarts Hall** Christ Church's impressive dining hall, with its hammerbeam roof, was used to film scenes from the *Harry Potter* films. The college opens to visitors almost every day. *See page 160.*
- **Pastoral walks** Few cities in Britain can offer such atmospheric walks among fields, grazing horses and birdlife – and all so close to the centre of town. *See page 202.*
- **Duke Humfrey's Library** Situated on the first floor of the ancient buildings of the Bodleian Library, this 15th-century interior – with its painted ceiling and leather-bound tomes – remains wonderfully intact. *See page 91.*
- **High Tea at the Randolph Hotel** Take tea the old-fashioned way in the Drawing Room of this historic hotel: scones with cream and jam, cakes galore, and maybe even a glass of champagne. *See page 165.*

OXFORD FOR FAMILIES

These attractions are popular with children, though not all will suits every age group.
- **Ghost Walks, Harry Potter Walks, and more** Take one of the themed walks organised by the Oxford Information Centre around the town and university. *See page 268.*
- **Take a Bus Ride** Open-top bus tours come with commentaries and are a good way of seeing the main sights. *See page 268.*
- **Take a Boat Trip** Get on the water with a Thames excursion up to Iffley or beyond from Folly Bridge. *See page 268.*
- **Hinksey Park** Just south of the city centre down Abingdon

Road, the park has an open-air swimming pool with splash feature. *See page 214.*
- **The Castle and Prison** The newly renovated prison complex will appeal to the ghoulish with tales of executions and ghostly hauntings. *See page 195.*
- **Botanic Garden** Familiar to fans of Philip Pullman's children's books, the garden also has a steamy and colourful tropical hothouse. *See page 122.*

LEFT: view of all All Souls College from St Mary's the Virgin.
ABOVE TOP: Magdalen College.
ABOVE: an afternoon's punting.

BEST PUBS

- **The King's Arms** The city-centre student haunt par excellence, with real ales and extensive menu. *See page 153.*
- **The Turf Tavern** Low ceilings, intimate bars and walled gardens provide real atmosphere. *See page 153.*
- **The Rose and Crown** Traditional pub set in a charming North Oxford street. *See page 191.*
- **The Eagle and Child** Once the haunt of Tolkien and other literary luminaries, it has avoided modernisation. *See page 176.*
- **The Trout Inn** A riverside pub in the nearby village of Wolvercote, the Trout is a perennial favourite with drinkers and diners alike. *See page 210.*
- **The Perch** Close to Port Meadow, this is an Oxford summertime institution, with large garden, good food and a healthy walk nearby. *See page 211.*
- **The Fishes** An up-and-coming gastropub. *See page 211.*

LEFT: pub lunch alfresco.
ABOVE: The Trout Inn, immortalised in TV's *Inspector Morse*.

TOP EVENTS

- **Eights Week** The annual drama of the fiercely competitive inter-college boat races, taking place over four days in late May. *See page 133.*
- **Encaenia** A colourful piece of academic pageantry held each June when visiting dignitaries walk through the streets to be awarded honorary degrees. *See page 133.*
- **Cowley Road Carnival** A day-long and often raucous celebration of East Oxford's cultural diversity that takes place on multiethnic Cowley Road in mid-June. *See page 27.*
- **St Giles' Fair** All the fun of the fair, with every type of hair-raising ride, in normally stately St Giles. *See page 172.*
- **Christmas Music** Carols are beautifully sung in the 12th-century Christ Church Cathedral in the run-up to Christmas. *See page 262.*

COLLEGE HIGHLIGHTS

- **Magdalen** Its bell tower, Chapel, Deer Park, Addison's Walk. *See page 108.*
- **Merton** Its Chapel with remarkable stained glass, and Mob Quad. *See page 119.*
- **Exeter** Its splendid High Gothic chapel by Sir George Gilbert Scott and the Fellows' Garden where Tolkien walked. *See page 142.*
- **St John's** Its expansive gardens and the statues in Canterbury Quad. *See page 178.*
- **Trinity** More fine gardens and a Baroque chapel. *See page 138.*
- **Worcester** a library by Hawksmoor, a fine chapel and hall by Wyatt and gardens that inspired Lewis Carroll's *Alice* adventures. *See page 169.*
- **Brasenose** Its famed door knocker and the startling views of the Radcliffe Camera and St Mary's from the Old Quad. *See page 95.*

LEFT: the Radcliffe Camera, at the hub of the university.
RIGHT: rowing at Oxford is fiercely competitive.

10

Best Walks

- **Christ Church Meadow** Oxford's city-centre rural retreat takes you into a surprisingly peaceful world of lush pasture land and Thameside paths. *See page 202.*
- **University Parks** The "green lung" of North

Oxford has a rich array of trees and shrubs as well as pleasant walks by the banks of the Cherwell. *See page 185.*

- **Addison's Walk** A tree-lined circuit within the grounds of Magdalen College gives views of the deer park, Cherwell and wild flowers. *See page 110.*
- **Thames Towpath** The stretch of towpath between Folly Bridge and Iffley is ideal for watching aspiring boat race contenders at practice. *See page 207.*
- **Mesopotamia Walk** Named after the land between the Tigris and Euphrates, this scenic walk follows the Cherwell over a number of bridges. *See page 207.*
- **Canal Walk** Leave busy Hythe Bridge Street to discover a picturesque world of prettily decorated canal boats and placid waterside gardens. *See page 196.*

Above: the Covered Market offers shopping as it used to be.
Left: pretty old mill in the grounds of Magdalen College.
Below: concert at New Theatre, the most spacious of venues.

Top Shopping

- **Food emporia at the Covered Market** Foodies will be in paradise here, faced with a bewildering array of high-class butchers, cheesemongers, delis and fishmongers. *See page 129.*
- **Wednesday Market** A weekly outdoor event in Gloucester Green, offering good value for money. *See page 198.*
- **Farmers' Market** Also held at Gloucester Green, on the first and third Thursday of every month. The emphasis is on local organic produce. *See page 198.*
- **Little Clarendon Street** Arguably the trendiest shopping street in Oxford. *See page 173.*
- **Cowley Road** A multi-ethnic cornucopia of Asian outlets and European delicatessens, punctuated by eateries. *See page 26.*
- **Turl Street** A medieval car-free lane, where you can browse in second-hand bookshops and consider buying top-quality shoes from Duckers. *See page 141.*

Best Music Venues

- **Sheldonian Theatre** Often used for concerts, Christopher Wren's magnificent auditorium seats 2,000, with unobscured views of the stage. *See page 88.*
- **Holywell Music Room** Sympathetically restored, this venerable 18th-century concert hall is famous for its chamber music. *See page 264.*
- **New Theatre** The city's most spacious

venue stages mainstream pop concerts as well as opera, comedy and an ever-popular Christmas pantomime. *See page 263.*
- **Jacqueline du Pré Music Building** A modern purpose-built auditorium in the grounds of St Hilda's College, it hosts an eclectic mix of medieval, classical and avant-garde performances. *See page 264.*

- **Jericho Tavern** Associated with Oxford bands such as Radiohead and Supergrass, this lively pub has a long association with local rock and folk music. *See page 265.*
- **The 02 Academy** The city's premier night spot (formerly known as The Zodiac) provides a high-octane mix of big-name acts, local talent and regular club nights. *See page 264.*

BEST MUSEUMS AND GALLERIES

- **Egyptian Mummies at the Ashmolean** Among the Ashmolean's many treasures is the Egyptian collection that includes even a pharoah's shrine, lifted wholesale from the Egyptian desert. *See page 165.*
- **Pitt Rivers Museum** Eccentric temple of ethnological exhibits where you'll find an amazing array of weird and wonderful objects from all over the world. *See page 184.*
- **Dinosaurs at the University Museum** The skeletons of prehistoric monsters soar up into the Gothic halls of the university's natural history museum. *See page 182.*
- **Museum of Oxford** A permanent exhibition traces the development of the town, with fascinating architectural exhibits. *See page 154.*
- **Modern Art Oxford** Oxford's own avant-garde modern art gallery for cutting-edge work. *See page 155.*
- **Christ Church Picture Gallery** Over 300 paintings on show in the college's private collection, with works by Veronese and Van Dyck. *See page 162.*

ABOVE: Richard Burton introduced Elizabeth Taylor to Oxford.
BELOW LETF: the University Museum's herd of dinosaurs.

BEST THEATRES AND CINEMAS

- **Oxford Playhouse** The city's most celebrated theatre, with many illustrious past members. Good range of drama, dance and opera. *See page 168.*
- **Burton Taylor Theatre** A 50-seater annex to the Playhouse, this studio theatre specialises in student productions and experimental small-scale drama. *See page 168.*
- **Old Fire Station Theatre** Bigger than the Burton Taylor but stages a similar programme of student-aimed performances. *See page 263.*
- **Pegasus Theatre** Located in East Oxford, the Pegasus runs a varied programme of events with an emphasis on youth theatre and community education. *See page 263.*
- **Ultimate Picture Palace** Cowley Road's relaxed art-house cinema shows films from around the world to a largely student audience. *See page 263.*
- **The Phoenix Picture House** Bohemian Jericho's fashionable cinema, where mainstream and indie films draw a faithful clientele. *See page 173.*

MONEY-SAVING TIPS

Access to the colleges The 39 colleges that make up the University of Oxford have very varied policies regarding visitors, ranging from the welcoming to the unfriendly. "Closed" signs are a common sight, especially in the mornings, and some colleges charge an entrance fee of up to £6. Groups are advised to book a visit in advance. The university website (www.ox.ac.uk/visitors) contains useful information. As a general rule it makes sense to use an official guide.

Knowledgeable guides can be booked through the Oxford Tourist Information Centre *(see page 275)* or can usually be found assembling customers in Broad Street, near Blackwell's bookshop. Disabled access is sometimes a problem in particular colleges.

University buildings Apart from the colleges, the university offers some stunning architectural and cultural treats in the form of libraries, museums and galleries. These are usually much more accessible to visitors than the colleges and often do not charge entrance fees.

College accommodation If you really want to experience what it is like to be a student at Oxford, you can actually stay in college rooms. The University Rooms scheme (www.oxfordrooms.co.uk) offers accommodation at some of the prettiest colleges at very reasonable rates. The greatest availability of rooms is during university vacations, though if you book well ahead, you can also secure accommodation in term-time.

A TALE OF TWO CITIES

While tomorrow's leaders are shaped within the university, today's cars roll off BMW's production lines. The historical tension between these two sides of Oxford – Town and Gown – is still potent

It is small wonder that Oxford is one of the world's most anthologised cities. Many famous writers, having attended its university, have tried to recapture on paper an experience that profoundly affected their lives. Often their feelings recall the relationship between child and parent: a complex cocktail of love and resentment, admiration and disdain.

Matthew Arnold, whose poetry immortalised Oxford as "that sweet city with her dreaming spires", captured this ambivalence in a letter to his mother in 1861: "I always like this place, and the intellectual life here is certainly much more intense than it used to be; but this has its disadvantages too, in the envies, hatreds, and jealousies that come with the activity of mind of most men." In *Wealth of Nations* (1776), Adam Smith was less equivocal, dismissing Oxford as "a sanctuary in which exploded systems and obsolete prejudices find shelter and protection after they have been hunted out of every corner of the world".

Those writers, of course, are equating Oxford with the university, and it is certainly the aura of learning that draws most visitors to the city. But there are many other sides to Oxford: it is a thriving market town, for example, as well as a pioneer of the latest bio-tech research. John Betjeman, an influential architectural critic as well as a poet, once lamented that the car factories

"could have been a model for the rest of England, so that visitors to the university [...] would have naturally hurried to see the living beauty of industrial Oxford after the dead glory of university architecture." The failure of such hopes led another poet, W. H. Auden, to moan: "Oxford city is sheer hell. Compared with New York, it's five times as crowded and the noise of the traffic is six times louder."

Yet even the complainers keep coming back. Oxford's allure is elusive, but its myths are powerful, offering visitors what the writer Peter Ackroyd called "a clutter of broken images" that demand to be seen again and again. ❑

PRECEDING PAGES: on the corner of St Mary the Virgin; Christ Church's dining hall, film location for the *Harry Potter* series. **LEFT:** meeting of minds in an Oxford quad. **ABOVE LEFT:** Cowley Road student bar. **ABOVE RIGHT:** the Sheldonian Theatre seen past the Clarendon Building.

THE ACADEMIC LIFE

Dons and students have always encouraged an image of effortless superiority. But to what extent is this assumption of elitism still justified?

The image of Oxford conveyed in countless films and books has given rise to two great myths. The first is the so-called "Brideshead" image, after Evelyn Waugh's 1945 novel *Brideshead Revisited*, which shows beautiful young aristocrats living a life of eternal summer and champagne in ancient ivy-clad colleges. The 1911 novel *Zuleika Dobson* by Max Beerbohm also paints a similar picture. The second myth is that of pale intellectuals and palaeolithic dons festering in crumbling cathedral-like libraries, their lives devoted to the study of Homer or Hegel.

Where once Oxford was the preserve of the upper-crust public schoolboy, today's reality is more complex – with students coming from a wide range of schools and backgrounds.

Both myths are outdated; but try as it might, the university cannot completely break free from its past. The world still regards it as a bastion of punting and privilege.

Fact or fiction?

Certainly, Oxford is very different from any other university in the world, except perhaps Cambridge – once referred to rather preciously in Oxford as "the other place". To differentiate itself, Oxford has its dons, scouts, tutorial system, Union, Boat Race and balls. But the people who inhabit the place are not, in reality, all that different from students elsewhere.

About 45 percent of applicants are still taken from the independent sector; however, the university is striving, with some record of achievement, to attract applicants from a diversity of backgrounds – both by making the selection process fairer and less weighted towards purely academic prowess and by offering a generous system of support for those from less wealthy families.

Women now account for approximately 47 percent of undergraduate admissions. Mixed

LEFT: detail from Edward Halliday's 1937 painting of Worcester's undergraduates – many were soon to die in service during World War II.

RIGHT: having a laugh on the Christ Church lawns.

ever. Academic concerns are still very much a priority; and, although Oxford no longer enjoys the pre-eminent status it once did, university departments find it relatively easy to attract funding from industry, especially in the sciences.

The academic life

Oxford's academic reputation is challenged only by Cambridge University in the UK, and in the US by Ivy League universities such as Harvard and Princeton. Nonetheless, its teaching is sometimes criticised for being too intense and too traditional. The intensity springs from the fact that terms are only eight weeks long compared to at least 10 at most other British universities (Michaelmas: 1 October to 17 December; Hilary: 7 January to 25 March or the Saturday before Palm Sunday, whichever is earlier; and Trinity: 20 April or the Wednesday after Easter, whichever is later, until 6 July); and, students are required to complete a minimum of one, and sometimes as many as two or three, essays or problem-sheets a week. Add to this the fact that the rigidly traditional nature of many of the courses is quite exceptional: for example, law students are required to study Roman Law, and English students must study Anglo-Saxon.

Conversely, the university's famous tutorial system means that most courses are quite unstructured. Science students may have compulsory lectures and practicals, but for arts undergraduates there is little formal teaching apart from the one hour a week spent with a tutor. Tutorials, which used to be mostly one-to-one, are now increasingly attended by two or three students, who are also taught in seminar

colleges were not introduced until the 1970s, and until recently Oxford was very much a male-dominated institution. Now, about 10 percent of professors are women, and about a quarter of all academic staff are female. The balance has also recently shifted in favour of postgraduate students, and the university is keen to develop research and graduate studies in line with other elite universities around the world.

The myth of Oxford as a book-lined ivory tower is not entirely without foundation, how-

ACTING, JOURNALISM AND POLITICS

Talented and/or ambitious students seek to climb quickly to the top of the organisations that control acting, journalism and politics in Oxford. This has been a traditional preparation for the assumption of real power in later life.

The clique-filled world of Oxford drama is presided over by OUDS, the Oxford University Dramatic Society. Many colleges also have their own theatre groups. The standard of productions varies, but the best are very good.

Oxford journalism has long been dominated by the weekly newspaper *Cherwell* (founded in 1920) and the literary magazine *Isis* (founded in 1897). Several national newspaper editors were former Cherwell editors – even

Rupert Murdoch once worked on the paper. The usual stereotypes are that *Cherwell* is frivolous and *Isis* pretentious; both regularly win national awards, though, and are worth looking at if you can get hold of a copy (they are both distributed in the colleges' lodges).

But it's the Oxford Union debating society, by turns frivolous and influential, which is by far the best-known student institution, even if Oxford students on the whole are quite apolitical. Five British prime ministers have been officers. The political clubs are also training grounds for future politicians: the Conservative Association can point to Margaret Thatcher as one of many ex-presidents to have made the big time.

In May each year, students take their university exams. You can often see them going into the Examination Schools building on the High Street, wearing their regulation black and white "sub-fusc" exam clothes.

groups. The system works brilliantly if the student and tutor are "compatible", but can backfire badly. The traditional picture of the tutorial – an ancient, book-lined study, an even more ancient don sipping sherry, a timorous student stumbling through his Aristotle – is now mostly the stuff of nostalgic fiction. However, the intensity of the student–tutor relationship is unlike that in other universities, and if an undergraduate dislikes his or her tutor (or vice versa) problems may arise.

Lectures were once solemn occasions, the students rising as the gown-clad don entered the lec-

ture hall. The don then, all too often, mumbled semi-coherently for an hour. The advent of lecture return forms, in which students evaluate the quality of a lecture course, have led to improvements in standards of lecturing, although the odd don still insists on wearing a gown.

Exams remain solemn – and terrifying. All students taking exams must wear "sub-fusc", a mode of dress descended from 13th-century ecclesiastical costume. It consists of dark suit, gown, white tie and mortar-board for men; gown, white blouse and black tie, skirt and stockings for women.

A matter of degree

Students sit a preliminary exam, called Mods or Prelims, in their first year. Finals, which were first set in 1807, are taken in the summer of the third year. Students are awarded a degree, or "Final Honour School", of either a First, 2:1, 2:2 or Third. Despite some moves to introduce dissertations and other course work into the final degree assessment, the system remains heavily weighted towards the dreaded final examination. Unlike other universities, exams are public – set centrally and marked by committees of academics from all colleges. This is very different from systems in which the tutor sets and

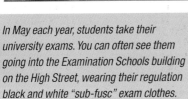

FAR LEFT: taking a perch in the ivory tower.
ABOVE TOP: students rely on pedal power to get from A to B.
ABOVE: an alfresco psychology tutorial gets underway at Balliol College. **FAR RIGHT:** on the way to an exam in the obligatory "sub-fusc".

marks the work submitted by those on his or her course.

Student life

The student's way of life has remained essentially unchanged for hundreds of years. Training for the ministry as an undergraduate's principal objective began to decline in the 19th century, and over the years new subjects have been added so that there are now 18 separate faculties. But all students' lives are still shaped by the fact that they are members of a college – and that is how they think of themselves, rather than as members of a faculty.

The college has always been much more than just a place of residence; lectures and exams are organised by the university, but the colleges are responsible for a student's weekly tutorials and classes. This is perhaps more the case for those studying arts degrees than for scientists, who spend much of their time in laboratories. In addition, the college is the centre of the student's social life. Every college has sports facilities and organised teams in most sports, plus a bar and a Junior Common Room, which usually provides newspapers and a TV room.

As well as the cost of accommodation (see panel), the cost of a student's social life is considerable: recent surveys have shown that most students expect to owe between £15,000 and £20,000 by the time they graduate. Concerns about the welfare of Oxford students are nothing new. The suicide rate has always been very high, and 43 percent of students claim to have suffered from bouts of depression or anxiety.

THE COST OF LIVING

Most colleges provide their students with accommodation for at least two years, some of it in modern buildings, but much of it in the college itself. Living in an ancient college room is a unique experience – romantic, stimulating and extremely draughty. Most students have to "live out" at some stage or another, usually sharing a house with other students. The average rent in Oxford is high (over £100 a week) and the rising price of college rooms has provoked some normally unmilitant students to stage rent strikes. In the face of pricey and scarce rented rooms, most colleges have decided to build or buy up accommodation in Oxford.

ABOVE: Matriculation Day.
RIGHT: the traditional image of a don in his study.

Donnish distinctions

All teaching at Oxford was originally conducted by clergymen, and its academics are still universally known as "dons". Not all dons actually do any teaching. Many students are taught by postgraduate students, or junior research fellows, who are in most cases appointed for a three-year period. The next step up is a lecturership, a permanent teaching post at a faculty attached to a particular college.

A lecturer can then become a reader, with fewer teaching duties and more opportunity to concentrate on his or her own research. Readers may become professors, who are responsible for overseeing a particular subject area, in which they are said to hold a "Chair". Professors give few or no undergraduate tutorials, while readers' tutorials are few and far between.

A comfortable existence

Oxford dons live a fairly comfortable life – although many would deny it. Most receive housing support from their college (ranging from a free house to a £1,000 income supplement), have the right to dine at High Table (though few do so regularly), and of course have long holidays. These, however, are the times when research must be pursued.

There are as many different types of don as there are student. Some dons never leave the library (the "old fogey"), while others appear regularly on television (the "trendy young don"). Then there is the "young fogey" – too untrendy to appear on TV but too youthful to be accepted as an academic. The "great and good don", who has the ear of the prime minister, is dying out, and in fact many feel the prestige of being a don is beginning to wane.

Recent years have witnessed huge changes in the way that most dons work. Largely gone is

Fewer graduates are seeking to become dons and, of those who do, many decide to leave for the private sector before they are 30, owing to poor prospects and salaries.

Scouts and porters

Aside from the don, the scout is probably the best-known Oxford figure. Scouts date back to the early 18th century and have traditionally been attached to a particular staircase of a particular college. As late as the 1950s they performed the role of a manservant, waking their students, cleaning their rooms, preparing light meals and running errands for them. Nowadays nearly all scouts are women and act only as cleaners or waiting staff in hall.

The other familiar college figure is the porter, who fulfills the duties of receptionist and

the old ethos of ivory tower exclusivity and cloistered college life, to be replaced by the pressures of chasing research grants and meeting exacting academic standards. Faculties now have to prove their worth to government and other funding agencies by producing quantifiable and quality-tested research in the form of books, articles and papers produced by their members.

The university currently has some 240 professors, 86 readers and 1,113 lecturers, but many Chairs have lain vacant through lack of funds.

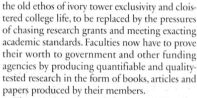

TOWN VERSUS GOWN

The relationship between the university and the city of Oxford has historically been one of hostility and mutual suspicion. In some ways Oxford is two cities, with certain shops, pubs and clubs never visited by students because they are "too townie", and others shunned by locals on the grounds that they are "too full of students".

Because of its cheap housing, the district of Cowley in the southeast of Oxford is popular with students living outside of college (most colleges are only able to provide accommodation on their own premises for two out of a student's three or four years in Oxford). But Cowley's student residents do not always mix well with the locals. With Cowley Road itself famous for its curry restaurants, the area's population includes many immigrants, plus a large "alternative", or bohemian, community *(see page 26)*.

There are some institutions however whose status doesn't quite fit the Town/Gown stereotype. Principal among these are the numerous secretarial and tutorial colleges, which find it easy to attract both students and teachers because of the proximity of the university. Students at secretarial colleges are universally known to Oxford University students as "seccies" and are often accused (in most cases unfairly) of coming to Oxford to snare an eligible bachelor than to perfect keyboarding skills.

security guard at the entrance to every college. They are involved in college discipline, and a minority are notorious for their obstinacy and rudeness. Each college is headed by what is variously titled the rector, master, principal, president, warden or provost, who is the supreme authority within the college, as well as the face the college presents to the outside world.

The Fresher experience

The chaotic first week of their first term is an experience no one forgets. First-year students or "Freshers", go through a hectic schedule dominated by Matriculation and Freshers' Fair.

The Matriculation ceremony is a ritual by which students are officially admitted as mem-

> *Most notorious among the exclusive, private dining societies is the Bullingdon Club, which counts Conservative politicians David Cameron and Boris Johnson as past members.*

bers of the university, and is conducted by the vice-chancellor in the Sheldonian Theatre. Students dress up in "sub-fusc" and listen to various Latin formulae. Other important first-week ceremonies include registering at the Bodleian Library, at which students have to swear not to "kindle flame" in the building.

In contrast, the Freshers' Fair is the craziest, most diverse event of the year. The Schools' building is invaded by stalls representing all the different university clubs and societies, hoping to sign up Freshers as new members. There are more than 200 clubs to choose from, ranging from the sensible (the Strategic Studies Group; the Industrial Society) to the surreal (the Pooh Sticks Club; the Heterosexual Decadence Society).

The social life

Although Oxford students predictably do most of their socialising at pubs and parties, for a few weeks every summer they indulge in the unashamed opulence of the summer balls.

Admission to the top balls costs the equiva-

lent of an average week's wages for a double dining ticket, sometimes anachronistically priced in guineas (£1.05) rather than pounds. Yet the vast majority of Oxford students go to at least one ball during their time at the university, considering them a harmless excuse for dressing up and having a good time.

Summer is the most active social season, as students go punting and roam the streets to raise money for charity during Rag Week. Long gone however are the extravagances of the 1930s when the "gilded youth" of Britain's great families supposedly squandered fortunes and flitted from lunch party to cocktail party to dinner party.

Private societies

Private dining societies with names like the Disraeli Society and the Ancien Régime still exist, although today's social scene tends to reflect the wider social mix of today's Oxford. Parties are generally unpretentious and alcoholic; they are also becoming more infrequent as increased academic pressure takes its toll.

However, Oxford is still alive at weekends with groups of students leaving their favourite pubs (the King's Arms, the Turf Tavern, the Bear or the White Horse) and heading for a party, easily recognisable by the alcoholic offerings they carry – today's party invitations invariably command: "Please Bring A Bottle." ❏

FAR LEFT: en route to an exam. **LEFT:** a college porter stands his ground outside the gates of Christ Church. **RIGHT:** purse-friendly socialising on the Cowley Road.

ALTERNATIVE OXFORD

For a place many automatically associate with elitism and conservatism, Oxford has a long and honourable history of nonconformism and radicalism – currently epitomised by the independent outlook of Cowley Road

test and a solid tradition of sheer bloodymindedness. Oxford people, as opposed to students, have often been at the forefront of movements pitted against the received wisdom of the day.

Cowley Road's "cool"

Nowhere is this story of "alternative" Oxford more clearly demonstrated than in the ordinary-seeming suburban thoroughfare known as Cowley Road. This street is simply different from its equivalents north, south and west.

Once a "respectable" white working-class suburb, inhabited in the first part of the 20th century by tradesmen and college "servants", Cowley Road developed into something quite different during the five decades that followed World War II. In the post-war period it was just another suburban street, with corner shops, pubs and a handful of churches and entertainment venues serving its mostly locally born population.

Over the centuries Oxford's colleges have turned out legions of Establishment figures, from politicians and civil servants to generals and high commissioners. But they have also produced their fair share of dissenters and agitators – political radicals, angry artists and critics of the existing order. From Wycliffe's 14th-century attempt to bring the Bible to ordinary people, through Ruskin's vision of labouring undergraduates, to the full-fledged revolutionary rage of Tariq Ali in the 1960s, the university has given us many proponents of social change.

The city, too, has not always been a model of genteel conformism. It has witnessed many a riot and demonstration, a good deal of organised pro-

> *Multiethnic Cowley Road has a reputation for being different, bohemian and, to the young, "cool".*

Then came the first wave of immigrants, attracted by employment at Cowley's car factory. People from the Caribbean began to settle on and around the road, followed by Pakistanis, Indians and Bangladeshis. As an Asian and West Indian community grew, it generated its own employment, and shops and restaurants began to open. By the 1960s the traditional "greasy spoon" was giving way to

the curry house – to the pleasure of residents of all ethnic backgrounds.

Next to arrive were large numbers of students, filling the houses that had once been family homes. They brought with them new and different tastes in food, music and fashion. As the area's property became relatively cheap, young couples bought homes. In those radical decades students found common cause with trade unionists and left-leaning Labour activists, and the street became a heartland of radical politics.

The New Age dawns

As the political fervour of the 1980s waned, Cowley Road remained both radical and different. The new politics of environmentalism quickly involved large numbers of locals, and Oxford's first Green councillors were elected in the area. Anti-war and anti-corporate thinking also spread widely, expressed in demonstrations.

More significantly perhaps, East Oxford's ethnic minorities began to make their presence felt in ways beyond restaurants and shops. Three mosques are now to be found in the area, with a magnificent gold-domed building completed in 2005. Cowley Road's multiethnic mix is today self-evident in the street decorations that celebrate Eid, the shops selling the latest Bollywood classics and the activism of community associations.

Cowley Road's claim to coolness was cemented with the opening in 1995 of the Zodiac (now officially called the O2 Academy), Oxford's premier non-mainstream music venue. Local bands Supergrass and Radiohead sponsored the initiative and have played there themselves.

FAR LEFT AND ABOVE RIGHT: not letting the rain dampen the Cowley Road Carnival spirit.

ABOVE: the flip side to Oxford's traditional face.

To some respectable citizens of north Oxford Cowley Road may represent too much of a walk on the wild side. There are occasional problems, often related to drugs, and the area is not entirely free of petty crime. But, on the whole, the street's risk reputation is wildly exaggerated.

This triumph of community relations – and celebration of alternative credibility – takes joyous form each June in the Cowley Road Carnival, a day-long street party that sees traffic banished and partying encouraged. ❑

THE ETHNIC MIX

Look at Cowley Road today and you will see Polish and Middle Eastern restaurants, Russian and Greek delicatessens, "Indian", Italian and Jamaican eating places, a sushi bar, Chinese takeaways, a huge number of Asian-run grocers' shops and (still going strong) Uhuru Wholefoods. Add to this the pubs, tapas bars, kebab and fish and chip shops and occasional surviving old-style café (the Exelsior, unchanged in 50 years) and you have one of the most varied range of eating options imaginable. Then there are the alternative shops and services: Chinese medicine, head massage, Brazilian artefacts, fair trade goods and much more. This ordinary looking suburban street is really very different.

DECISIVE DATES

c.1130
Henry I builds his Palace of
Beaumont just outside the
north gate, setting the seal
on the town's rising importance.

1199
King John grants the town
his royal charter, and local
government, based on the
guilds, is free to develop
independently.

1500 BC onwards
Bronze Age cattle herders
and farmers build large,
round grave mounds on
Port Meadow. During the
Iron Age the landscape is
dotted with small, mixed
farms.

3rd century AD
The Romans establish
important potteries in the
area.

400
Migrants from Germany
and Saxon mercenaries in
the Roman army forcibly
settle local farms; their
descendants live there as
peaceable tenant farmers.

730
According to legend,
Oxford's first abbey is
founded by St Frideswide
on the site of present-day
Christ Church. This may
have been the core of the
original town.

912
The first written reference
to Oxford in the *Anglo-*

Saxon Chronicle during
the reign of King Edward
the Elder, son of King
Alfred, who fortifies the
town to guard the river
crossing into Wessex and
protect the surrounding
countryside against the
Danes.

1071
Robert d'Oilly, Oxford's Norman governor, erects a
castle to the west of town.

12th century
Oxford attracts scholarly
clerics from far and wide.
Monasteries bring prosperity and stability. The
Thames provides power for
the mills, and the economy
is based on cloth and
leather as well as the
trades spawned by the
emerging university.

1129
Osney Abbey built on an
island in the west. It
becomes one of the larg-
est and most important
Augustinian monasteries
in England.

1200
By this time an
association of scholars
has been established in
the city.

13th century
Friars form the various
major orders teaching in
Oxford. Their students live
and work in academic
halls dotted around the
city. The first colleges are
founded by powerful bish-
ops; they are noted for
their exclusivity and
wealth and cater only for
graduates.

1226–40
The city wall is extended
and rebuilt.

1349
The Black Death kills one
in three people.

1355
St Scholastica's Day. A
pub brawl turns into a
massacre of dozens of
scholars. This event has
dire consequences for the
future of the town.

1361
John Wycliffe, Master of Balliol, speaks out against corruption within the church. His teachings resonate throughout Europe.

1379
New College is founded as the first college to accept undergraduates. From now on the balance of learning in the town gradually shifts from the academic halls to the colleges.

1400
Oxford is one of the largest towns in England with a population of some 6,000. There are 1,500 students.

1426
Work begins on the Divinity School.

1478
First book (the Bible) printed in Oxford.

1488
Duke Humfrey's Library opened.

1490s
Erasmus and Thomas Moore in Oxford, developing Humanist ideas.

1525
Cardinal Wolsey founds Cardinal College (later to be known as Christ Church)

on the site of St Frideswide's Monastery.

1536
The university is brought to the brink of destruction by the Dissolution of the Monasteries, but Henry VIII saves the colleges by adopting them to train the state's most loyal supporters.

1542
Creation of the Diocese of Oxford, with its cathedral at Christ Church.

1555–6
The Protestant Martyrs Latimer and Ridley are burned at the stake in the city ditch (later Broad Street) on 16 October. Six months later, Thomas Cranmer suffers the same fate.

1558–1603
Reign of Elizabeth I. The city is transformed as a new civic pride

emerges with increased trade and prosperity. The university expands greatly.

17th century
Prosperity is fuelled by the famous glovers and cutlers of Oxford. University buildings begin to dominate the central area.

1602
Duke Humfrey's Library reopened to the public as the Bodleian Library.

1613
Work begins on the Old Schools Quadrangle extension to the Bodleian Library.

1621
The Physic Garden, which was later developed to

Above Left: a Bronze Age hill figure in chalk – the Uffington White Horse. Above Right: the bishops Hugh Latimer and Nicholas Ridley prepare to be burnt at the stake in 1555. Right: Cardinal Wolsey, from a portrait in the Bodleian Library.

become the Botanic Garden, is established on the site of the old Jewish cemetery opposite Magdalen Tower.

1642–5
Civil War. Oxford is the royal capital and headquarters of the king's army.

1646
Oxford besieged by General Fairfax and his Parliamentary army. Charles I escapes in disguise and the city surrenders.

1650s
A group of mathematicians and scientists, including Christopher Wren and Robert Boyle, meet regularly in Wadham College, before moving to London in 1658 to found the Royal Society.

1664–8
The Sheldonian Theatre, designed by Christopher Wren, is built.

1670s onwards
Glove and cutlery industries in decline. The university provides new additions to the already famous Oxford skyline; many existing colleges are radically altered or rebuilt.

1715
Hawksmoor's Clarendon Building completed for the Oxford University Press.

1748
The Radcliffe Camera built according to a design by James Gibbs.

1771
Paving Commission established. Much of old Oxford is destroyed to allow traffic easier access to the city centre.

1790
The Oxford Canal arrives from Coventry bringing cheap coal from the Midlands.

1830
The Oxford University Press moves to its present site on Walton Street. The suburb of Jericho, with its terraced housing, is built to house the Press workers.

1833
John Keble preaches his famous sermon on national apostasy, leading to the foundation of the Oxford Movement.

1844
A branch railway line connects Oxford with Didcot.

1853
University Commission is established to reform the university.

1860
The University Museum opens.

1878–9
The first two women's colleges, Lady Margaret Hall and Somerville, open.

1913
William Morris establishes his car plant at Cowley. In the 1930s, as Lord Nuffield, he becomes the university's most celebrated benefactor in the fields of medicine and science.

1956
A "green belt" is created around Oxford, putting an end to the haphazard development that surrounded the city.

1960s
Plans for a link road across Christ Church Meadow are abolished.

1996
Syrian-born businessman Wafic Saïd offers the university £20 million for the establishment of the Oxford Business School.

1999
Cornmarket Street is

pedestrianised as part of a controversial new road scheme.

2000
The first Cowley Road Carnival is held.

2003
A 1,000-strong crowd gathers in Cornmarket to protest against the Iraq war.

2005
Oxford is rated fourth best

university (after Harvard, MIT and Cambridge) by 20,000 academics around the world.

2006
St Hilda's, Oxford's last women-only college, votes to accept men.

2009
£60-million redevelopment of the Ashmolean Museum complex is completed.

ABOVE LEFT: Wadham College, as seen by the noted artist Rudolph Ackermann. **LEFT:** the architect James Gibbs. **ABOVE RIGHT:** new horsepower in the Morris works. **RIGHT:** a student at Somerville College, one of the first two women's colleges, pictured here in 1895.

THE MAKING OF OXFORD

The site was first settled in Saxon times, and was named after its oxen ford. In the 1640s Oxford played a central role in the Civil War, and through the centuries a less bloody civil war continued between Town and Gown

Oxford was a late starter. Shunned by Stone Age tribes and avoided by the Romans, it had to wait for the Saxons, who always lived and moved by water, to launch it in importance as one of England's great defensive and cultural centres. If that is a simplistic view of local history, then the evidence to the contrary is thin on the ground – and, indeed, in the museums. A few axe-heads, some bronze tools and perhaps the burial mounds of farmers and cattle herders in Port Meadow by the river and in the University Parks are all that remain to span thousands of years.

It is not difficult to see why the site of Oxford was unattractive to settlers. It was low-lying and traversed by the deep streams of the Thames and Cherwell. The Romans, who hated clay soil for their roads and never settled at fords, bypassed the site to the east and north, building their villas away from the rivers.

The Middle Ages

Assorted worthies were credited with founding Oxford – a legendary King Memphric in 1000 BC, Brutus bringing Greek scholars after the fall of Troy, and, more credibly, Alfred the Great. Offa, king of Mercia from 757 to 796, may have built the oxen ford across the river that gave the settlement its name.

Those dates are narrowly beaten for the founder's stakes by the persistent legend of St Frideswide. Daughter of a Mercian king, the vir-

ginal Frideswide seems to have resisted the unwelcome attentions of a princely suitor by blinding him with the aid of a well-aimed thunderbolt. Relenting, she restored his sight with water from her own private holy well by the river. At Binsey, to the west of the fringes of Oxford, that well still exists in the churchyard, and is credited by a notice posted on the church door with being "the very beginning of anything at Oxford".

Frideswide, vowed to celibacy, went on to found a priory on a site near the present cathedral. The time: the early 8th century. The place: a gravel spit near where the Thames and Cherwell rivers meet. Nothing except an obituary is recorded of the 400 years of the priory's existence.

INVASION AND CONQUEST

The natural barriers of the Thames and Cherwell rivers helped Oxford develop as a strategic frontier town in England's battles against Danish invaders. Gradually, some Danes settled in the town, but this uneasy integration was brought to a bloody conclusion in 1002 by the king's order to massacre all Danes living in Oxford. Seven years later the Danish army sacked the town as a reprisal, which may account for the derelict condition of much of the town and its suburbs outside the walls.

The Norman Conquest in 1066 ushered in an even bigger physical change. Robert d'Oilly, the town's governor, upgraded the defensive works by building a castle, which destroyed an entire western suburb and involved the diversion of the road to the west. Keep and mound were raised and a moat fed from the Thames. Walls were extended to include the castle and the eastern suburb near the River Cherwell. As with the Tower of London, the Normans believed in symbolising their power in stone.

It is also likely that d'Oilly built Grandpont, the first stone bridge (where Folly Bridge now stands). Within the castle walls d'Oilly erected a chapel to St George, one of the first-known dedications to the patron saint of England, and in the founding of the Secular Canons of St George we can anticipate the beginnings of the university itself.

It was burned down during a massacre of the Danes in 1002.

In the cathedral that replaced the priory, between the choir and the north aisle, is the shrine of St Frideswide. Stand near it and you are at Oxford's heart and Oxford's beginning. From the fragmented canopy of stone, faces peer through sculptured leaves of ivy and sycamore, oak and vine, a medieval mason's interpretation of the virgin princess's escape from her tormenter to the safety of the forest.

Fact or fiction, St Frideswide is remembered every year on 19 October in a service at the cathedral attended by both town and university. The body of the saint is no longer there; it disappeared during the upheavals of the Reformation in the 16th century.

The town developed as a sort of Saxon conference centre, and even became attractive to monarchs in spite of St Frideswide's curse on royalty. At Henry I's great palace of Beaumont, just beyond where the Ashmolean is now, Rich-

LEFT: the Battle of Hastings decided England's future.
ABOVE: King Edward II, remembered for being the first monarch to establish colleges within Oxford University.
RIGHT: scholars depicted in the mid-14th-century manuscript *Romance of Alexander* (Bodleian art archive).

la outre voel paſſer
auoec ce notonier
ſi menrai auoec moi
mon neueu gadifier

ard the Lionheart and probably King John were born. Henry had also built a palace – or, more likely, a hunting lodge – at Woodstock, 8 miles (13km) from Oxford in the forest of Wychwood.

Trade brings prosperity

Following a decline in the 11th century, the fortunes of the town were rescued by the growth of the trade in wool and cloth. This brought the formation of trade guilds, of which the weavers and corvesers (shoemakers) were the earliest, and provided the embryo of civic rule. The right to produce, sell and buy goods was strictly controlled. No one could set up a loom within 15 miles (24km) of Oxford or sell leather without the guild's consent. The weekly market was held under similarly strict protectionism.

The scholars arrive

The university was the product of the pursuit of knowledge fusing with the convenience of physical and spiritual community that Oxford provided. From the early 12th century, English scholars, all of them clerks in holy orders, customarily went to the University of Paris to complete their education, but, following an unresolved quarrel with the king of France in 1167,

King Henry II summarily ordered them home.

Oxford was a natural place for these outcasts to settle. There were already centres of learning in the Augustinian monasteries of St Frideswide's Priory and Osney Abbey, and they were close to power. Henry, from his palace at Beaumont could readily select public servants from this pool of academic talent.

Life for the early students at Oxford was organised along the lines of the tradesmen's guilds. Like apprentices, they lived and studied for seven

TOWN VERSUS GOWN

Tensions between the scholars and the citizenry have a long history. In 1209 a woman was killed by scholars, and two of them were hanged in revenge. Traders were often accused of overcharging scholars. Town and Gown took their differences into the 17th century, spilling less blood but spending more money on legal arguments over an ever-increasing number of issues. In 1609 the city complained of proctors' high-handed treatment of citizens, the excessive number of alehouses licensed by the university and the drunkenness and bad manners of its members. Little was resolved, but legal fees accounted for half the city's income.

years with their masters in "Halls". After four years they took their Bachelor of Arts degree, and at the end of the course their Master's degree, which entitled them to lecture. Those who chose to do so hired houses, boarding and teaching their students under one roof. Beam Hall in Merton Street is one of these halls. Most disappeared as colleges gradually took their place.

The first colleges

As the university had no buildings, Congregation, the governing body, met in the church of St Mary the Virgin. There were no students either. The first colleges were founded by bishops, catered only for graduates and were exclusively for the wealthy. They were organised like monasteries, with a hall, chapel, lodgings, kitchen and quarters for the master; the pattern is the same today.

The atmosphere of a medieval college is most nearly captured in Merton. Founded in 1264 by Walter de Merton, it shares the "oldest" title with University and Balliol colleges.

A cuckoo in the nest

From the 13th century, Oxford's 6,000 people became increasingly dependent on the growing

university. The most important trades – weavers and cloth merchants, shoemakers, masons, metalworkers, artists in stained glass, manuscript painters and scribes – prospered.

As the university's star moved into the ascendant, so that of the town waned. Relegated to the status of a country and market town, it became more and more subservient to the university's needs. As a cuckoo in the town's nest, puffed up with self-importance and royal patronage, the university forced trades and residents out as more and more sites in the central area were acquired for colleges. Houses were demolished wholesale.

The plight of the Oxford townsfolk is vividly illustrated in the fortunes of the weavers, whose guild was one of the earliest in England. In the 12th century there were 60 members. By 1270, 15 remained. Fifty years later there were none.

Poverty and poor living conditions bred disease; in 1348 a quarter of the townspeople succumbed to the plague. Labour became scarce and an attempt was made by both chancellor and mayor to control wages. Widespread dissatisfaction led to popular demonstrations against authority.

Brasenose was founded by another Bishop of Lincoln in 1517, and Corpus Christi by yet another Bishop of Winchester in 1525. Trinity was set up by a civil servant in 1555, and St John's, also in 1555, by a lord mayor of London.

Because colleges were by now accepting undergraduates as well as graduates, rich men could buy their sons a university education, and clever scholars could get assisted places.

Henry versus the Church

The severing of the link between the established Church and the Pope in Rome by Henry VIII's assumption of leadership of the Church of England brought the university to the brink of destruction. The colleges' wealth and their essentially ecclesiastical nature made them a prime target when parliament authorised the dissolution of the monasteries in 1536, and their property and revenues were made over to the Crown.

As Franciscans and Carmelites, Cistercians and Benedictines were expelled, the door closed on medieval Oxford. Their property was dispersed among the colleges, and the sites were greedily developed.

The pressure on Henry grew as his advisers urged that the university should follow the

Building the colleges

For the next 200 years, the history of Oxford is the history of the university. New colleges were founded by bishops investing in learning as an insurance for the future power and influence of the Church, king and realm. "Men of learning, fruitful to the Church" was the prescription of William of Wykeham, Bishop of Winchester, for his students when founding New College in 1379. With the land went part of the 12th-century city wall and an obligation to keep it in good repair that still conserves this valuable link with the city's past.

A clutch of colleges followed: Lincoln in 1427, founded by the Bishop of Lincoln; All Souls, by the Archbishop of Canterbury with Henry VI as co-founder in 1438; Magdalen in 1458 by another Bishop of Winchester. The aims were always the same: to sustain the material superiority of the aristocracy.

Far Left: William of Wykeham, founder of New College.
Above Left: New College's 100 clerics c.1453.
Above: Sir Thomas Bodley, a diplomat whose efforts founded the Bodleian Library in 1602.
Right: Richard Foxe, Bishop of Winchester and founder of Corpus Christi.

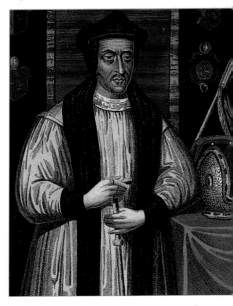

same fate as the monasteries, but Henry was a scholar and had a personal reason for wishing to see it survive. In 1532 Wolsey, his chancellor, had founded Cardinal College on the site of St Frideswide's Priory.

After Wolsey's dismissal Henry refounded it as Henry VIII College and after the suppression the college re-emerged as Christ Church. The remnant of the priory church became Oxford Cathedral and went on to enjoy a double life as the college chapel. Henry's epitaph on the outcome was to be: "No land in England is better bestowed than that which is given to our universities."

The age of privilege

The spread of the New Learning and the Protestant Reformation continued under Henry's son, Edward VI. Translations of the Bible into English began to appear in churches and the services themselves were conducted wholly in English.

Queen Mary's death brought the burnings of Protestant martyrs to an end in the cooling-off period of Elizabeth I's reign from 1558 to 1603 (*see panel below*). The Church became Protestant again, this time permanently.

In this climate of tolerance, learning flourished and the city's population and prosperity increased. While theology was still predominant, other subjects became popular as careers in public life and the professions led well-off parents to choose the university for their sons' education. The age of privilege had arrived.

The university's power

In the early 17th century came the last of the great charters reinforcing the university's pow-

ers and incidentally breeding fresh disputes. The university gained the right to appoint its own coroners and the chancellor was given the right to veto new building in the town. Dunghills and poor paving would attract fines, and the right to police the streets was bandied about between mayor and chancellor.

Behind the walls of their colleges, gardeners drew their battle lines with spade and fork. On the banks of the Cherwell, opposite Magdalen Tower, they created in 1621 Britain's

---

THE OXFORD MARTYRS

In 1549 the first Book of Common Prayer was issued and Protestants could now worship in their own faith. But it was a short honeymoon. When the boy king Edward VI died, his successor, Queen Mary, brought what can only be described as a burning zeal to the reintroduction of Roman Catholicism. Between 1555 and 1558, following the repeal of anti-papal legislation by a compliant parliament, 300 people were burnt at the stake for heresy.

Mary chose the streets of Oxford for the public humiliation of the three most influential and resistant of the Protestant leaders – bishops Ridley and Latimer and Archbishop Cranmer. At first held in the Golden Cross Inn, then in the

Bocardo Prison by Northgate, Latimer and Ridley went to the stake in Broad Street. Cranmer, it is said, was forced to watch from his cell as attempts were made to get him to recant. This he did, but when fastened to the stake his courage and his faith returned, and he thrust into the flames the hand that had signed the recantation.

Oxford's memorial to the martyrs today faces the threat of traffic in St Giles, where a Victorian Eleanor Cross has Cranmer in a niche holding his Bible. A cross in Broad Street marks the scene of the burnings, and in Balliol College nearby a door blackened by the fire that consumed the flesh of three brave men is preserved.

first botanic garden, called "Physick" Garden because it produced herbs and plants for medicine and was linked with the scientific studies of the Faculty of Medicine.

Civil War capital

In the struggle ahead Oxford was to be the stage, and king and parliament merely players. Charles I's connection with Oxford thrust it into the forefront of the conflict between Crown and State that erupted in civil war in 1642. The miracle is that the city emerged virtually unscathed from the extensive works undertaken to put it in readiness for assault, and from the siege that subsequently took place but which was abandoned, without the expected battle ever happening.

The king already had strong support at the university. Nearly all the dons and scholars were sympathetic to the Royalist cause. But the towns-

people deeply resented the university's control over their affairs and so supported parliament.

A surprise visit in 1642 from a troop of Royalist cavalry under Sir John Byron brought the citizens out onto the streets and a half-hearted attempt was made to close the gates. After some confusion the Royalists were welcomed in by the scholars. Eleven days later the cavalry went, leaving a divided city to receive a Parliamentary force with Lord Saye at the head. The university was disarmed, the towns-people armed, the head was shot off the Virgin on the porch of St Mary's, and the troops left for what was to be the first great battle of the Civil War.

The Battle of Edgehill made Charles look for a new headquarters, now that London was in the hands of parliament. Oxford's central position, natural defences and accessibility to areas of support in the west and north made it an obvious choice, and an accommodating Christ Church provided a good substitute palace for the king.

The king departs

The Parliamentarians seem to have made rather ineffectual attempts to contain Charles

Above Left: an early university procession, produced by the celebrated print-maker Rudolph Ackermann.
Above: Ackermann's *Kitchen at Christ Church*.
Inset: the Triple Unite coin was only produced at King Charles I's mint in Oxford during the English Civil War.

in Oxford. The elusive king was able to escape after the decisive battle of the war at Naseby, returning to Oxford and hoping to plan a renewed siege. Looking for guidance in his predicament, he decided to borrow a book on other civil wars from the Bodleian Library, sending a peremptory note. His request was refused: the library *never* lends books, not even to kings.

The last Oxford saw of Charles, who had decided on escape and surrender to the Scots, was as a humble servant with short hair riding out on horseback over Magdalen Bridge in the middle of the night. For the garrison, surrender was near. With the king's assent, conditions were formally agreed and the soldiers marched out on 25 June 1646. The war was over and Oxford was saved.

War wounds

Picking up the pieces was not easy for the university. There were few scholars, but the college

---

A CITY UNDER SIEGE

During the Civil War, ditches were dug and ramparts raised in Oxford by the reluctant citizens and enthusiastic students, guided by a Dutch engineer. The halls and colleges became warehouses for food and supplies, factories for the manufacture of gunpowder and uniforms, and foundries for the cannon. The townspeople looked on aghast as Magdalen Bridge was demolished and a drawbridge erected in its place, and watched with disbelief as cannon so heavy that they needed 15 horses and 26 men to pull them were brought to the parks near Magdalen.

All this and the maintenance of the garrison required money. The king's answer was to make it. The Royal Mint was brought to New Inn Hall Street, and college plate was pillaged for silver and gold to turn into coin. Unfortunately it did not make enough. City and university were asked for cash "contributions".

The burden put on accommodation by the influx of more than 5,000 soldiers with their wives and camp followers can easily be imagined. It was inevitable that disease should breed in the filthy conditions of streets and sewers, and there were outbreaks of camp fever and plague. Just as inevitable was the danger of fire. In 1644 the centre of the city was devastated by a blaze that began in a kitchen and destroyed hundreds of houses.

buildings and the churches were undamaged. Farmers and landowners in the immediate vicinity of Oxford complained of damage by Royalist troops to their houses, woods and cattle, and of the loss of income from not being able to grow crops. They found the university inflexible, however, as did those in the city who had suffered during the occupation, and negotiations were abandoned.

Business in Oxford settled down slowly to its only real trade: selling to the university. With this obvious limitation, small shopkeepers were kept small and the only growth was in poverty. The city persisted in its attempts to extend its powers but made little progress.

> During the Civil War, Oxford became a centre for the Royalists: for a time King Charles made Christ Church his home, while the Queen took up residence in Merton College.

Idle students

After the monarchy was restored, the Puritan influence evaporated from Oxford and serious scholars, as so often in subsequent years, bemoaned the behaviour of their students. Anthony Wood, in his *Life and Times, 1631–95*, wrote: "Why doth solid and serious learning decline, and few or none follow it now in the university? Answer: because of coffee-houses, where they spend all their time; and in entertainments at their chambers, where their studies are become places for victualers, also great drinking at taverns and ale-houses (Dr Lampshire told me there were 370 in Oxford), spending their time in common chambers whole afternoons, and thence to the coffee-house."

But the university also began devoting its attentions to building. A place for grand ceremonial was provided in Wren's Sheldonian Theatre, and a place for the bell from Osney Abbey in Tom Tower. The Clarendon Building formed a new home for the Oxford University

Press, and the fantastic curiosities collected by Elias Ashmole joined experimental science in the Old Ashmolean Museum.

There followed Gibbs' masterpiece, the Radcliffe Camera, the world's first library in the round, and the unique evocation of the Tower of the Winds in the Radcliffe Observatory. Sir Nicholas Hawksmoor contributed the twin towers of All Souls College, Gothic outside and classical within. Palladian architecture jos-

FAR LEFT: Oliver Cromwell, who overthrew Charles I.
ABOVE LEFT: Lord Fairfax, Parliamentarian general during the English Civil War, at his camp before Oxford.
RIGHT: Elias Ashmole, 17th-century collector of curiosities that are now to be found in the Ashmolean Museum.

tled medieval, and stone came to replace brick.

The glory of Oxford was assured; the university's academic achievement anything but. Student sons of the wealthy drank much and learned little. Exams became a farce. The seeds of 19th-century reform and revival were sown in this climate of stagnation.

Housing boom

New enterprises brought workers to the area and a consequent demand for new housing. When the Oxford University Press moved to Walton Street in 1830 it became the principal employer, its employees finding homes nearby in the new suburb of Jericho.

Towards the end of the 18th century the main streets around Carfax were still cluttered with market stalls, just as they had been in medieval times, impeding the free movement of traffic, unhygienic and untidy. Both city and university agreed that a market building was the answer, and in 1774 meat, fish and vegetables were moved to an area behind the High Street.

The new market, open every day, was extended and roofed over in the Victorian "iron" age, the preponderance of butchers then a barometer of prosperity. It was also an indica-

TRANSPORT CONTROVERSIES

Opened in 1790, the Oxford Canal, which brought cheap coal from the Midlands, survived competition from the Grand Junction Canal but was killed off by the railway, suffering a final indignity when its terminal was filled in and became the site of Nuffield College in 1937. The city and university were less inviting to the railway pioneers. A proposed terminus for the Great Western Railway at Magdalen Bridge in 1837 was rejected. Opponents feared what might happen if the lower classes could move about more freely and said that students' morals would be corrupted. Concessions were made, however, and the railway steamed into Oxford in 1844.

tion that Oxford's population was increasing rapidly. In the first 40 years of the 19th century it doubled to 24,000. The character of shopping was also changing. Earlier restrictions on the sale of goods other than those produced locally were abandoned. Factory-made goods were being brought in from London and the Midlands by railway and canal, ousting the work of all except for the specialised craftsmen. Choice became wider, credit was no longer given, and price fixing and tickets replaced bargaining.

Unfortunately for the growing number of retailers, the student population halved in the first half of the 19th century and many shopkeepers found themselves in economic difficulties as a result.

A time of change

Between 1830 and 1850 one question engaged members of the university to the exclusion of everything else. In the words of a contemporary scholar, Mark Pattison, it "entirely diverted our thoughts from the true business of the place". Such was the Oxford Movement, which started with a church sermon and left Oxford, with its protagonists, to be debated elsewhere.

It all began on 14 July 1833 when John Keble, Fellow of Oriel and Professor of Poetry, preached the Assize Sermon in the University Church. It stimulated the publication of the controversial *Tracts for the Times*, which gave the movement the alternative title of "Tractarian". The main thrust of the arguments put forward was in support of a "Catholic" church, but not Roman Catholic, and the most tangible outcome was the revival of ceremonial in Anglican churches.

One in particular, St Barnabas, built to serve the growing working-class suburb of Jericho, was visited by the Rev. Francis Kilvert in 1876. He noted in his celebrated *Diary* that the priest wore "a biretta and a chasuble stiff with gold. The poor humble Roman Church hard by is quite plain, simple and Low Church in its ritual."

Of the leading churchmen associated with the movement, John Newman, vicar of St Mary's at the time, addressed his readers of the first tract as "Fellow-Labourers". After the last tract appeared he left Oxford, embraced the Roman Catholic Church, and was made a cardinal in 1879.

John Keble's posthumous contribution to Oxford was the college named after him in 1870. The intention was to provide people of small means with an academic education

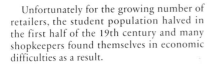

LEFT: an artist's impression of Christ Church College in the 17th century.
ABOVE TOP: Keble College, a striking example of the Gothic Revival style.
ABOVE: the Grand Junction Canal, 1900, which brought factory-made goods to Oxford.
ABOVE RIGHT: John Keble.

based on the principles of the Church of England. The chosen architect was William Butterfield, a follower of the movement, who produced a building in Gothic Revival style.

When the sun fell on its patterned brick, John Betjeman thought it appeared at its worst. Norman Shaw saw Butterfield as "paddling in a boat of his own". His building is certainly unique and striking.

Diversity is the essential element of the growth of Oxford throughout the 60 years of

---

THE ASHMOLEAN MUSEUM

At the beginning of Queen Victoria's reign in the 1840s, the collection of rarities of the dubiously acquired inheritance of Elias Ashmole was still installed, neglected and deteriorating, in the Old Ashmolean building in Broad Street. Thanks to two timely bequests, a suitable home was found for the display of these and the university's treasures and works of art. In 1841 Charles Robert Cockerell designed the neoclassical Ashmolean Museum which today so magnificently displays the wonderful diversity of its contents. The most compelling of the exhibits is the Alfred Jewel *(see page 167)* – the Alfred who could have been the university's founder.

Queen Victoria's reign, a diversity of demand from an expanding city that ranged from books to breweries, marmalade to melodrama and town houses to trams.

The tram to North Oxford

There is a romantic idea that the development of the area north of the Martyrs' Memorial that is North Oxford came about when the university allowed dons to marry. The need for large family housing, however, was earlier felt by the city's wealthy merchants and traders.

No doubt St John's College, which had acquired the land as early as the 16th century, was alive to its potential for development as well. Gothic was the flavour of university architecture; red and yellow brick its chosen medium; gables and gardens characterised the style. Keble College and the Parks' Museum welcomed the villas like hens with chickens. By 1880 most of the houses had been completed, and after 1877 the dons began moving in with their families.

ABOVE: a dead heat at the end of the 1877 Oxford–Cambridge Boat Race.

RIGHT: Blackwell's bookshop, part and parcel of Oxford.

Five years later North Oxford's first trams followed them up the Banbury Road all the way from Carfax for one penny. The horse-drawn single deckers on 4ft (1.3-metre) gauge rails also ran from east to west over a specially widened Magdalen Bridge, up the High Street and out to Jericho via Walton Street. Speed was limited to 8 miles (13km) an hour and further restricted if confronted with a herd of cattle. Worse, a flock of sheep called for a dead stop.

It was the turn of the century before an electric tramway was mooted, and 1913 before the idea was effectively scotched by the motorbus. William Morris, later Lord Nuffield, was refused a licence by the city to run these, but tickets for a ride could be bought in shops. The Tramway Company followed suit, but with buses instead of trams, and eventually won exclusive rights to run Oxford's first official bus service.

Books and boats

Blackwell's bookshop *(see page 145)* is such an Oxford's institution that you expect it to go back further than 1879, yet it was only then that Benjamin Henry Blackwell started the business at his house in Holywell Street. Bigger premises were soon needed.

Down on the river at Folly Bridge, Salter Bros had been quietly contributing to Oxford's sporting prowess and public pleasure since they established the firm in 1858. Boats and college barges were built here, including the eights that took the university to victory over Cambridge, and in 1886 the firm began the steamer trips that have opened Oxford's waters to millions.   ❑

The 19th century in Oxford was a time of root-and-branch university reform, of controversy over the direction of the Church of England and of development of large residential suburbs.

WOMEN? WHO LET THEM IN?

The seeds of the slow and grudging acceptance of the equal right of women to higher education were sown not by the university authorities but by central government through the Parliamentary Commissions of 1850 and 1874. Oxford came a conspicuous second to Cambridge in admitting women more freely. As early as 1863 examinations had been open to girls at Cambridge, and Girton became the first residential college for women in 1869.

But it was nine years before Oxford followed suit with Lady Margaret Hall, for Church of England girls, and Somerville College, in 1879, the first to place no religious requirements on its entrants (both are now mixed). St

Hugh's joined them in 1886 and St Hilda's Hall in 1893, founded by the principal of Cheltenham Ladies' College for women going up to Oxford from that college.

Concessions were slow in coming. Examinations were opened to women in 1884, but degrees and equal status for women's colleges had to wait until the 20th century.

Male chauvinism took many forms. At Brasenose College, the Moosehunters were a group of young men who strapped antlers to their heads and crashed around in pursuit of young maidens. One Junior Common Room debated a motion that: "Women should be hired out on the same basis as college punts."

Oxford's Motoring Heritage

Given its current traffic problems, it's ironic that the city helped pioneer motor manufacturing in Britain. The much-loved Morris Minor was built here, and so is today's BMW-produced Mini

The career of William Richard Morris, Viscount Nuffield, has been described by British industrial historians as the biggest success story of the 20th century. His achievement had a profound effect on Oxford and the surrounding area, for it was through Morris's efforts that a major industry – motor manufacturing – was added to what had been a predominantly academic city. He was also one of the great benefactors of his time, distributing some £30 million to various charitable causes before he died in l963 at the age of 85.

The William Morris story

William Morris was born in Worcester in 1877, but his parents were from Oxford and the family moved back to the city when he was a young child. He attended the Church School in Cowley, leaving at the age of 14 to become apprenticed to a bicycle repairer. Within months, and with just £4 capital, he had established his own cycle repair business in a shed behind his parents' house in James Street, Cowley St John.

Rebuilding old bicycles soon led to building new ones, the first order being for an abnormally large frame to suit the towering rector of nearby St Clement's Church. Next came Morris motorcycles, or what would today be called mopeds.

Morris became an agent for a number of British car and motorcycle manufacturers. By 1910 he had given up making two-wheelers and built a new garage on the Longwall site with a view to producing a car of his own. It would be a small car of high quality, made in large numbers and sold at a low price. His strategy was to reduce the cost of design and manufacture by purchasing all the major components from outside companies and simply assembling the cars in Oxford. Longwall was not big enough, so Morris moved out to the suburb of Cowley.

Appropriately, this first car, delivered in 1913, was called the Morris Oxford. It cost £175 and was the first of the "Bullnose" Morrises, so-called because of the rounded shape of their brass radiators. Morris sold 393 Oxfords in the first year and over 900 in 1914; this represented the beginning of mass production in Britain. After

Left: Lord Nuffield in his later years.
Above Right: a man fixes balloon tyres to wheels at the Morris Motors automobile factory in Cowley.
Above Far Right: motoring heritage – a vintage poster from 1930.

MORRIS OXFORD
SIX CYLINDER · FABRIC SALOON · PRICE £268 EX WORKS

From humble beginnings, William Morris went on to become Lord Nuffield, one of the wealthiest industrialists in Britain. His title became extinct on his death.

World War I, production increased sharply but so did costs and therefore prices. Then came the slump. By 1921, 60 cars a week were coming out of Cowley – but sales had reduced to a trickle. Faced with a stockpile of cars, William Morris took the bold step of slashing prices by as much as £200 a car – a lot of money then. While others scoffed, he said that sales would double – and he was right. By 1923 Morris was selling 20,000 cars a year; in 1925 demand reached 55,000.

New blood

One of Morris's managers, Cecil Kimber, also had ambitions as a car-maker and designed special, more rakish, bodies for the Morris Oxford and Cowley which were then sold as MG (for "Morris Garages") and carried the distinctive octagonal badge. The MG Super Sports models were so successful that by 1929 a separate MG factory was set up, first in Cowley and then Abingdon, from where the best-selling Midget sports cars emerged. It was the T-series successors to these that, 20 years later, converted a generation of young Americans to lightweight British sports cars.

Money for medicine

Lord Nuffield (as he became in 1938) and his wife Elizabeth had no children and he was determined not to leave his fortune to be depleted by death duties. Medicine was a lifelong interest and

A MAN OF SIMPLE TASTES

Though rich beyond dreams, he was a man of simple tastes. He used the same small and modestly furnished office upstairs in the old school building at Cowley for 50 years. His desk had a pile of neatly sliced used envelopes to use as notepaper and he would unknot string from parcels for future use – habits inherited from his father and his own poorer days as a child. Asked to comment on his wealth, he once said: "You can only wear one suit at a time." His own luxuries were specially made cigarettes and long sea voyages to distant lands – a taste he acquired when he visited America to study Henry Ford's production methods.

in the 1920s he donated sums of money to various hospitals. In 1937, he put up £900,000 to establish a new university establishment, Nuffield College, to the west of the city (its foundation stone was not laid until after the war, in 1949).

Although he loved Oxford, William Morris had not, in his earlier years, enjoyed friendly relations with the city authorities or the university. He was suspicious of graduates in business and for a long time would not employ anyone who had been through the university. Disagreement with the city council went back to 1913, when he had proposed buses as an alternative to trams to replace Oxford's horse-drawn trams. The council rejected the idea, so Morris bought a fleet of six buses and put them into operation illegally. His audacity paid off, for the bus service was popular, the city was spared ugly and disruptive trams, and he eventually sold the vehicles to the council.

Merger mania

During World War II, the Cowley plant produced battle tanks, repaired aeroplanes, and made Tiger

Moth trainers, as well as engines for military aircraft. An airstrip was built on the factory site.

In 1952 the company merged with arch-rival Austin to form the British Motor Corporation. Lord Nuffield, by then 75, was appointed chairman but retired after six months. In 1968, after further mergers, BMC became British Leyland.

The unremarkable 1971 Morris Marina was the last car to carry the Morris name. Eventually, after a troubled period of heavy losses that led to government control, British Leyland became the Rover Group and, in 1988, a division of British Aerospace. The new owners concentrated Rover executive car production in the Cowley body plant and shut down Cowley North and South, which included Morris's original buildings. With the help of Honda, Rover's fortunes were reversed. But the Japanese, after heavy investment, were shocked when British Aerospace abruptly sold the company to BMW.

The BMW years

BMW's arrival at Cowley in 2000 sparked a further revival in Oxford's car-manufacturing fortunes, as the German company decided to base the new Mini production line there. Investment totalling £280 million between 2000 and 2004 saw employment at the plant rise to 4,500 after years of decline. By 2005 Cowley was turning out some 4,000 Minis a week, making it the third most productive car plant in the UK, and a new streamlined version of the car was unveiled in 2006. Visits to the car plant can be arranged by calling 01865-825 842 (see page 214). ❏

THE MINI

In August 1999, 70,000 people and 5,000 Minis from all over the world converged at Silverstone racing circuit to celebrate the 40th anniversary of this legendary car. The Mini was reputedly designed on a restaurant tablecloth by Sir Alec Issigonis as a blueprint for the smallest car for four adults. At its launch, it cost a mere £500. Since then more than 5.3 million have been sold. It became a fashion icon in the 1960s, associated with such stars as Twiggy and Peter Sellers, and starred with Michael Caine in the 1969 film The Italian Job. Production stopped at Cowley in 1968, but the car was restyled and brought back to Cowley by BMW in 2000.

ABOVE LEFT: production line at the Morris Motors Cowley factory, 1946; the target was 2,500 cars a week.
ABOVE RIGHT: the Mini in production at BMW Cowley.

Oxford University Press

Another of the city's major employers is Oxford University Press, the world's largest university press, known widely as OUP.

Oxford University Press publishes more than 3,000 new titles a year, employs some 3,000 people worldwide and achieves a yearly turnover of over £300 million (US$480 million).

Among its most important publications is the *Oxford English Dictionary*, first published in 12 volumes and dedicated to Queen Victoria. Today it has four supplements and has been republished in 20 volumes. It also comes in a much-praised CD-Rom version.

As the beginning of each of its books reminds us, "Oxford University Press is a department of the University of Oxford. It furthers the university's objective of excellence in research, scholarship and education by publishing worldwide." OUP has no board of directors but is controlled by a body of senior Oxford scholars – the Delegates of the Press – and a finance committee. Like any university press, it serves education and research, but unlike others it has to pay its own way. OUP is very international in its outlook, maintaining branches and promotion offices in more than 50 countries, many with their own substantial publishing programmes.

It is more than 500 years since the first book was printed in Oxford, though the date in Roman numerals on that first title page actually reads 1468 instead of 1478 – an unfortunate beginning for a press renowned for its high standards of accuracy.

OUP has had a succession of homes, including the Sheldonian Theatre and the Clarendon Building, the latter partly financed by the profits from the first edition of Lord Clarendon's *History of the Great Rebellion*. In 1830 it moved to its present home in Walton Street, a series of elegant buildings grouped, in true Oxford fashion, round a quadrangle complete with ornamental pond, lawn and copper beech. It has frequently had a London presence, too: a Bible warehouse in Paternoster Row, and later offices in nearby Amen House. All publishing is now based in Oxford.

Promoting music

One of OUP's unusual features is a flourishing music department. This not only publishes sheet music and major editions of classical works, but promotes the performance, recording and hire of the work of more than 20 contemporary composers.

Although OUP played a major role in the history of printing, including being the first

printers in Britain to use the beautifully designed "Fell types", brought over from the Netherlands by Dr Fell in the 17th century, its own printing works closed in the late 1980s. The company now outsources all printing, although many artefacts and papers relating to its history are preserved for posterity in the OUP Museum (visits by appointment, tel: 01865-556 767). ❑

RIGHT: the days when OUP printed its own books.

MODERN OXFORD

As Oxford developed in the 20th century from a sleepy market town into an important industrial centre, it faced a new range of social and economic problems

Vera Brittain, author of *Testament of Youth*, went up to Somerville College in 1914, an innocent former debutante who had been born into "that unparalleled age of rich materialism and tranquil comfort", the Edwardian age. The Oxford that she discovered in the first year of World War I still basked in that mellow security more than a decade into the new century.

This was the Oxford of Zuleika Dobson, the eponymous heroine of Max Beerbohm's novel who caused titled undergraduates, besotted with her, to drown themselves in the Isis. Around the stately quadrangles were narrow, medieval streets containing small businesses and close-

> *Colleges dominated the university, and the university controlled the city that existed to service it.*

knit communities. Public transport was still by horse-drawn trams that were advertised as meeting every train at the sleepy station. In the North Oxford suburb, built to house the large Victorian families of the dons, croquet was played on the lawns, and afternoon tea served with ceremony.

Death in the trenches

In 1915, Vera Brittain left Oxford to train as a nurse. In 1919 she returned to Somerville. "It seemed unbearable that everything should be

exactly the same when all my life was so much changed." She had lost her brother, her lover, and many friends; 2,700 Oxford men had died in the trenches.

It is invidious to select one name from these thousands, but H.G.J. (Harry) Moseley, who was killed at Gallipoli in 1915, had graduated from Trinity College and was the most promising physicist of his generation. His work on atomic structure using the relatively new X-rays was in four years already enough for a Nobel prize to be predicted. His classic equipment has an honoured place in the Museum of the History of Science.

LEFT: Oxford women did all kinds of jobs in World War I; here they are working as ticket collectors.
RIGHT: Vera Brittain, Somerville College alumnus.

In every college the memorial slabs went up, and the ancient buildings were haunted for those who had survived. The great eccentric William Spooner, Warden of New College (*see page 150*), had a plaque erected in the chapel to record the names of college members who had died fighting on the enemy side: "In memory of the men of this college who coming from a foreign land entered into the inheritance of this place and returning fought and died for their country in the war 1914–1919."

FEMALE EMANCIPATION

Women, admitted to lectures of the university in 1880, and permitted to take exams in 1884, were first given degrees – the ultimate equality – in 1920. Four women's colleges had been founded between 1878 and 1893, so the academic groundwork was well established. It was post-war emancipation that was to free female undergraduates to take a more active part in university life.

Christopher Hobhouse, a traditionalist, did not welcome the invasion, and wrote caustically: "They are perpetually awheel. They bicycle in droves from lecture to lecture, capped and gowned, handlebars laden with notebooks and notebooks crammed with notes."

> *Between the wars, as the "Brideshead generation" of students lived lives of indolent privilege, the rest of Oxford was becoming an industrial powerhouse.*

But life went on, and for many the top priority was to live it as on a roller coaster, for as much excitement and risk as possible. Between the wars, Oxford University, so often an exaggeration of the contemporary mood, experienced the excesses of hearties and aesthetes.

Evelyn Waugh's 1945 novel *Brideshead Revisited* offered the fictional version of this lifestyle, and Vera Brittain wrote of her contemporaries: "One and all combined to create that 'eat-drink-and-be-merry-for-tomorrow-we-die' atmosphere which seemed to have drifted from the trenches via the Paris hotels and London nightclubs into Oxford colleges."

Tenacious traditions

The invasion of Oxford by women (*see panel*) made little impact on male undergraduate life

no longer a sleepy market town, but an important industrial centre. As early as 1898, William Morris had opened his garage, and the first Morris car came off the line in 1913. By 1923, the Cowley factory's production was more than 20,000 vehicles a year *(see pages 46–48)*.

The area east of Magdalen Bridge had become a town in its own right, owing no allegiance to the university. The industrial age in Oxford had finally arrived.

Between 1911 and 1951, the population of Oxford grew from 62,000 to 97,000, mostly due to the immigration of industrial workers. Many of these came from the Welsh valleys, creating a strong and obstinately self-contained Welsh community in Cowley, that made its own social life, complete with choirs. The villages close to Oxford – Headington, Marston, Iffley, Wolvercote – also became suburbs of the city.

The industrial expansion of the town caused dismay to many for whom Oxford was Matthew Arnold's "sweet city with her dreaming spires". In 1928, Dr H.A.L. Fisher, warden of New College, was the prime mover in establishing the Oxford Preservation Trust, whose first act was to raise the money to buy land on Boars Hill and at Marston, in the Cherwell valley, to safeguard

in the interwar years. Traditional sports and clubs continued. Eights Week still brought throngs of families and girlfriends to cheer on the boat races and socialise on the picturesque college barges lining the river bank.

Many of the clubs remained exclusively male, notably the Oxford Union debating society, which was founded in 1823 and by mid-century occupied its own premises between Cornmarket and New Inn Hall Street. Its debates were the nursery of a glittering succession of politicians, lawyers and clerics, the most famous of whom were always ready to return in later life as guest speakers. The union resisted admitting women as members until after World War II. The many other clubs were gradually opened to women, but the majority of male undergraduates had little contact with their female counterparts.

Equally far-reaching changes had been happening to the city of Oxford. By the 1920s, it was

Above Left: Godley's Own Oxford Volunteers march past the Emperors' Heads on Broad Street in World War I.
Above: Miss Ivy Williams, the first woman to receive an Oxford degree, 1920.
Right: Oxford women at work in World War I as unpaid social workers.

these areas from development. The trust, still active today, owns 350 acres (140 hectares) of land in and around Oxford, and campaigns to preserve the Green Belt so that the historic city, in its ring of hills, may retain its special setting, free of urban sprawl.

A new look

The architectural face of Oxford changed greatly between the wars. There were some undoubted improvements in the city centre. The elegant new Elliston & Cavell store was built in Magdalen Street, and the corner of Broad Street and Cornmarket was dignified by the pillared curve of William Baker's furniture shop. Beaumont Street, with its fine 18th-century facades,

---

---

suffered little from the inclusion of the Playhouse, a piece of infill in the very best of taste. The New Theatre in George Street, spacious inside and simple outside, was also welcome.

For the university, there was much new building in the Parks Road area. The Radcliffe Science Library filled with dignity the northern corner of South Parks Road. Opposite, an eccentricity was designed by Sir Herbert Baker: Rhodes House, headquarters of the Rhodes Trust and its scholars. This was aptly described by the writer Christopher Hobhouse as "a Cotswold manor house with a circular temple of heroic scale deposited in its forecourt". Where Parks Road joins Broad Street, another corner site accommodated the New Bodleian Library, a curiously uninteresting building above ground, but fascinating below, where the vast book stacks are linked by conveyor belt underneath the street to the subterranean reaches of the Bodleian proper.

The commercial building of the 1930s shows how prosperous Oxford had become, even during the Depression, thanks to the motor industry. The university, too, was expanding with the advent of science and medicine, much of the expansion due to the patronage of Lord Nuffield. He endowed poorer colleges, created a medical

---

Above: the Oxford men, known as "the cabbage patch recruits", who dug air raid shelters during the war.
Right: leading the way in biochemistry – Sir Howard Florey, Sir Percival Hartley and Sir Alexander Fleming, 1946.

institute, and in 1936 gave the university £1.25 million for medical research. More funding was poured into the physical sciences, and social science came to Oxford for the first time with the foundation in 1937 of Nuffield College.

The new boys

The university was gradually changing its character in the 1930s as an increasing number of undergraduates entered with the aid of scholarships. By 1939, about half the student population was grant-aided, leading to a profound change of attitude to studying. For the scholarship boy, Oxford was a place reached through luck and hard work, carrying the obligation to strive for the best degree possible.

Yet, despite these changes, public schools still provided the majority of students. The criterion of selection was by no means only intellectual ability. A college had to have its quota of sportsmen and gentlemen, irrespective of their academic quality. As Ronald Knox put it: "They don't do much harm, and when they've finished playing here, they can go out like good little boys and govern the Empire."

But in 1939, Oxford again sent out its young men to fight in another war, at the end of which running the Empire was no longer an option. The Oxford University Air Squadron contributed its quota to the Few who fought the Battle of Britain, among whom was Richard Hilary, author of that great war book *The Last Enemy*.

Medical breakthrough

Oxford made many contributions to the war effort, of which the most dramatic was the discovery of penicillin, which founded the science of antibiotics. Penicillin was described and named in 1929 by Alexander Fleming, but he was not able to make it chemically stable. This was the achievement of Howard Florey and his team, who first used penicillin on a patient in the Radcliffe Infirmary in 1941, the start of a breakthrough in healing of the greatest magnitude. The discovery is commemorated in a formal rose garden between Oxford's Botanic Garden and the High Street, the gift of the American Lasker Foundation in 1953.

Another Oxford contribution to the war was the work of Professor F.A. Lindemann, later Lord Cherwell, Churchill's controversial scientific adviser. He made his home in Oxford, and laid a significant part of the foundations of modern physics at the Clarendon Laboratory.

As Oxford entered another post-war period, the same uneasy mixture of ex-servicemen and women and youngsters straight from school was being shaped through three years in the university's old, inimitable way. It was at this time that the city, having grown to an unwieldy

size, began to realise that traffic was a major problem. A planning consultant, Thomas Sharp, was engaged for three years by the City Council to produce a detailed study, which was published in 1948 under the title *Oxford Replanned*. More than 40 years on, one marvels at its confident comprehensiveness, and thinks, if only it were as simple as that to manage the growth of a city.

Protecting the Meadow

Sharp's study has deservedly become a classic, but its fame rests largely on one of its proposals, the Meadow Road. Sharp wrote: "In the case of Oxford one piece of surgery is required to release the city from a pressure on its spinal column which will otherwise eventually paralyse it." The spinal column was the admired

---

The Brewing Tradition That Died

Oxford had a head start when it came to brewing: it was in the middle of malting barley country and had easy access to pure well water found deep beneath the Thames. From the Middle Ages most of the monasteries and some of the colleges brewed their own beer, those without brewhouses obtaining permission to use the facilities of those that had. Queen's was founded with a brewer among the servants, and brewing was carried on until 1939. Changes in taste and a new building spelt the end of college-produced beer and left a clear field to the professional brewer. Time was eventually called even on the latter, however, and Oxford's last brewery, Morrell's, produced its final pint in 1998.

High Street, then ruined by traffic; the surgery was to create a new east–west relief road, running through Christ Church Meadow to cross the river by a new bridge south of Magdalen Bridge. The patient being a city of such fame, the storm that greeted Sharp's proposal was of international proportions, and rumbled on ill-temperedly for the next 25 years.

After a period of shock, the battle lines were drawn. Christ Church, and behind it the university, refused to consider a Meadow Road. But the idea of a relief road, once mooted, continued to occupy the planners' minds: another route, further south, called the Eastwyke Farm Road, was proposed in the 1960s.

At this point it was the turn of Oxford's citizens to protest. A Civic Society was formed, a best-selling booklet called *Let's Live in Oxford* was published, and vigorous opposition was mounted to the motorway scheme at a Public Inquiry. A combination of political factors, lack of money, and public protest caused the Eastwyke Farm scheme to be abandoned. A couple of years later, a Labour City Council devised the Balanced Transport Policy, using reduced car-parking, improved public transport and a park-and-ride scheme to contain city-centre traffic.

Attempts to rid Oxford's medieval central streets of ever-growing volumes of traffic culminated in the Oxford Transport Strategy, introduced by the City Council in 1999. This scheme has at last emptied Cornmarket Street of all traffic, even the buses, and drastically reduced car access along the High Street and Broad Street. Is it a success? If you like fresh air and a car-free stroll along Cornmarket, you'll probably say yes. But several traders claim that stopping the flow of cars has impeded the flow of customers. The debate is far from over.

The wreckers move in

Although urban motorways did not bring about the wholesale destruction of housing, the new-buildings-for-old enthusiasm of the 1960s produced what some now see as the tragic destruction of the old Oxford as huge

---

Above Left: students in Oxford attending a beer party in the 1930s.

Right: the modernisation of Oxford University takes form with the construction of the organic chemistry building.

shopping centres and a multistorey car park replaced ancient buildings. In the 1980s, the Clarendon Centre, another shopping centre, was built to link Cornmarket with Queen Street, a sensible idea marred by crude and inappropriate execution.

But conservation policies did gain credence, and more sites were treated with sensitivity. On the corner of Ship Street, for example, a medieval building was restored by Jesus College.

University upheavals

Changes in the university after World War II were no less significant and controversial. With its usual capacity for pulling a rabbit out of the hat, Oxford suddenly produced a sporting star of international magnitude in Dr Roger Bannister (now Sir Roger, and formerly master of Pembroke College), who famously used his knowledge of physiology to run the first four-minute mile on the Iffley Road track in June 1954.

There was a strong feeling that the university must modernise its administration or find itself forced to do so by outside forces. The result was the establishment of a committee under the chairmanship of Lord Franks, whose report led to far-reaching changes in the university's structure. The achievements of the 1960s were extraordinary in financial and practical terms. The Historic Buildings Appeal raised over £2 million, making it possible for the grime of centuries to be removed from Oxford's stone, and restoration work on a huge scale to be done.

The College Contributions scheme, which required the richer colleges to provide funds for the poorer, as well as generous outside funding, enabled new building work to the value of £11 million to be carried out. Six new colleges were established: St Catherine's for undergraduates, on the pattern of the older colleges, and another five for graduates only. The science area burgeoned, with 4,000 undergraduates and graduate students working there.

Surviving the 1960s

Oxford suffered less than many of the newer universities from the student unrest that was a feature of the 1960s. But it did not escape entirely, and its reaction was predictable: a committee on relations with junior members, the Hart Committee, was set up, leading to the creation of a Student Representative Council. Pressure for mixed colleges built up all through that radical decade, and this change was implemented from

1970. Today, all the former men's colleges take male and female undergraduates, and the last remaining all-female college, St Hilda's, voted in 2006 to accept male undergraduates. The ratio of men to women in the university as a whole is three to two.

The 1980s saw none of the spectacular spending of the previous two decades. All academic expenditure was restricted by the Conservative

After World War II, Oxford's major battles were about traffic congestion, urban sprawl and university funding – and these remain pressing issues into the 21st century.

Government, and Oxford found itself at odds with Margaret Thatcher, despite the fact that the then prime minister was herself an Oxford graduate (Somerville College). An attempt to award her an honorary degree was actually voted down. No such snub was delivered to US President Bill Clinton, however. In 1994, a quarter of a century after he had completed his time at Oxford as a Rhodes Scholar, he was

awarded his honorary doctorate with great pomp and ceremony.

Fundraising for a new future

Severe spending restrictions remain in force from the government, and the university, keen to expand into new fields of study, is continuously raising money, both at home and abroad. Colleges rely on donations because the income from fees and lodging charges covers scarcely more than half the costs of teaching, housing and maintenance. The annual deficit stands at more than £90 million. Oxford's Development Programme, however – which was established in 1988 – has already offset these costs by raising more than £350 million from philanthropic gifts.

But what of the city? The battle is still on between the conservationists, who insist that at least something of the old city should remain intact, and the pressure for more jobs and housing.

Before 1991, few outsiders had ever heard of the Blackbird Leys estate, barely 3 miles (5km) along the Cowley Road from Oxford's famously dreaming spires. In that year the estate achieved national notoriety as law and order broke down and the habit of joy-riding

THE VIVISECTION WARS

The old university has also witnessed bitter conflict, particularly with regard to the issue of vivisection and animal testing in scientific research. From the late 1990s onwards, Professor Colin Blakemore, an eminent neuroscientist, became a target for animal rights protestors who argued that his experiments involved unacceptable cruelty towards laboratory animals.

The controversy intensified with the university's decision to construct a new £18-million research facility in the South Parks Road science area. The planned laboratory was alleged by the Animal Liberation Front to be intended for animal experiments.

The ensuing struggle pitted pro-animal extremists against the university's scientific establishment, who argued that animal testing was necessary for clinical advances. After death threats were issued against contractors, and university staff were intimidated, the construction of the new facility continued behind screens to protect the identity of the builders.

The passions raised over the new laboratory may not have been shared by most students or citizens of Oxford, but they showed that the city, and particularly its venerable academic institution, had lost none of its ability to raise the big ethical questions of the day.

became firmly established as a popular pastime in deprived areas of Britain.

The anarchy at Blackbird Leys did not last long, but it did highlight the fact that even Oxford has its fair share of economic and social problems. Money worries, accommodation worries and employment worries are nothing new here – not even among students.

Development versus conservation

If the City Fathers have had some success in stemming the tide of cars, they have been less able, or willing, to prevent the gradual in-filling of Oxford's green spaces by new building. Population pressure, the booming Thames Valley economy and the rapid expansion of Brookes University have all fuelled demand for new housing and business premises.

Some of the new developments are welcome. New university buildings such as the Saïd Business School by the railway station grace formerly run-down areas, while the modern Oxford Business Park, built on what used to be the sprawling industrial site of Cowley's car factory, is a pleasant, if unexceptional, collection of landscaped office accommodation. Where possible, city planners have insisted on the redevelopment of "brown field" areas.

But much of the once-picturesque canalside area of North Oxford and Jericho has been concreted over with bland residential developments. Halls of residence for students have sprouted throughout East Oxford, sometimes on what was previously open land. Residents and conservationists are engaged in almost daily battle with developers. ❏

LEFT: the Senior Common Room at St John's College.
ABOVE: Wolfson College and its punts.
RIGHT: Bill Clinton receives an honorary doctorate.

OXFORD COLLEGES: A WHO'S WHO

Football fans can seem restrained compared to supporters
of individual colleges. We cut through the snobbery
to assess their strengths and weaknesses

Oxford University consists of 38 colleges and six permanent private halls (originally religious institutions), each of which is financially independent and self-governing and responsible for the tutoring, feeding and housing of its students. Of the 38 colleges, seven are for graduates only and one of these (All Souls) is exclusively for fellows. This chapter profiles the undergraduate colleges and, because of its academic and architectural importance, also includes All Souls. It charts the political persuasions, sporting accolades and passions of students past and present, and lists architectural and historical highlights as well as other key characteristics of each college.

For each entry, we cite the number of undergraduates and graduates (eg *300/100*) as well as famous alumni. Frequent reference is made to the Norrington Table, Oxford's unofficial academic ranking system, which classes the colleges according to the annual results in the final-year undergraduate examinations.

ALL SOULS

Founded: 1437
Number of students: varies, graduate students only.
Alumni: Sir Isaiah Berlin, T.E. Lawrence, John Redwood, William Waldegrave.
All Souls, a research-oriented college for fellows only, stands on the High Street but can also be reached from Radcliffe Square, from where its spectacular twin towers are best viewed. The Front Quad has remained virtually unchanged since the college's foundation, as has the chapel, and there is a sundial designed by Christopher Wren, a former All Souls bursar. To be elected a fellow of All Souls is perhaps the highest academic honour in the university: each year the top finalists are invited to sit an examination to apply, and only two are actually elected to fellowship.

BALLIOL

Founded: 1263
Number of students: 422/221
Alumni: H.H. Asquith, Hilaire Belloc, Graham Greene, Denis Healey, Edward Heath, Aldous Huxley,

ABOVE: scarves bearing the colours of individual colleges.

Roy Jenkins, Boris Johnson, Harold Macmillan, Howard Marks, Chris Patten, Siegfried Sassoon.

Occupying a huge area between Broad Street and Magdalen Street, Balliol is one of the oldest, biggest, wealthiest, highest-achieving and most prestigious colleges in the university. The college has a strong political tradition, and went through an especially radical phase in the 1960s. Formal Hall, the saying of Grace and the wearing of gowns have all been abolished, and students are even allowed to walk on the college grass – an activity deemed a crime in most colleges. Balliol was also one of the first colleges to begin accepting large numbers of non-public school-educated and overseas students, fostering a refreshingly cosmopolitan atmosphere. There is long-standing rivalry between Balliol and its Broad Street neighbour Trinity.

BRASENOSE

Founded: 1509
Number of students: 362/176
Alumni: John Buchan, David Cameron, Colin Cowdrey, William Golding, Michael Palin, Robert Runcie.

"BNC" tends to be overshadowed by the splendour of the nearby Bodleian Library and Radcliffe Camera, although the attractive Old Quadrangle is noted for its colourful sundial. Historically "middle-of-the-road", Brasenose has a good reputation for sport – mostly rowing – and on the academic side it has a distinguished

tradition in law. It acquired its name from a rather unusual door-knocker ("brazen nose"), which now hangs in the hall.

CHRIST CHURCH

Founded: 1546
Number of students: 426/154
Alumni: W.H. Auden, Lewis Carroll, Alan Clark, Richard Curtis, Anthony Eden, Albert Einstein, William Gladstone, Lord Hailsham, Sir Robert Peel, Auberon Waugh, John Wesley, Sir Christopher Wren.

Originally founded in 1525 by Cardinal Wolsey and re-founded by Henry VIII in 1546, "The House" is Oxford's largest and best-known college as well as being one of the top colleges both academically and in sport. It is the one college *every* tourist visits, despite the entrance charge and the risk of being shouted at by the bowler-hatted "bulldogs" on duty there. The grandiose architecture is imposing to the point of being intimidating, especially Sir Christopher Wren's Tom Quad, with its famous tower and fountain – and the college even has its own cathedral, picture gallery and meadow. The college architecture may be familiar to some from the *Harry Potter* films.

For many years the cradle of the British aristocracy, Christ Church still produces its fair share of bishops and MPs, though there is a slightly wider social mix at the college today; women were first admitted in 1980.

HOW THE COLLEGES ARE GOVERNED

All undergraduate colleges have a governing body of fellows in charge of all aspects of college life. Some fellows are more important than others, although key posts, such as senior tutor or dean, are normally filled by one fellow for two or three years only. The senior tutor is concerned with academic achievement, while the dean has the unenviable task of enforcing discipline. The other top jobs are the bursar, responsible for finances, and the principal (or warden, master, provost, president, dean or rector). The head of house is elected by all the fellows and is recruited on the strength of his or her expertise and connections.

The governing body meets regularly to discuss the day-to-day running of the college. Some subcommittees, such as those supervising the college gardens or the wine cellar, tend to be more popular than those dealing with

investments or building works. Votes are taken on all issues.

One of the governing body's duties is to sit in judgment on students in trouble. Those who fail exams are usually given a further test, with the threat of expulsion if the exam is failed again. The old punishments of "gating" (confinement to college) and "rustication" (sending out of residence for a term or two) are obsolete, as are the arcane rules that made attendance at chapel compulsory or imposed curfews. Nowadays, serious disciplinary matters are more likely to involve vandalism or other forms of anti-social behaviour, and students will be "sent down" (expelled) only for serious misdemeanours.

Undergraduates also have regular meetings, under the auspices of the Junior Common Room (JCR). Motions, some serious and others frivolous, are debated, with budding politicians trying out their oratorical skills.

CORPUS CHRISTI

Founded: 1517
Number of students: 246/115
Alumni: Matthew Arnold, Sir Isaiah Berlin, David Miliband, Vikram Seth.

Corpus is the smallest undergraduate college but has a main quad that is among the most beautiful in Oxford, its most notable feature being the Pelican Sundial. Academic standards are traditionally high, but the college is also known for its tolerance and friendliness. It is also the home of the annual tortoise races, the slowest spectator sport in the university.

EXETER

Founded: 1314
Number of students: 328/177
Alumni: Martin Amis, Roger Bannister, Alan Bennett, Edward Burne-Jones, Richard Burton, William Morris, Philip Pullman, Will Self, Ned Sherrin, J.R.R. Tolkien.

One of the three Turl Street colleges (along with Jesus and Lincoln), Exeter is an architectural mish-mash of styles, as bits were added on over the centuries. Highlights include the Gothic chapel, with its vast spire, and the tiny garden at the back of the college, with beautiful views over the Bodleian and Radcliffe Camera. Exeter has traditionally been known as an unpretentious, slightly unremarkable, even apathetic college, although feelings have traditionally been strong regarding the college food (dreadful) and the bar (excellent).

HARRIS MANCHESTER

Founded: 1786
Number of students: 108/150
Alumni: James Martineau.

Originally established by English Presbyterians in Manchester in 1786, "HMC" moved to Oxford in 1889 and was given full college status only in 1996, making it the university's newest college. It's also the only one to cater solely for mature students – candidates must be at least 21 to apply, although there is no upper age limit. Architectural highlights include the stained-glass windows by William Morris and Edward Burne-Jones in the chapel.

HERTFORD

Founded: 1740
Number of students: 370/220
Alumni: John Donne, Charles James Fox, Thomas Hobbes, Jonathan Swift, Evelyn Waugh.

A hall for students known as "Hart Hall" was established as long ago as 1282, but Hertford College has had a chequered history and has been plagued by financial problems, which remain to this day. The most remarkable and attractive feature of this close-knit, medium-sized college is the famous Bridge of Sighs (an echo of the one in Venice), which connects its two halves. This attracts hordes of tourists, partly because of its proximity to the Bodleian.

JESUS

Founded: 1571
Number of students: 330/130
Alumni: T.E. Lawrence (of Arabia), Magnus Magnusson, Harold Wilson.

Jesus was founded by Queen Elizabeth I, but much of the money behind the foundation was provided by a Welshman called Hugh Price, and the college retains very strong links with Wales – the college newspaper is entitled *The Sheepshagger*. Architecturally the least interesting of the Turl Street colleges (the other two are Exeter and Lincoln), Jesus has fallen over backwards to keep a low profile over the years – except in 1974, when it became one of the first of the previously all-male colleges to admit women.

KEBLE

Founded: 1870
Number of students: 422/235
Alumni: Imran Khan, Peter Pears, Chad Varah, Andreas Whittam-Smith.

Keble was originally founded with the intention of making an Oxford education more accessible to people from different social backgrounds. Links with the Church (John Keble was a leading figure of the Oxford Movement, *see pages 43 and 98*) ensure that the college retains a strong social conscience. It's a dynamic place, active in sport and politics, with academic achievement especially strong in the sciences.

Keble's buildings have aroused enormous controversy. The main quad is a neo-Gothic palace of red-and-white chequered bricks, with the appearance of a Victorian mental institution. Other buildings are modern glass-and-steel affairs – the bar often being compared to a space ship. Local rival St John's has a "Demolish Keble Society", the membership requirement of which is to bring along a brick removed from Keble to your first meeting.

LADY MARGARET HALL

Founded: 1878
Number of students: 424/148
Alumnae: Benazir Bhutto, Antonia Fraser, Nigella Lawson, Ann Widdecombe.

Its out-of-town location (15 minutes on foot from St Giles) and 12 acres (5 hectares) of beautiful grounds make this college idyllic in summer, though it does look like a prison from the front. LMH was the first "academic hall" for women at Oxford – it became a full college only in 1960 and went mixed in 1978. It is known for its general tolerance, though it has been radical enough to stage an anti-pornography protest.

LINCOLN

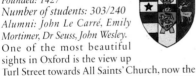

Founded: 1427
Number of students: 303/240
Alumni: John Le Carré, Emily Mortimer, Dr Seuss, John Wesley.
One of the most beautiful sights in Oxford is the view up Turl Street towards All Saints' Church, now the Lincoln College library. The college itself is rather small, but very picturesque. It was originally founded as a "small college" in order to create a friendly, cosy atmosphere – a tradition that is still strongly adhered to. Lincoln enjoys long-standing rivalry with the other Turl Street colleges, Exeter and Jesus.

MAGDALEN

Founded: 1458
Number of students: 389/235
Alumni: Sir John Betjeman, William Hague, Ian Hislop, Martha Lane Fox, C.S. Lewis, Dudley Moore, Ivor Novello, Oscar Wilde, Cardinal Wolsey.

Pronounced "maudlin", Magdalen's academic traditions are as fine as its romantic architecture. Its buildings include the 15th-century tower overlooking Magdalen Bridge from which its acclaimed choir sings on May Morning, Cloister Quad and the Regency New Buildings. The gardens are just as impressive, with over a mile of riverside walks and a Deer Park. Magdalen probably captures the spirit of Evelyn Waugh's *Brideshead Revisited* more than any other college.

MANSFIELD

Founded: 1886
Number of students: 191/51
Alumni: C.H. Dodd, Nathaniel Micklem.
Originally a Congregationalist theological college, diminutive Mansfield has the advantage of beautiful and tranquil surroundings in a fairly central location off Holywell Street. The college is historically short of cash and strong in the arts. In undergraduate life, it contributes more than its fair share to journalism, and its Women's Group has been active. Pool is another college forte.

MERTON

Founded: 1264
Number of students: 309/212
Alumni: Andy Cato (half of Groove Armada), T.S. Eliot, Jeremy Isaacs, Kris Kristofferson, Robert Morley, John Wycliffe.
Merton has the oldest quad in the university, beautiful gardens and a fine academic pedigree. From the cobblestones of Merton Street to the medieval library in Mob Quad to the old city wall that borders the pretty garden, this college constantly delights the eye. It is noted for extremely high academic standards, its inexpensive but top-notch food, its students' musical talents and for holding the only Winter Ball in Oxford. The college also hosts an annual Arts Festival during Trinity Term. During the English Civil War, Henrietta Maria, wife of Charles I, set up house at Merton in what is now the Queen's Room, while her husband was more grandly installed at nearby Christ Church, which neatly filled in as a substitute palace.

NEW

Founded: 1379
Number of students: 420/180
Alumni: Kate Beckinsale, Tony Benn, Gyles Brandreth, Richard Crossman, John Fowles, Hugh Gaitskell, John Galsworthy, Hugh Grant, Dennis Potter, Rick Stein.
New College looks anything but new. In fact, it's one of the oldest colleges in the university, and many of the buildings, including the front quad, dining hall, chapel and cloisters, have survived from the original foundations and look positively medieval. The college has a kind of austere beauty – certainly it is difficult not to be impressed by its size and sheer solidity. It's a prestigious and well-known college, with well-established links to the Civil Service and to Winchester (it was founded by William of Wykeham). Strong in sport (especially rowing), academia and music, New is currently considered to be one of the main social centres of university life.

ORIEL

Founded: 1326
Number of students: 304/158
Alumni: Beau Brummell, John Keble, Cardinal Newman, Sir Walter Raleigh, Cecil Rhodes, A.J.P Taylor.
Oriel was the last college to remain all-male, admitting women only in 1985. Traditional in more ways than one, it is also known for the right-wing leanings of its students, having the only Junior Common Room that refuses to subscribe to the Oxford University Student Union. It has a strong rowing tradition, with the college having long dominated the river. Oriel is in a lovely location, just off the High Street – the wonderfully picturesque Oriel Square has become one of the most-filmed locations in Oxford.

PEMBROKE

Founded: 1624
Number of students: 416/112
Alumni: Sir Rocco Forte, William Fulbright, Michael Heseltine, Samuel Johnson.
Compact, unassuming Pembroke is tucked away behind Carfax and suf-

fers somewhat from being opposite the far more grandiose Christ Church. Academically it's a pretty middle-of-the-road place, and the laid-back atmosphere in college reflects this. Pembroke is anything but apathetic when it comes to sport, however, with both its men's and women's rowing teams consistently close to the top of the university rowing charts. Music is also a strong area in the college.

QUEEN'S

Founded: 1341
Number of students: 304/133
Alumni: Rowan Atkinson, Tim Berners-Lee, Edmund Halley.
This college is named after Philippa, wife of Edward III, whose chaplain, Robert Eglesfield, founded it. But the statue above the main gate, overlooking the High Street, is of Queen Caroline, wife of George II, who in the mid-18th century funded the building of its two unusual and impressive Baroque quads. The college has links with the north of England and is traditionally a sporting college, being especially strong in rugby (with appropriate beer cellar).

ST ANNE'S

Founded: 1893
Number of students: 437/187
Alumnae: Sister Wendy Beckett, Edwina Currie, Helen Fielding, Zoë Heller, Penelope Lively, Iris Murdoch.
This former women's college, which looks like a 1970s polytechnic, now has equal numbers of men and women. One of Oxford's more "unpretentious" colleges, "Stan's" also does its bit for student drama and journalism. Academic standards have been on the up recently, with the college making the top 10 of the Norrington Table three times since 2002.

ST CATHERINE'S

Founded: 1963
Number of students: 447/187
Alumni: J. Paul Getty, Joseph Heller, Peter Mandelson, A.A. Milne, Eric Partridge, Matthew Pinsent, Jeanette Winterson.
"Catz" is viewed either as an architectural masterpiece or a sprawling modern monstrosity.

Designed by Danish architect Arne Jacobsen, even down to the cutlery used by the tutors, and situated out of town by the River Cherwell, it is lovely in summer. It has yet to perform a feat remarkable enough to attract the attention of the rest of the university, but its liberal establishment (for example, it has no chapel – the only Oxford college without one) makes it popular with students.

ST EDMUND HALL

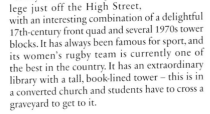

Founded: c.1278
Number of students: 400/150
Alumni: Sir Robin Day, Amitav Ghosh, Terry Jones, Al Murray.
"Teddy Hall" is a compact college just off the High Street, with an interesting combination of a delightful 17th-century front quad and several 1970s tower blocks. It has always been famous for sport, and its women's rugby team is currently one of the best in the country. It has an extraordinary library with a tall, book-lined tower – this is in a converted church and students have to cross a graveyard to get to it.

ST HILDA'S

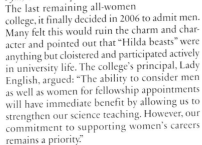

Founded: 1893
Number of students: 419/116
Alumnae: Monica Ali, Susan Blackmore, Wendy Cope, Barbara Pym, Gillian Shepherd.
The last remaining all-women college, it finally decided in 2006 to admit men. Many felt this would ruin the charm and character and pointed out that "Hilda beasts" were anything but cloistered and participated actively in university life. The college's principal, Lady English, argued: "The ability to consider men as well as women for fellowship appointments will have immediate benefit by allowing us to strengthen our science teaching. However, our commitment to supporting women's careers remains a priority."

ST HUGH'S

Founded: 1886
Number of students: 419/226
Alumnae: Kate Adie, Brigid Brophy, Barbara Castle, Theresa May, Joanna Trollope.
St Hugh's is a close-knit former

women's college, founded by Elizabeth Wordsworth, great-niece of the poet. Mixed since 1986, it is sited far out in North Oxford, on the extreme edge of the university area. The college's 14-acre (6-hectare) grounds are said to be quite pleasant, but the joke goes that no one except St Hugh's students have actually seen them.

ST JOHN'S

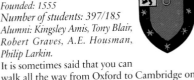

Founded: 1555
Number of students: 397/185
Alumni: Kingsley Amis, Tony Blair, Robert Graves, A.E. Housman, Philip Larkin.
It is sometimes said that you can walk all the way from Oxford to Cambridge on land owned by St John's. It is the richest Oxford college and is believed to own a fair chunk of Switzerland as well as large tracts of London's West End. The college's extreme wealth means glorious buildings and luxurious accommodation for the students (there are even rumours of jacuzzis). Only a modern block – dubbed "a fish tank on stilts" – lets things down. Situated on St Giles (which the college owns and under which is reportedly a highly impressive wine cellar), St John's has traditionally been the most academically successful college.

ST PETER'S

Founded: 1929
Number of students: 390/125
Alumni: Edward Akufo Addo, Ken Loach, Peter Wright.
"St Pete's" has long been considered a backwater of Oxford. Situated next to the former Oxford Prison and rooted firmly to the bottom of the Norrington Table, it is mostly noted for the ugliness of its buildings and the beer-drinking exploits of its students. Highlights, however, include the snazzy set of automatic doors at the entrance to the main quad, the only pair of its kind in an Oxford college.

SOMERVILLE

Founded: 1879
Number of students: 370/102
Alumnae: Indira Gandhi, Iris Murdoch, Esther Rantzen, Dorothy L. Sayers, Margaret Thatcher, Shirley Williams.

Baroness Thatcher's old college is not overly proud of its most illustrious graduate – in 1989 a bust of the Supreme Leader had to be taken off display and stored in a broom cupboard after being repeatedly daubed with graffiti. The college site up the Woodstock Road is grassy and pleasant, and its members are sociable and outward-looking. Long an all-women college, it went mixed in 1994 and now has equal numbers of men and women. Like Trinity, Somerville houses some keen croquet players.

TRINITY

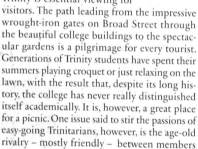

Founded: 1554–5
Number of students: 297/121
Alumni: Anthony Crosland, Miles Kington, William Pitt the Elder, Terence Rattigan, Jeremy Thorpe.
Trinity is essential viewing for visitors. The path leading from the impressive wrought-iron gates on Broad Street through the beautiful college buildings to the spectacular gardens is a pilgrimage for every tourist. Generations of Trinity students have spent their summers playing croquet or just relaxing on the lawn, with the result that, despite its long history, the college has never really distinguished itself academically. It is, however, a great place for a picnic. One issue said to stir the passions of easy-going Trinitarians, however, is the age-old rivalry – mostly friendly – between members of this college and their wealthy Broad Street neighbour Balliol.

UNIVERSITY

Founded: 1249
Number of students: 420/144
Alumni: Clement Attlee, Bill Clinton, Chelsea Clinton, Stephen Hawking, V.S. Naipaul, Percy Bysshe Shelley.
"Univ" is said to have been founded by King Alfred the Great in 812, but this is disputed. What is certain is that "Univ" was the first Oxford college to be founded, and has never ceased to set high standards for its students, whether in the library or on the games field. The college has a strong reputation in the sciences, and its students have always been very active in university life – perhaps in order to escape the architecture of their own college, which has been likened by some to an Alcatraz on the High Street.

WADHAM

Founded: 1610
Number of students: 480/190
Alumni: Sir Thomas Beecham, Melvyn Bragg, Michael Checkland, Cecil Day Lewis, Michael Foot, Rosamund Pike, Sir Christopher Wren.
Once nicknamed the "People's Republic of Wadham", this college has always been a centre for radical thought. In its early days it was the meeting place for the leading figures of the Scientific Revolution, who went on to form the Royal Society. It was later one of the first colleges to admit women. The Parks Road college has a long tradition of political activism – it is the only college to have its own student union rather than a Junior Common Room and remains fiercely left wing. The college buildings are attractive, especially the original front quad, but the notoriously trendy Wadhamites are more likely to be found in the neighbouring King's Arms than in college.

WORCESTER

Founded: 1714
Number of students: 413/185
Alumni: Richard Adams, Sir Alastair Burnett, Richard Lovelace, Rupert Murdoch, Thomas de Quincey, Lord Sainsbury.
Secluded Worcester College is set in 26 acres (10 hectares) of beautiful grounds on the western edge of the university area – something that you might not realise from its forbidding, grim even, entrance located on Walton Street. It stands on the site of the former Gloucester Hall, a Benedictine foundation of 1283 that was dissolved during the suppression of the monasteries. The college's unusually spacious front quad isn't really a quad at all – the money ran out after only three sides had been finished.

Worcester is the only Oxford college to possess its own lake – complete with ducks – next to which outdoor drama is held in summer by the college's thriving "Buskins" theatre group. Other highlights include the acclaimed food at Formal Hall and the recently renovated chapel, of which Oscar Wilde wrote: "as a piece of simple decorative and beautiful art it is perfect, and the windows very artistic." ❑

Oxford Brookes University

Although Oxford is synonymous with its medieval university, the city contains another centre of academic excellence: Oxford Brookes University.

Oxford Brookes University, at the top of Headington Hill, can claim little of the longevity of its illustrious neighbour, but it has its own claims to fame and a burgeoning student population – estimated at over 18,500 in 2009.

The institution's history involves many a change of name and site. Originally the Oxford School of Art, housed in the Taylor Institution in St Giles, it became the Oxford City Technical School and moved to St Ebbes in 1894. These premises were soon judged inadequate, but it took a further 50 years before the land on Headington Hill was acquired. During that time the school spread into different buildings, at one stage being scattered over 19 separate sites.

The vision of John Brookes

The modern-day university was named after John Brookes, whose vision was of a single college on a single campus, offering a mix of academic and vocational courses. Under his inspirational stewardship from 1928 to 1956 the college not only found its physical home but also began to develop a high reputation in disciplines such as architecture and catering. Brookes also persuaded well-known academics and experts to lecture at the school.

After its official opening in 1963, the College of Technology (as it was now called) started offering degree-level courses. As part of the nationwide trend towards the creation of a network of polytechnics, it was then renamed Oxford Polytechnic in 1970. With an emphasis on vocational and professional courses, it continued to excel in training architects

as well as pioneering work in publishing and hospitality. The polytechnic's size and range of academic options were further increased with the merger in 1976 with the Lady Spencer Churchill teacher training college in nearby Wheatley. The Oxford School of Nursing also came into the polytechnic fold in 1988.

Full university status was acquired in 1992. With new funding, Brookes built much-needed student accommodation and took over the 14-acre (5.7-hectare) Headington Hill Hall site.

Today Brookes attracts an eclectic mix of students from the UK and further afield to a wide and often imaginative range of courses. The modular system allows for a greater choice within academic fields than conventional degree courses, while degrees and post-graduate qualifications

in the established subjects of architecture and publishing remain highly sought-after. A mixture of innovation and established academic prowess means that Brookes has on several occasions won the coveted best new university award judged and published by *The Times*.

Brookes is also proud of its sporting and social facilities. A state-of-the-art sports centre rivals anything the old university has to offer, while Brookes rowers are proud to point out that they have more than once beaten their venerable rival on the river. And with its own top-quality restaurant *(see page 217)*, the newer university has some attractions that the older one, for all its heritage, cannot hope to match. ❑

RIGHT: the School of Social Sciences and Law has a vibrant postgraduate research culture.

LITERARY OXFORD

The university has nurtured writers and given them a place in which to develop their craft, but it has also made enemies of men and women of letters

And that sweet city with her dreaming spires,
She needs not June for beauty's heightening.

–Matthew Arnold

The waiting list for the single "local author" review slot in the weekly *Oxford Times* must be one of the longest literary queues in the world. Sometimes it seems that almost everyone in Oxford is an author (when they're not working in publishing or a bookshop), and parts of genteel North Oxford must surely echo to the sound of clattering keyboards. Look at the browser in Blackwell's bookshop surreptitiously turning a book face outwards; he or she is a local author.

Oxford has always been a mecca for writers,

> The popular perception of Oxford has been largely moulded by the city's depiction in literary fiction. The image created by *Brideshead Revisited, in particular, has proved hard to shake off.*

partly because of its proximity to the literary heartland of London, partly because of its cultural buzz, but mostly because of the old university. Countless novelists, poets and playwrights have passed through its colleges, some with more success than others, while a good many others have stayed on to find a day job in academia.

The Athens of England

The university literary connection goes back to medieval times, and in Chaucer's *Canterbury Tales* (*c.*1387) we read of the Clerke of Oxenforde, an unworldly and impoverished bookworm – and a prototype for generations of students to come. The Middle Ages witnessed the heyday of the university's religious institutions, and much writing was of a theological or philosophical nature. It was not until Elizabethan times that the city – and university – developed a reputation as a centre of aesthetic excellence. The historian William Camden made a bold claim for Oxford's cultural status in 1586 when he wrote of "Our most noble Athens, the seat of the English Muses."

Muses or not, a succession of eminent writers passed through Oxford from the 16th century onwards. Some, like Shakespeare, were just en route to somewhere else, but others stayed,

adopting the almost monastic life that university dons had to endure until the reforms of the 19th century. Robert Burton, author of *The Anatomy of Melancholy* (1621), taught and studied at Christ Church, where he claimed: "I have liv'd a silent, sedentary, solitary, private life."

Nothing could have been further away from the gregarious, excessive and distinctly non-monastic lives led by the sons of the rich as the university became a finishing school for England's social elite during the 18th century. Men of letters did attend the university, but many were scathing about its dons and students. The poet Robert Southey (1774–1843) lambasted his tutors as "a waste of wigs and want of wisdom", while the great historian Edward Gibbon thought the time spent at Magdalen to have been "the most idle and unprofitable of my whole life".

The long-overdue reforms that swept through the university from the 1830s were bound up with religious debate but also with new directions in literature. Dons such as Walter Pater at Brasenose and Mark Pattison at Lincoln were inspirational leaders of movements devoted to the development of the intellectual life and the pursuit of "art for art's sake". As Oxford lost both its clerical and aristocratic dominance, the city's literary prestige rose accordingly. The Romantic period saw Oxford eulogised by Wordsworth and, in the 1860s, by Matthew Arnold, a fellow of Oriel College and professor of poetry. To Arnold we owe the immortal phrases "city of dreaming spires" (later wittily transformed into "city of perspiring dreams") and "home of lost causes".

LEFT: the oft-quoted Matthew Arnold.
ABOVE: the 1981 TV adaptation of *Brideshead Revisited* conveyed a sybaritic view of Oxford life.

WRITERS WITH RESERVATIONS

Not all Oxford-educated writers have been enamoured with the place. The most famous rebel to be thrown out was Percy Bysshe Shelley *(see right)*, whose sojourn at University College came to an end in 1811 when he was expelled for publishing a pamphlet in defence of atheism. "Mad Shelley" later complained that "I never met with such unworthy treatment." Another poet to be shown the door (in his case of Magdalen) was John Betjeman, who failed an exam in 1927, while poor Samuel Johnson was sent down in 1729 because he couldn't pay his bills.

Literary associations

Prominent among writers who have loved and celebrated the university were Charles Dodgson, aka Lewis Carroll, and fellow of Christ Church, William Morris of pre-Raphaelite fame, the aesthete John Ruskin and T. E. Lawrence "of Arabia". The first half of the 20th century marked the golden age of Oxford's literary associations, as the city and university featured in classic novels such as Max Beerbohm's *Zuleika Dobson* (1911) and Evelyn Waugh's *Brideshead Revisited* (1945). The

terrible death toll of the Great War encouraged a mythic image of prewar Oxford and the generation of gilded young men who did not return.

Many Oxford writers, such as C.S. Lewis and J.R.R. Tolkien, have chosen not to write about Oxford. Others have written about the place in coded form. Thomas Hardy's *Jude the Obscure* (1896), for instance, is set in "Christminster", a thinly disguised version of Oxford. Increasing numbers, moreover, have set their work beyond the cloistered confines of the university and have used the "real" city as the backdrop for their work. This was the case with Hardy, but more recently John Wain, in his trilogy *Where the Rivers Meet*, and writers such as A.S. Byatt and Barbara Trapido have dealt with non-university Oxford.

Women writers

Literary Oxford, like academic Oxford, was long a male monopoly, but now the coveted local author slot is as likely to be occupied by one of the many women writers who live in the city. Pre-eminent among them until her death in 1999 was Iris Murdoch, a philosophy don at St Anne's before becoming an acclaimed novelist. Other women authors with an Oxford University pedigree include Vera Brittain (famous for *Testament of Youth*, 1933), Dorothy L. Sayers, Barbara Pym and Penelope Lively.

Nowadays, Oxford's love affair with the book takes many forms, from a plethora of local reading groups to the prestigious annual Oxford Literary Festival. Authors such as Ian McEwan live in the city, while the university attracts poets of the calibre of Craig Raine, James Fenton and David Constantine. ❏

MURDEROUS INTENT

The city is thankfully not a crime hot spot, but detective novels and murder mysteries abound. Millions of readers have been introduced to Oxford via Colin Dexter's ingenious Inspector Morse novels and John Thaw's popular portrayal of Morse on television kept camera crews busy around the city for years. Morse follows in a line of Oxford sleuths, starting with Dorothy L. Sayers' Harriet Vane in *Gaudy Night* (1935) and including the investigative creations of Michael Innes, Michael Dibdin and Veronica Stallwood. To read these, you might be excused for thinking that every college quadrangle and city street is fraught with murderous danger.

ABOVE LEFT: *Lord of the Rings* creator, J.R.R. Tolkien.
ABOVE: Iris Murdoch, philosophy don turned novelist.

Lewis Carroll

Another literary figure inextricably linked with Oxford is Lewis Carroll, famous author of *Alice's Adventures in Wonderland*.

Lewis Carroll was born Charles Lutwidge Dodgson in Christ Church rectory, Lincolnshire, and entered Oxford's Christ Church at the age of 18 in 1850. He went on to become a lecturer in mathematics, was ordained deacon, and remained in Oxford until his death in 1898. Outside his academic studies he was a keen photographer, developing his own plates in a darkroom he built on the roof of his rooms overlooking Tom Quad.

Extremely shy, he was most at ease with children and they became his favourite subjects. It was in the Deanery gardens at Christ Church that Dodgson first met Alice, the dean's daughter. There to photograph the Cathedral, his attention was constantly diverted by Alice and her sisters, who insisted on getting into the frame.

Getting to know Alice

The friendship with the girls grew, and soon they were posing for his camera in his rooms. Dressed in Chinese costumes or the rags of beggar waifs from the cupboards in his dressing-room, the children began their games of "Let's pretend", and Alice's adventures were about to begin.

During the summer Dodgson took the children on the river, making up stories that lived and died "like summer midges". One expedition, on 4 July 1862, took them upstream to Godstow. The children, as always, pressed their friend for more stories and, when they returned to the Deanery, Alice implored him to write down her adventures. Dodgson began the carefully hand-

written book with his own illustrations and gave it to her as a Christmas gift.

Alice's Adventures were so well thought of that Dodgson agreed to their publication, and, on the advice of John Ruskin, the artist and social reformer, to have them illustrated by a professional artist. John Tenniel was chosen, and the author's name changed to Lewis Carroll (Lewis from Lutwidge, Carroll from Charles).

A second book, *Through the Looking Glass*, was published in 1871. The relationship had ended with the end of her childhood, and Alice was now 19. She married a Christ Church man and went to live at Lyndhurst.

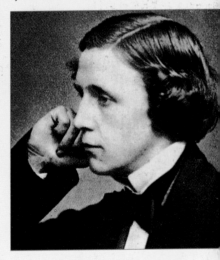

From the moment Alice clutches the jar of "orange marmalade" Lewis Carroll starts an intriguing guessing game in identifying Oxford references and characters. Dodgson was currently advertising for sale his brother's orange marmalade. The Cheshire cat is Dinah, Alice's tabby. The Rev. Robinson Duckworth, a friend of Lewis Carroll's, becomes, affectionately, the Duck. The Dodo is the author himself, and was derived from visits to the new University Museum. The Dormouse's story of three children living at the bottom of a treacle-well leads us to the healing well at Binsey. ❑

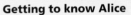

ABOVE: cover of the 1916 edition, published by Cassell. **RIGHT:** Lewis Carroll, afflicted by shyness.

Architecture

For more than a thousand years, the rich and powerful in Oxford have employed top architects to create showpiece buildings in which to live, study, work and worship. The result is a three-dimensional catalogue of all that's best in British architecture

Not much remains of Oxford's earliest architecture, the only surviving Saxon relic being the tower of the church of St Michael at the Northgate, which was built as a lookout tower against the Danes. From the Norman era there is the fine crypt of St Peter in the East, as well as St George's Tower, part of the castle. The abbeys which played such a pivotal role in establishing the city as a centre of learning were almost completely destroyed during the Reformation, although most of the Augustinian priory church built on the site of St Frideswide's priory was saved, and subsequently became Christ Church Cathedral.

Both St Michael's and St George's towers are constructed of the coral rag limestone quarried in the Cumnor hills, a stone so tough it could not be shaped into regular blocks, thus accounting for their rough-cast look. When the great abbeys and early colleges were built, the builders preferred the more manageable Jurassic limestone found in great quantity in Headington and to the west of Oxford. Like some modern polymer, it came out of the ground "soft", and was easily cut and carved but, once in place, it weathered into a tough hard-wearing stone.

College blueprints

Founded by rich and powerful bishops, Oxford's first medieval colleges were a stark contrast to the cramped academic halls in which most students lived and worked. Their creators could afford to construct fine buildings for the college members. Components included a chapel, a grand dining hall, accommodation set around an intimate quadrangle (much in the style of a medieval cloister or inn) and a library to house the priceless manuscripts. The colleges were private places looking inwards, with few external windows and only one great gateway giving entrance.

While we can see the blueprint for some of these features in the surviving Mob Quad and chapel at Merton, it wasn't until the foundation of New College in 1379 that all of them were combined for the first time into a unified whole, with the chapel and hall and library all occupying space within the main quadrangle.

Medieval miracles

Gothic architecture transformed the city. By the early 14th century, the spire of the University

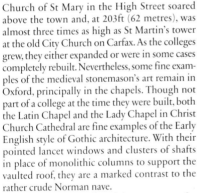

Church of St Mary in the High Street soared above the town and, at 203ft (62 metres), was almost three times as high as St Martin's tower at the old City Church on Carfax. As the colleges grew, they either expanded or were in some cases completely rebuilt. Nevertheless, some fine examples of the medieval stonemason's art remain in Oxford, principally in the chapels. Though not part of a college at the time they were built, both the Latin Chapel and the Lady Chapel in Christ Church Cathedral are fine examples of the Early English style of Gothic architecture. With their pointed lancet windows and clusters of shafts in place of monolithic columns to support the vaulted roof, they are a marked contrast to the rather crude Norman nave.

Merton College Chapel demonstrates the transition to the Decorated style that took place in the early 14th century. With its flowing and curvaceous tracery, the chapel's huge east window is one of the finest examples in England.

Left: *Brazen Nose College,* an engraving by Rudolph Ackermann.
Above Top: Wren's Tom Tower at Christ Church.
Above: the Mob Quad at Merton College.
Right: Radcliffe Camera seen from the Bodleian Library.

As the university grew in stature, it needed more of its own buildings, independent of the colleges. The first major step in this direction was the all-important Divinity School. Completed in 1488, it is a fine example of Perpendicular Gothic, with its intricate fan or lierne vaulting. Further examples of this form of vaulting include the Christ Church choir.

Later overlays

During the reign of Elizabeth I, college and university buildings began to dominate the central area. But the Elizabethan era and the first half of the 17th century also brought enormous changes to the town. Streets were extended and lined with three- and four-storey houses, mainly of timber-framed construction, of which several notable examples remain, including Kemp Hall just off the High Street. Medieval courtyard inns expanded to take up much space in the central streets; parts of such an inn remain in the Golden Cross off Cornmarket and The Mitre on High Street.

The 17th century also saw the emergence of Oxford's very own style of architecture, the Jacobean Gothic, incorporating a tentative mixture of Gothic and classical features and motifs and

> *Oxford is particularly noted for its examples of neo-Gothic architecture, of which Exeter College Chapel and the University Museum are particularly successful examples.*

best exemplified by the magnificent Old Schools Quadrangle. But less than 100 years later, classical architecture began to alter the Oxford skyline, with fine university buildings being erected in the central area, including Wren's Sheldonian Theatre (1668), Hawksmoor's Clarendon Building (1715) and Gibbs' Radcliffe Camera (1748).

Magnificent though they are, these buildings did not destroy the essentially medieval face of Oxford. Even when they were rebuilt, most colleges remained very conservative. The ancient-looking frontage of University College was completed at the same time as the Clarendon Building. Hawksmoor submitted plans for a neoclassical rebuilding of All Souls, but these were not accepted; nor were the designs of Sir John Soane for Brasenose, whose medieval High Street facade wasn't completed until the early 20th century.

Gothic revivalism

Oxford and Gothic go naturally together; that was the feeling of the influential Oxford Architectural Society, which from the 1830s tried to influence anyone building in the city. Oxford became a bastion of Gothic Revivalism, apparent in Sir George Gilbert Scott's Martyrs' Memorial, completed in 1843, and the impressive chapel of Exeter College, built in 1854–60 by the same architect and almost an exact copy of Sainte-Chapelle in Paris. Gothic forms and motifs were also used for secular buildings, the most notable example of which is the University Museum (1855).

The founder of the Oxford Movement, John Keble, is remembered in Keble College, which was founded in 1868. However, William Butterfield's daring design transgressed Oxford's hallowed traditions, for it was built not of stone, but of a Byzantine riot of red, yellow and blue brick. Oxford had seen nothing like the polychromatic patterning and, while the under-

LEFT: an unforgettable example of the classical style, Gibbs' Radcliffe Camera.
ABOVE: Merton Street retains a medieval feel.
RIGHT: All Souls College, open to fellows only.

WREN'S ROLE IN OXFORD

When the monarchy was restored in 1660, Oxford was rewarded for its Royalist loyalty by extended patronage, and money flowed back for new building projects. The favoured style now was classical and the University found the ideal architect in its young professor of astronomy, Christopher Wren. The Sheldonian Theatre was his first building. His U-shaped design was based on the antique Theatre of Marcellus in Rome. However, whereas the classical equivalent was safely left open to the elements, Wren had to cover the 72ft (22-metre) span with a permanent roof and couldn't spoil the audience's view with pillars. His complicated series of trusses taking the strain from the roof to the outside walls is hidden from spectators by a great painted ceiling but can be seen by those who visit the cupola on the roof.

Wren was booked for more architectural work at Trinity and Queen's colleges, though he was also rebuilding the churches lost in the Great Fire of London when he came back to complete his other Oxford landmark, Tom Tower at Christ Church. The great master of the classical style agreed to work in Gothic form to fit in with the existing gatehouse, built in Henry VIII's time. The ogee-shaped dome on the tower and the smaller gate turrets are a masterly touch, harking back to early Tudor architecture.

graduates treated it as a joke, older members of the university were outraged.

Geological harmony

Oxford is home to a profusion of architectural styles, and the fact that, by and large, these appear to hang together so harmoniously is largely down to the local limestone, of which most of the older buildings are constructed (*see page 72*). Nowhere is the harmonising power of the Oxford stone more evident than in Radcliffe Square, whose buildings were all built at different times but nevertheless combine to form one of the most magnificent architectural ensembles in Europe. And if you cross the High Street, the facade of Brasenose College (19th–20th-centuries), the spire of St Mary's (14th-century) and the portal of St Mary's (16th-century Baroque) all appear to be part of the same intricate scheme.

Stained glass

There are many fine examples of stained glass in Oxford, much of it, including the magnificent

east window of Merton Chapel, the handiwork of local medieval craftsmen. But foreign artists, too, played their part, the most prolific being the German Abraham von Linge, who arrived in the city in 1629. His exquisite craftsmanship and intense colours can be admired in the chapel of The Queen's College, as well as at Lincoln.

Later contributions came from William Morris and Edward Burne-Jones, who met while studying at Exeter College in the 1850s and were influenced by the ideas of John Ruskin and the Pre-Raphaelites. Exeter College chapel houses one of their tapestries of the Adoration of the Magi, but it was in stained glass that they left their most notable mark on Oxford, particularly in the chapels and choir of Christ Church.

Atmospheric streets

In the end, though, more than the details of great buildings, it's the overall effect of the city that most visitors remember. There are places where one can escape the 21st century and recapture the past. New College Lane has hardly changed since 1400, cobbled Merton Street maintains a quiet medieval air and Holywell Street, built in the early 17th century to rehouse those displaced by the building of the Bodleian, seems almost untouched. The lack of traffic in these streets helps. Walk down any of them at daybreak or dusk and the magic multiplies. ❑

MODERN CONTROVERSIES

Throughout the 20th century, controversy regularly courted new building plans, from the "Cotswold domestic" style of Nuffield College to what was seen as the totally alien International Style of Arne Jacobsen's St Catherine's College. Worcester College's Colditz-style watchtowers overlooking Hythe Bridge Street and the city council's nautical-themed Ice Rink apparently moored by the Thames in Oxpens both seemed out of place and, in the 21st century, the dull box that is the Saïd Business School and the exotic luxury of the Islamic Studies centre in Marston Road have both had their vociferous detractors.

LEFT: the Divinity School's lierne vaulted ceiling.
ABOVE TOP: Bath Place, a cobbled alley tucked off Holywell Street.
ABOVE LEFT AND RIGHT: this stained glass by Edward Burne-Jones can be admired at Christ Church.

Gargoyles

It's worth carrying binoculars to appreciate the intricacies of some of the countless carved heads gazing down on passers-by from Oxford's ancient buildings.

The carvings looking down at you from Oxford's buildings are a reminder of the university's medieval origins, yet many are quite modern, their faces inspired not by the piety of a Christian saint but by the lugubrious expression of some contemporary don or even the managing director of the firm that created the stone sculptures.

Although today's faces are purely ornamental, their original purpose was rigorously functional. Rainwater, channelled into them from roofs, was ejected through their mouths. This projected the water away from a building, stopping it running down the exterior walls, discolouring and decaying them. It was this "gargling" function that gave them the name gargoyles – probably after the French *gargouille* (throat). Carvings that don't have this purpose are more properly termed grotesques.

Vices and virtues

Animal-shaped waterspouts can be traced back to the ancient Egyptians and Etruscans, and the gargoyles that decorated Europe's Gothic cathedrals from the 12th century constituted a medieval bestiary. Gradually, human heads joined those of the beasts, and their creators' sense of mischief gave them an individuality that painters of the day seldom conveyed. Because facial subtleties could not easily be seen from ground level, there was a tendency to exaggerate features to the point of caricature.

The allegorical meaning of many gargoyles is a source of endless debate. Some obviously portray vices and virtues, from lust to temperance, reminding the citizenry

of the ever-present evils that tempt most mortals. But the majority of gargoyles may have been designed simply to entertain. Today's taste for horror movies and Tolkein's hobbits may once have been satisfied by the imagination that turned decorative waterspouts into works of art.

Wear and tear

Some original 13th-century carvings, such as those in Merton College's chapel and Christ Church Cathedral, have been preserved. But wind, rain and modern pollu-

tion are the enemies of outdoor carvings. The so-called Emperors' Heads in front of the Sheldonian Theatre, for example, were replaced in 1868 and then again between 1970 and 1972. The heads adorning New College are all modern.

For their own safety, the stone carvers create the replacement grotesques not *in situ* but in their yards and studios. The large blocks of which the heads form part are then hoisted into position. As is true of so many areas of knowledge, medieval stone-carving skills are kept alive in Oxford. ❑

RIGHT: extraordinary carved heads that look down at you with expressions ranging from joy to disgust.

PLACES

A detailed guide to the city, with the
principal sites clearly cross-referenced
by number to the maps

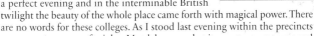

What, precisely, gives Oxford its special appeal? In 1856 the American writer Nathaniel Hawthorne, in his *English Note-Books*, put forward a theory: "The quality of the stone has a great deal to do with the apparent antiquity. It is a stone found in the neighbourhood of Oxford, and very soon begins to crumble and decay superficially, when exposed to the weather; so that 20 years do the work of a 100, so far as appearances go. If you strike one of the old walls with a stick, a portion of it comes powdering down. The effect of this decay is very picturesque."

Despite the subsequent destructive emissions of the internal combustion engine, Oxford's walls have yet to fall down. But the city retains its allure, seldom better expressed than by another 19th-century American writer, Henry James: "I walked along, thro' the lovely Christ Church meadow, by the river side and back through the town. It was a perfect evening and in the interminable British twilight the beauty of the whole place came forth with magical power. There are no words for these colleges. As I stood last evening within the precincts

of mighty Magdalen, gazed at its great serene tower and uncapped my throbbing brow in the wild dimness of its courts, I thought that the heart of me would crack with the fulness of satisfied desire."

The setting is equally magical. Oxford is not a large town and you don't need to climb far up one of the dreaming spires in order to spy the green countryside that encircles it. Beyond the town centre traffic jams and the undistinguished suburbs beckon the Cotswolds and their showpiece villages. For some, Stratford-upon-Avon will be a place of essential pilgrimage. For others, the sleepy Thames-side towns hold more attractions.

As Nathaniel Hawthorne put it: "The world, surely, has not another place like Oxford; it is a despair to see such a place and ever to leave it." ❏

PRECEDING PAGES: the pleasures of punting on the Cherwell; the classic "dreaming spires". **LEFT:** the Radcliffe Camera and its surroundings from the air. **ABOVE LEFT:** the Bridge of Sighs, a whimsical span between two sections of Hertford College.
ABOVE RIGHT: history perfectly preserved in an alleyway close to Brasenose.

Central Oxford

Woodstock

Banbury

Radcliffe Infirmary

Old Parsonage Hotel

Science & Nuclear Physics Faculties

Woodstock Road

Banbury Road

Parks Road

Keble Road

JERICHO

Oxford Canal

Juxon Street

Cranham Terrace

Cranham Street

Walton Street

Alvain St

Jericho St

Victor Street

Albert Street

Hart Street

Great Clarendon Street

St Giles'

St Aloysius

Keble Road

Blackhall Road

Kebl Colle

Somerville College

Oxford University Press

Cardigan St

Wellington St

Little Clarendon Street

Dartington House

University Offices

St Giles'

War Memorial

Queen Elizabeth House

St Barnabas

Cardigan

Canal Street

St Barnabas Street

Albert St

Walton Crescent

Walton Street

St Benet's Hall

Lamb & Flag

Museum

Nelson Street

Richmond Road

Walton Lane

Square

Wellington

Kellogg College

Regent's Park College

Pusey Street

Pusey House

St Cross College

St John's College

Sainsbury Building

Worcester Place

Ruskin College

Beaumont Buildings

Pusey Lane

St John Street

Blackfriars

Oriental Institute

Blackfriars College

WORCESTER COLLEGE CRICKET GROUND

Worcester College Lake

Ashmolean Museum

Taylor Institute

Worcester College

Beaumont Street

Randolph Hotel

Martyrs' Memorial

Balli Colle

Oxford Playhouse

St Mary Magdalen

Oxford Canal

Castle Mill Stream

Worcester St

Friars' Entry

Gloucester Street

New Theatre Oxford

Broad Stre

Gloucester Green

Bus Station

Magdalen St

Buck Stream

Said Business School

Hythe Bridge Street

Hythe Bridge

George Street

St Michael's St

St Michael-at-the-Northgate

Ship St

Oxford Union Society

Jes Col

Railway Station

Cripley Road

Bewley Rd

George St Mews

New Inn Hall Street

Cornmarket Street

Ma

Botley

Botley Road

Park End Street

Royal Oxford Hotel

Worcester St

Nuffield College

St Peter's College

Frewin Hall

Clarendon Centre

Tidmarsh Lane

Bulwarks Lane

Frewin Court

Shoe La.

Carfax Tower

New Road

Mill Street

St Thomas the Martyr

Hollybush Row

Woodbine Pl.

St Thomas Street

St George's Tower

Castle (remains)

Castle St

County Hall

Library

Queen Street

Tow Ha

Osney Lane

Paradise Square

Malmaison Hotel

Oxford Castle Unlocked

Westgate Shopping Centre

Modern Art Oxford (MAO)

Paradise Street

St Ebbe's Street

Pembroke St

St Alc

Beef Lane

ST EBBE'S

Pembroke College

Old Greyfriars Street

Norfolk Street

Oxford & Cherwell Valley College

Oxpens Road

Castle

Littlegate Street

Roger Bacon Lane

Campion Hall

Brewer St

Rose P

Albion Place

Street

Coach Station

Oxford Ice Rink

Mill Stream

Trinity St

Thames Street

Speedwell

Street S

Thames

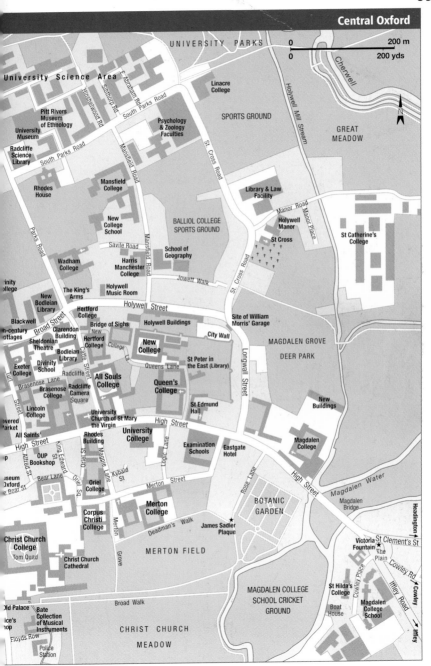

UNIVERSITY PARKS

0   200 m
0   200 yds

Cherwell

University Science Area

E. Abraham Rd

Sibthorp Rd

Husshwood Rd

South Parks Road

Linacre College

SPORTS GROUND

Holywell Mill Stream

GREAT MEADOW

Pitt Rivers Museum of Ethnology

University Museum

Radcliffe Science Library

South Parks Road

Psychology & Zoology Faculties

St. Cross Road

Mansfield Road

Rhodes House

Mansfield College

Library & Law Facility

Manor Road

Manor Place

St Catherine's College

New College School

BALLIOL COLLEGE SPORTS GROUND

Holywell Manor

Parks Road

Savile Road

School of Geography

St Cross

Wadham College

Harris Manchester College

Jowett Walk

St. Cross Road

inity ollege

New Bodleian Library

The King's Arms

Holywell Music Room

Holywell Street

Site of William Morris' Garage

MAGDALEN GROVE DEER PARK

Blackwell

Broad Street

Hertford College

Bridge of Sighs

Holywell Buildings

City Wall

Longwall Street

n-century ottages

Clarendon Building

Sheldonian Theatre

New Hertford College

College

New College

City Wall

Exeter College

Bodleian Library

Divinity School

Radcliffe

St Peter in the East (Library)

Brasenose Lane

Brasenose College

Radcliffe Camera Square

All Souls College

Queens Lane

Queen's College

St Edmund Hall

New Buildings

Lincoln College

University Church of St Mary the Virgin

High Street

Magdalen College

overed arket

All Saints'

Rhodes Building

University College

High Street

Examination Schools

Eastgate Hotel

Rose Lane

OUP Bookshop

King Edward St

Alfred St

Bear Lane

Magpie Lane

Kybald St

Logic Lane

High Street

Magdalen Water

useum Oxford e Boat

Oriel Sq

Oriel College

Merton Street

Magdalen Bridge

Headington

Corpus Christi College

Merton

Merton College

Deadman's Walk

James Sadler Plaque

BOTANIC GARDEN

Victoria Fountain

St Clement's St

The Plain

Cowley Rd

Christ Church College

Tom Quad

Christ Church Cathedral

Grove

MERTON FIELD

St Hilda's College

Cowley Place

Iffley Road

Cowley

Iffley

ld Palace

ice's hop

Bate Collection of Musical Instruments

Broad Walk

MAGDALEN COLLEGE SCHOOL CRICKET GROUND

Boat House

Magdalen College School

Floyds Row

Police Station

CHRIST CHURCH MEADOW

THE HUB OF THE UNIVERSITY

One area of town can be described as the heart of the university. Lying between the High Street and Broad Street, it includes the Bodleian Library, the Sheldonian Theatre and the Radcliffe Camera

Main Attractions

THE EMPERORS' HEADS
SHELDONIAN THEATRE
BODLEIAN LIBRARY
DIVINITY SCHOOL
DUKE HUMFREY'S LIBRARY
RADCLIFFE CAMERA
ALL SOULS COLLEGE
BRASENOSE COLLEGE
CHURCH OF ST MARY THE
VIRGIN

Maps and Listings

MAP OF THE HUB OF THE
UNIVERSITY, PAGE 88
ACCOMMODATION, PAGES
256–7

A precious and rather feeble Oxford joke is sometimes told about the American tourist who stops an undergraduate in the High Street and asks to be directed to the university. At this point, those in the know are supposed to chuckle over their port for – "as every educated person is aware" – Oxford does not have a central university campus. Along with Cambridge, these two ancient universities differ from others in Britain in that they constitute a federation of independent colleges.

Yet, if our American tourist had stopped a helpful student instead of a prig, he would have been directed down Broad Street to the heart of Oxford, where an impressive group of buildings might loosely be termed "the university" – in the sense that they provide central facilities for all college members.

The Emperors' Heads

Walking east down **Broad Street**, the eye is drawn to the curious set of railings that separate "the town" from the realm of ceremony and scholarship. Towering above the railings is a series of 13 outsize stone busts, the **Emperors' Heads**, or Bearded Ones ❶. They follow the curve of the apsidal end of the Sheldonian Theatre, and were put up in 1669, the year the theatre was completed.

Armless busts like these have been used to surmount gateposts since antiquity, and are called "terms", from the Latin terminus, a boundary, or "herms" if they represent Hermes, the messenger of the gods. Nobody knows what these splendid giants represent. Max Beerbohm, in his 1911 Oxford-based novel *Zuleika Dobson*,

LEFT: an archway at the Bodleian Library leads through to Radcliffe Camera.
RIGHT: chancellor and beadle on the way to a ceremony at the Sheldonian Theatre.

wrote that "they are, by American visitors, frequently mistaken for the Twelve Apostles" – having yet another dig at the poor, untutored tourist from the New World. He also calls them "the faceless Caesars", and perhaps from that developed the current nickname, the Emperors.

Faceless they were until recently; the original terms were replaced in 1868 but with such poor-quality stone that time and the weather soon reduced their features to what John Betjeman called "illustrations in a medical textbook on skin diseases". In 1970, and despite Henry Moore's objection that the eroded heads had their own awesome power, the Oxford sculptor Michael Black was commissioned to carve new heads. After completing the work in 1972, and following exhaustive research into the form of the original heads, Michael Black added his own theory, that the 13 represent the history of fashions in beards.

ABOVE: the Emperors' Heads are also known as the Bearded Ones.
BELOW: The Sheldonian Theatre

The Sheldonian Theatre ❷

Tel: 01865-277 299
Opening Hrs: Mar–Oct Mon–Sat 10am–12.30pm, 2–4.30pm, Nov–Feb until 3.30pm; closed Sat afternoon on performance days and for university events
Entrance Fee: Charge

In any event, the Sheldonian terms make an impressive approach to the buildings beyond, starting with the **Sheldonian Theatre**. The theatre was commissioned by Gilbert Sheldon, chancellor (or honorary head) of the university, in 1662. Sheldon chose as his architect, the young Christopher Wren, who was then 30. Wren had been appointed Professor of Astronomy the previous year and was regarded as one of the most brilliant mathematicians of his day. He had not yet, however, designed any buildings, and the Sheldonian Theatre was the first commission to launch his architectural career.

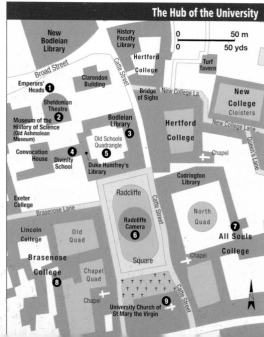

The Hub of the University

New Bodleian Library
History Faculty Library
Broad Street
Hertford College
Turf Tavern
0   50 m
0   50 yds
Emperors' Heads ❶
Clarendon Building
Bridge of Sighs
New College La.
New College Cloisters
Sheldonian Theatre ❷
Bodleian Library ❸
New College Lane
Museum of the History of Science (Old Ashmolean Museum)
Old Schools Quadrangle
Hertford College
Convocation House ❹
Divinity School
Duke Humfrey's Library ❺
Chapel
Codrington Library
Exeter College
Radcliffe
Catte Street
North Quad
Brasenose Lane
Lincoln College
Old Quad
Radcliffe Camera ❻
All Souls College ❼
Brasenose College ❽
Chapel Quad
Square
Chapel
University Church of St Mary the Virgin ❾
Catte Street

It is fashionable among art historians to describe the theatre as the work of a young amateur, but most of us would give this exuberant building, with its rich, honey-gold coloured stone, far higher praise. It was also revolutionary in its time, for Wren rejected the popular Jacobean-Gothic style and chose instead to follow classical antecedents.

Wren modelled the Sheldonian on the antique open-air Theatre of Marcellus, in Rome. The English weather made it necessary to give it a roof, however, so Wren devised an ingenious timber structure (since replaced) that dispensed with pillars and allowed all 2,000 spectators an uninterrupted view of the proceedings. In place of the open sky, Robert Streeter was commissioned, in 1669, to paint the ceiling with a depiction of the *Triumph of Religion, Arts and Science over Envy, Hate and Malice*.

The Sheldonian was built for university ceremonials, rather than for stage drama, and is still used for this purpose, as well as for concerts and lectures. Here, successful students receive their degrees and, at the "Encaenia" ceremony in June, scarlet-gowned dons meet to honour the university founders and bestow honorary degrees upon the worthy and famous *(see also pages 132–3)*.

At other times of the year the theatre is open to the public and is well worth visiting for the original woodwork of the chancellor's throne and the two orators' pulpits – but most of all for the fine views over the heart of Oxford from the rooftop cupola.

The Clarendon Building

On the other side of the Sheldonian is the **Clarendon Building**, created to provide the first permanent home for Oxford University Press. Originally, the Press occupied odd rooms in the Sheldonian Theatre – an inconvenient arrangement.

Between 1702 and 1704 the Press published the Earl of Clarendon's account of the English Civil War, and this three-volume *History of the Great Rebellion* proved to be a best-seller. Despite the fact that some of the profits were embezzled by the university vice-chancellor, sales of Clarendon's work were sufficient to

ABOVE: rare leather-bound books in Duke Humfrey's Library.
BELOW: a degree ceremony in the Sheldonian.

As a copyright library, the Bodleian is obliged to accept a copy of every book and journal published in the UK. The result is that space for books is rapidly running out, despite the more than 80 miles (130km) of shelving that have been installed just a few feet beneath the surface of Radcliffe Square.

provide the Press with a new home next door.

The Clarendon, a rather severe classical building, was designed by Nicholas Hawksmoor, Christopher Wren's brilliant pupil, and completed in 1715. The Earl of Clarendon himself occupies a niche on the west wall, where he gesticulates proudly at the building he paid for. Around the roofline are gracious figures, by James Thornhill, of the nine Muses (1717); seven are cast in lead but two are fibre-glass replicas, made in 1974 to replace the originals that had blown down.

The Press moved out of the Clarendon Building in 1830 and the space vacated by the compositors and printers is now filled by part of the Bodleian Library's vast collection of books.

The Bodleian Library ❸

Tel: 01865-277 2924
Opening Hrs: guided tours included in Divinity School tour. Tour of Divinity School, Convocation House and Duke Humfrey's Library: Mon–Sat 10.30am, 11.30am, 2pm and 3pm, university ceremonies permitting. Divinity School

BELOW: the Clarendon Building.

only: Mon–Fri 9am–5pm, Sat 10am–4.30pm
Entrance Fee: Charge

To the south of the Sheldonian lies the **Bodleian Library**, which is entered through a small opening into Old Schools Quadrangle. Before admiring this beautiful courtyard in too much detail, first journey back in time by entering the doors behind the 17th-century bronze statue by Le Sueur of the Earl of Pembroke (a university chancellor) and proceeding through the vestibule into the much older Divinity School.

Divinity School

Regarded by many as the finest interior in Oxford, work began on this central school of theology known as **Divinity School** ❹ *(see above for guided tours)* in 1426, following an appeal for funds by the university. As it was the most important of all faculties, Divinity required a suitable space, but money kept running out and the room took almost 60 years to complete.

Its crowning glory is the lierne-vaulted ceiling, which was added in

Thomas Bodley

Thomas Bodley (1545–1613) spent his youth in Geneva, since as a member of a Protestant family he was liable to religious persecution under the reign of Mary I. When Elizabeth I came to the throne, he returned to England, where, after studying at Oxford, he became a diplomat and was briefly an MP. On his return to Oxford as a fellow of Merton College, the now knighted Sir Thomas Bodley resolved in 1598 to take action to restore Duke Humfrey's Library, wrecked during the reign of Edward VI. He established a collection of 2,000 books, some captured during the 1596 plundering of Cádiz by the Earl of Essex, and the new library opened in 1602. In 1604 it was named the Bodleian.

and the coats of arms of university benefactors.

Candidates for degrees of Bachelor and Doctor of Divinity were not the only people to demonstrate their dialectical skill under this glorious ceiling. It was here that the Oxford Martyrs – Latimer, Ridley and Cranmer – were cross-examined by the Papal Commissioner in 1554, then condemned as Protestant heretics.

Now it is empty, except for an iron-bound chest, with its elaborate lock mechanism, that once belonged to Thomas Bodley, the library's founder. The chest is used to collect donations towards a £10-million appeal for vital restoration work that will eventually allow books back on display in a temperature and humidity-controlled environment. In the meantime, there is a small display of exhibits, ranging from early copies of Chaucer's *Canterbury Tales* to Victorian playbills, in the School of Natural Philosophy, on the south side of Old Schools Quad.

1478, after the university received a gift from Thomas Kemp, the bishop of London. Completed by local mason William Orchard, the ceiling is adorned with sculpted figures and 455 bosses carved with biblical subjects, real and mythical beasts,

Duke Humfrey's Library

In around 1440, a substantial collection of manuscripts was donated

ABOVE LEFT: arriving at the Bodleian.
ABOVE: the Earl of Pembroke's statue in the Old Schools Quadrangle. **BELOW:** Duke Humfrey's Library

ABOVE: the Old Schools Quadrangle, in the Jacobean-Gothic style.

The New Bodleian
The Bodleian Library has always been a reading library, from which no book could ever be borrowed. In 1939, the New Bodleian was completed to take some of the overspill. This fortress-like building opposite the Clarendon, on the corner of Broad Street and Parks Road, has three floors of underground storage beneath Blackwell's bookshop. A conveyor belt beneath Broad Street links the new and old libraries.

to the university by Humfrey, Duke of Gloucester, the younger brother of Henry V. The walls of the Divinity School were built up to create a second storey for **Duke Humfrey's Library,** now the centrepiece of what is overall the Bodleian Library *(see page 90 for guided tours)*. Duke Humfrey's Library, with its magnificent beamed ceiling, was first opened to readers in 1488, but was defunct by 1550, largely as a result of neglect and the emergence of book printing (which rendered manuscripts redundant), but also due to the depredations of the King's Commissioners after the dissolution.

It was while he was a student at Magdalen College that Thomas Bodley became aware of this sad state of affairs and resolved to take action *(see panel on page 90)*. The library he founded in 1602 was soon extended with an "Arts End" and, around 1650, by the "Selden End", named after John Selden, who gave 8,000 volumes to the library. Both

the "Ends" have beautiful panelled and painted ceilings.

Today visitors can see original leather-bound books dating from the 17th century, some of them turned spine inwards so that chaining them to the shelves (a common practice) would cause less damage. Sometimes visitors are also shown the top floor of the library, with its painted frieze of 200 famous men, which dates from around 1620 but was only rediscovered in the 1960s.

Old Schools Quadrangle

In 1610, an agreement was made whereby the library would receive a copy of every single book registered at Stationers' Hall. Soon Bodley's collection had grown so large that a major extension was required, hence the **Old Schools Quadrangle ⑤**. This magnificent piece of architecture is designed in Jacobean-Gothic style (a style that characterises many Oxford buildings of the early 17th century). The quadrangle has a wonderful serenity, and despite being built much higher than college quads it is still light and airy.

The complex was designed to provide lecture rooms on the lower floors, and library space above. Above the ground-floor doorways, painted in letters of gold, are the names of the original schools, or faculties, of the university. Note that the Divinity School facade, covered in panel tracery, is considerably more ornate than the rest of Old Schools Quad – appropriately enough, as Divinity, or Theology, was the principal subject at Oxford until well into the 19th century and the subject for which all other studies were merely a preparation.

Three sides of the quad are regular in composition. James I was on the throne when the building was completed in 1624, and the monarch sits in a niche between allegorical figures representing fame and the university, in the gate-tower at the east end. This splendidly carved work is called the **Tower of the Five Orders** because it is ornamented with columns and capitals

of each of the five orders of classical architecture – Doric, Tuscan, Ionic, Corinthian and Composite – in ascending order.

You will find many more heads (binoculars are essential to appreciate them fully) carved in stone all around the battlement line of Old Schools Quad – grotesques and demons, angels and men, all convincingly medieval in appearance but, in fact, the inspired work of masons who restored these buildings in the 1950s. At ground-floor level as you pass through the passageway between the schools of Music and Natural Philosophy, look for the portraits of two recent librarians, carved into the stone.

The Radcliffe Camera

Emerging to the south of the Old Schools Quadrangle, the splendid sight of the **Radcliffe Camera** ❻ rising from a perfect green lawn meets the eye. "Camera" simply means chamber, and John Radcliffe was the physician who, despite his renowned ill temper, made a huge fortune by treating the wealthy –

ABOVE: a medieval window at All Souls College captures St Etheldreda.
BELOW: The Radcliffe Camera.

including the monarch, William III. The Radcliffe Camera was built after his death in 1714 to house a library devoted to the sciences – just one of the Oxford projects that was funded from his estate.

The gracious round form of the Camera was suggested by Nicholas Hawksmoor, but it was another great 18th-century architect, James Gibbs, who was asked to produce the detailed designs.

The building was completed in 1748 and absorbed as a reading room of the Bodleian in 1860. The Radcliffe Camera was just part of a grand 18th-century scheme to open up this part of the city as a public square, to replace the existing jumble of medieval houses.

All Souls College ❼

Tel: 01865-279 379
Opening Hrs: Mon–Fri 2–4pm; parties of more than six need permission from the bursar
Entrance Fee: Free

BELOW: the porch of Brasenose College chapel.

Hawksmoor did, eventually, get his fair share of Oxford commissions, including the great North Quad

of **All Souls College.** This college, founded in 1438, is unique: it does not admit undergraduates, nor even graduate students in the conventional way. Instead, it retains the medieval tradition of restricting membership to "fellows".

There are several means of entry: distinguished scholars from all over the world may be elected as visiting fellows, while others sit a highly competitive examination. The system is, in theory, designed to provide facilities for the brightest and best minds to pursue their research, but it has not always been so, and in the 16th century fellowships were bought and sold, and the college was notorious for the drunkenness and corruption of its members.

A century or so later, the winds of reform swept through the college and, as if in a symbolic break with the past, the medieval cloister was cleared away, and new accommodation planned. Then, in 1710, before the work began, Christopher Codrington, a fellow and governor of the Leeward Islands, died, leaving much of his sugar wealth to the col-

lege, as well as a large collection of books. Thus the building plans were changed, and Hawksmoor designed the grand library block and the imposing twin towers of the east side of the North Quad.

The **Codrington Library** (viewing times same as All Souls College) is an ingenious piece of work; outside it is all Gothic, while the interior is fully classical – even the windows are Venetian within but with lancets and tracery on the outside. The sundial on the library wall, moved from the chapel, is renowned for its accuracy; Christopher Wren is reputed to be the designer.

The chapel is essentially 15th-century, with its original hammer-beam roof carved with gilded angels and misericords, which include depictions of a mermaid and a man playing the bagpipes. The floor-to-ceiling reredos is a *tour de force*, although the statues are all replacements, installed in 1870, for those smashed by Puritan iconoclasts. The surviving 15th-century niches were once brightly painted and even now a few have traces of the original pigment.

Brasenose College ⓑ

Tel: 01865-277 830
Opening Hrs: daily 2–4.30pm
Entrance Fee: Charge for groups only

On the opposite (west) side of the

ABOVE: the North Quad of All Souls.
BELOW LEFT: Brasenose College.

How Brasenose Got Its Name

The college is named after the "brazen nose", a bronze door knocker that once hung on the gates of Brasenose Hall. Anyone fleeing from the law could claim sanctuary within the hall if they could get their hands firmly round the ring of the knocker.

Perhaps because of the protective powers of the brazen nose, a group of students stole the ring in the 1330s and took it with them to Stamford where they intended to establish a rival university. Edward II refused to sanction the breakaway institution, but while some students settled in Cambridge, others returned to Oxford and the brazen nose got left behind. Here it remained, serving as a door knocker, until Brasenose House in Stamford came on the market in 1890. Even then, the college had to buy the whole house to secure the return of the symbolic piece of bronze – now hung behind the High Table in the dining hall.

Meanwhile, a new knocker was commissioned for Brasenose, on the occasion of its official foundation as a college, as distinct from the pre-existing academic hall, in 1509. Shaped like a human head, this is now fixed at the apex of the main gate of the college.

square is **Brasenose College**. Passing through the entrance, you reach the Old Quad with its Tudor buildings, completed shortly after the foundation; the third storey, with its fine dormer windows, was added in the early 17th century. The sundial on the right-hand side was painted in 1719.

The dining hall, on the left side, is usually open, so that the original brazen nose (*see panel on previous page*) can be viewed. First mentioned in a document of 1279, the Romanesque feline head and ring could have been made as early as the 12th century.

A passageway in the southeastern corner leads into Chapel Quad, with its delightful library, carved with a frieze of exuberant swags, and lit below by pairs of oval windows. This work dates to the mid-17th century and is surprisingly innovative for its date, foreshadowing the 18th-century's Baroque style.

- The chapel is of the same date and mixes Gothic with classical motifs. The unusual fan-vaulted and painted roof is made of plaster. In the ante-chapel is a bronze plaque with a Greek inscription celebrating Walter Pater (died 1894), the writer and aesthete. He is portrayed at the centre of a tree whose other branches bear portrait medallions of Plato, Dante, Leonardo da Vinci and Michelangelo. The implication that Pater deserved to stand alongside these great artists reminds us that his precious and overblown style was once deemed the epitome of fine writing.

As you turn to leave the college, you realise what a splendid view the students and fellows enjoy, being so close to Radcliffe Square. The huge dome of the Radcliffe Camera looms above the entrance tower and the spire of St Mary's church to the right.

St Mary the Virgin

Returning to Radcliffe Square, the huge university church of **St Mary the Virgin** fronts on to the High Street. In its grandeur it rivals many cathedrals and can be regarded as the

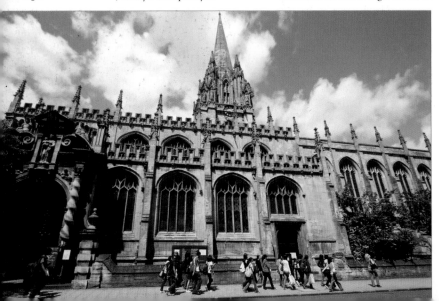

(Mon–Sat 9am–5pm, Sun 11.45am–5pm; charge), which dates to the late 13th and early 14th centuries. You need to be fit: there are 127 steps and the last few form a narrow spiral staircase.

The gangway at the base of the spire offers a magnificent view, revealing not only the layout of the city and many of the colleges, but just how much green space there is in the heart of Oxford.

The rest of the church was rebuilt in Perpendicular style in the early 16th century and is really rather dull, except for the eccentric south porch at the High Street side, added in 1637 and designed by Nicholas Stone. Fat barley-sugar columns support the curvaceous pediment, and angels surround the central niche containing a statue of the Virgin and Child. Perhaps the Virgin's rather startled look is a legacy of the English Civil War, for her head was shot off by a soldier in 1642 – but replaced 20 years later.

original hub of the university, for it was here in the 13th century that the first university meetings and ceremonies were held, and all the administrative documents kept.

Before entering via its north door, you'll see the sign to the **Vaults & Garden Coffee House**. There can be few cafés with such a history, for it occupies the space of the former Convocation House, an annex built in 1320 specifically to house the university governing body, which continued to meet here until 1534 when the administration moved to Convocation House at the Divinity School.

A library was installed above it, but this was later replaced by Duke Humfrey's Library. The café serves wholesome soups, sandwiches and cakes, and the garden, sheltered by shrubs, is delightful in summer.

Now, instead of disputatious students sharpening their wits in learned debate, the church is often full of visitors queuing to climb the 188ft (62-metre) spire-topped **Tower**

ABOVE LEFT: Brasenose's sundial.
ABOVE: view of the High Street from St Mary's.
BELOW RIGHT: the nave of St Mary the Virgin.

Inside the church, the pillar opposite the pulpit in the north side of the nave has been cut away; this was done to build a platform for the final trial of Thomas Cranmer, archbishop of Canterbury, in 1556. His fellow martyrs, Nicholas Ridley, bishop of London, and Hugh Latimer, bishop of Worcester, had both been executed at the stake the previous year for their support of the Protestant Reforma-

tion. Cranmer, however, was given leave to appeal against his sentence, and signed several statements recanting his earlier beliefs.

Burnt at the stake

This was not sufficient for his accusers, the Pope's commissioners and the zealous supporters of the Catholic Queen Mary. Cranmer was brought to St Mary's to make a public statement of his errors, but he refused to do so, and instead retracted his former recantations. Like Ridley and Latimer before him, having been dragged from St Mary's Church he was burned at the stake in Broad Street (he was imprisoned first at Bocardo Prison, by the church of St Michael at the North Gate, and brought to St Mary's for the final verdict).

Return along Catte Street, looking back to admire Radcliffe Square. The view is at its most splendid from opposite the Bridge of Sighs (*see page 147*). The gateway to the Old Schools Quadrangle, the dome of the Radcliffe Camera and the spire of St Mary's create one of the finest urban panoramas in Europe. ❏

Opposite this point near the Cross in the middle of Broad Street HUGH LATIMER one time Bishop of Worcester, NICHOLAS RIDLEY Bishop of London, and THOMAS CRANMER Archbishop of Canterbury, were burnt for their faith in 1555 and 1556.

H.H.

The Oxford Movement

In 1833 John Keble preached a famous sermon in St Mary the Virgin, leading to the foundation of the Oxford Movement. John Henry Newman, then Vicar of St Mary's and a leading supporter of the movement, brought down a storm of indignation for his increasingly pro-Catholic views; his sillier supporters affected an ascetic appearance, fasted on toast and water and smoked Spanish (Catholic) cigars – while some colleges altered the times of compulsory chapel services to keep students away from Newman's sermons. In the end, he resigned, became a Catholic and ended up a cardinal. To this day Oxford remains a centre of High Church Anglo-Catholicism.

They Studied Here

Oxford has been a centre of teaching since the 12th century, and numerous are the heads of state, writers, scientists and other luminaries who have studied here.

The catalogue of the Great, the Good and the Notorious who have attended Oxford University is a lengthy one. Part of the fun of exploring the city lies in knowing that so many of the world's most illustrious people also once walked those same cobbled streets.

Prime ministers

Two dozen British prime ministers have been educated at Oxford. In recent times they have included Clement Attlee, Sir Anthony Eden, Harold Macmillan, Sir Alec Douglas-Home, Harold Wilson, Edward Heath, Margaret Thatcher and Tony Blair.

Writers

John Ruskin (1819–1900), who was at Christ Church until 1836, became a renowned art critic and author. The poet Percy Bysshe Shelley (1792–1822) was sent down from Oxford for his pamphlet *The Necessity of Atheism*. Other literary luminaries include the lexicographer Dr Samuel Johnson (Pembroke 1728); Oscar Wilde (Magdalen 1874); Robert Browning (1812–89), who attended Balliol; and Lewis Carroll (Charles Dodgson), a mathematics don at Christ Church and author of *Alice in Wonderland*. More recent names include J.R.R. Tolkien, W.H. Auden, Robert Graves, Graham Greene, Evelyn Waugh and T.S. Eliot.

Philosophers

These include Thomas Hobbes (Magdalen Hall, 1603), who published *The Leviathan* in 1651; John Locke (Christ Church, c.1654) and Jeremy Bentham (Queen's, 1760).

Top Left: Clement Attlee.
Bottom Right: Indira Gandhi.

Scientists

Roger Bacon first studied arts at Oxford in 1231, then devoted himself to experimental science, especially alchemy and optics. Founder of English philosophy, he became a Franciscan friar in 1257. Robert Boyle (in Oxford 1654–68) with Robert Hooke (1635–1708) laid the foundation for chemistry and physics. The Astronomer Royal, Edmund Halley, (1656–1742) was at Queen's, 1673. He was the first to predict the return of a comet and his meteorological observations led to his publication of the first map of the winds of the globe (1686).

In 1945 Oxford scientists Howard Walter Florey and E.B. Chain shared the Nobel Prize with Alexander Fleming for the clinical development of penicillin. The most widely used antibiotic today, cephalosporin, was discovered in 1955 by Edward Abraham, working in a University laboratory.

Men of religion

The poet John Donne (1572–1631) attended Hart Hall (now Hertford College). John Wesley (1703–91) was at Christ Church. John Henry Newman (1801–90), best remembered for his *Apologia pro Vita Sua*, tracing the development of his religious thought, graduated from Trinity.

Women graduates

Well-known women graduates are mostly writers or politicians: Dorothy L. Sayers (Somerville, 1920), Indira Gandhi, Dame Iris Murdoch (both Somerville, 1938), and Benazir Bhutto (Lady Margaret Hall, 1973).

Musicians

Famous musicians from Christ Church are Sir William Walton and Sir Adrian Boult. Sir Thomas Beecham was at Wadham.

Young students

Some precocious students just couldn't wait to attend Oxford. Ruth Lawrence, born in 1971, came up to Oxford when she was 11 and graduated with First-Class Honours in mathematics at 13. ❑

THE HIGH

High Street, known as "The High", has a grace and elegance unmatched elsewhere in the city, inspiring Nikolaus Pevsner to describe it as "one of the world's greatest streets"

Main Attractions

UNIVERSITY COLLEGE
SHELLEY'S MONUMENT
QUEEN'S COLLEGE
EXAMINATION SCHOOLS
MAGDALEN COLLEGE
MAGDALEN GROVE (DEER PARK)
ST HILDA'S COLLEGE

Maps and Listings

MAP OF THE HIGH, PAGE 102
RESTAURANTS, CAFÉS, PUBS AND BARS, PAGE 113
ACCOMMODATION, PAGES 256–7

The High Street is different from other streets in central Oxford in that it is curved. This is because the layout of the original Saxon town was out of alignment with the crossing point of the River Cherwell to the east, at the site of Magdalen Bridge. So beyond the original east gate (where St Mary the Virgin church now stands) the road, then nothing more than a track, began a gentle curve down to the river. Over the centuries, not only colleges but also inns and shops were built, resulting in the charming street we see today.

History in the making

The High Street has always been busy with local and long-distance traffic. In the 18th and 19th centuries, the coach-and-four to London departed with ever-increasing rapidity from coaching inns such as the Angel and the Mitre. Since the car arrived, there have been attempts to limit the numbers of vehicles, including a radical (but abandoned) scheme to construct a link road from St Ebbe's across Christ Church Meadow. In 1999, the most radical shake-up of Oxford's

transport scheme in decades closed the western end of the High as far as Longwall Street to all traffic except delivery vans and buses.

The Carfax end is the commercial end, mostly taken up by shops and the facade of the Covered Market *(see page 129)*. But there are interesting details worth examining. Starting on the south side, at No. 137, is Savory's fragrant pipe and tobacco shop, in a medieval building that was once the Fox Inn. Also take a look at the sign above the silversmiths at **No. 131**, a

LEFT: the High Street, not far from the countryside.
RIGHT: detail from J.M.W. Turner's portrait of the High Street.

white dog with a giant watch in its mouth. Just here, a small alley – one of many that delineated the original medieval plots along this part of the street – leads down to the Chequers Inn, a tavern dating from the 15th century with many interesting features. The next alley along is signposted to the Chiang Mai Kitchen, a Thai restaurant housed in the beautiful **Kemp Hall ❶**. Built by an Oxford alderman in 1637, this is a fine example of the numerous timber-framed houses that sprang up all over Oxford during the great rebuilding of the city in the 16th and 17th centuries. The timber door with its projecting canopy is original, as are many of the windows; the interior is also very well preserved.

Back on the High Street, the next building of interest is **No. 126**. With its elegantly curved windows and fine proportions, this is the best preserved example of a 17th-century facade in Oxford. But the building itself actu-

ABOVE: outside the Mitre, on the High Street.

ally dates back a lot further, for it is known to have been owned by a bell founder before being taken over by St Frideswide's Abbey in 1350. This is the story of many of the buildings along the High Street – medieval in origin but given new facades later.

The Mitre

Cross the road at the traffic lights to arrive at the **Mitre ❷**, now housing a restaurant and tearoom but once a popular student inn. It was built in about 1600 over a 13th-century vault, which sadly can no longer be visited. Nevertheless, the Mitre remains full of history, enlivened by anecdotes of ale-supping clergy.

The German clergyman Pastor Moritz relates in his *Travels in England* (1795) that he was taken there by a companion and found it full of convivial parsons debating whether or not a passage in the *Book of Judges* ("wine cheereth God and man") meant literally that God was a wine

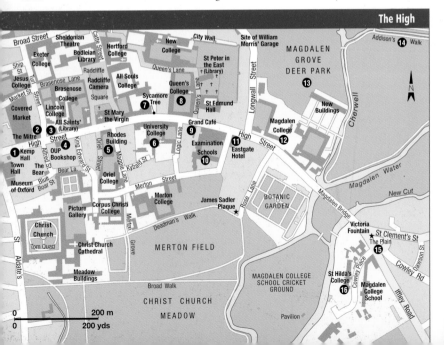

The High

tippler. A sign in the lobby recalls the Mitre's role as a coaching inn.

The Mitre stands on the corner of Turl Street *(see page 141)*, and on the opposite corner stands the former **All Saints' Church** ❸, now used as a library by Lincoln College. The splendid tower was rebuilt, partly to the designs of Nicholas Hawksmoor, after the original tower collapsed in 1700. Beyond this is the High Street frontage to Brasenose College *(see page 96)*, which, despite looking positively medieval, was built only in the latter part of the 19th and early 20th centuries.

On the south side is a fine run of buildings with 18th-century facades. The Regency bow-fronted shop window of Ede and Ravenscroft, University Tailors, is used to display silk-lined academic gowns and clothing embroidered with multicoloured college crests. **No. 117/118** has a fine Art-Nouveau shop window, while next door at No. 116 are the premises of the **Oxford University Press Bookshop** ❹ (Mon–Sat 9am–6pm), which sells only the books that the Press publishes. Further down, beyond

King Edward Street, **Nos 106** and **107** (The University of Oxford Shop and A-Plan Insurance) are particularly interesting. Together they were originally **Tackley's Inn**, built in 1320 and subsequently rented out for use as an academic hall. A-Plan may allow you through to the back of their premises to see the 16th-century roof structure of the hall as well as a large medieval window. The cellar is regarded as the best medieval cellar in Oxford.

The Rhodes Building

On the other side of Oriel Street, opposite the University Church of St Mary the Virgin *(see page 96)*, is the **Rhodes Building** ❺ of Oriel College, built in 1910 from funds bequeathed by Cecil Rhodes, the South African statesman who made a fortune in Southern Africa after completing his education at Oriel and ultimately gave his name to Rhodesia (now Zimbabwe). Rhodes also endowed Rhodes Scholarships at Oxford, one of the most notable beneficiaries being Bill Clinton.

Continue along the south side, cross Magpie Lane past the former

ABOVE: Oxford University Press.
BELOW: the Rhodes Building.

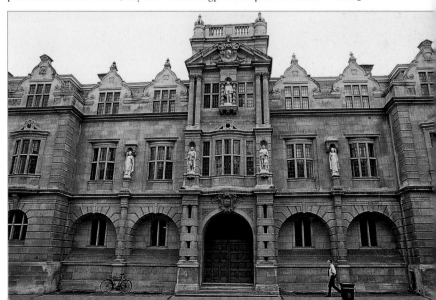

Barclays Bank buildings, now the Old Bank Hotel and Quod restaurant. Opposite is All Souls College *(see page 94)*. Dating from the 14th century, this is the oldest surviving part of the college, though it was refaced in the 19th century. A line of grotesque sculptures runs beneath the parapet.

University College ⑥

Tel: 01865-276 602
Opening Hrs: enquire at the porter's lodge for permission to enter
Entrance Fee: Free

Still on the south side, we now come to the long frontage of **University College**. The claim that "Univ" was founded by King Alfred was invented by medieval lawyers, but it did not stop the college celebrating its millennium in 1874. Even without this fiction, Univ is respectably ancient: William of Durham, who had fled from Paris after a row between the kings of France and England, left funds for its foundation in 1249, and on this basis it can claim to be the oldest college. None of the original buildings remain, however, the college having been rebuilt from substantial benefactions in the 17th century in the now familiar Oxford Jacobean-Gothic style.

The range facing The High is in two parts: first the **Front Quad** (with main entrance), completed in the 1670s, and beyond, the **Radcliffe Quad**, almost an exact copy, completed 40 years later. The gate towers contain, respectively, the statues of Queen Anne (which replaced a statue of King Alfred in 1700) and Queen Mary. On the inner face of the front quad is a statue of James II, wearing a toga, one of only two statues in England of this unpopular Catholic king. It was erected in 1676 by the then master, Obadiah Walker, who supported the monarch's religious views.

Shelley's Monument

Before reaching the main range, you may have noticed a small dome peeping above the wall. This covers the **memorial to Percy Bysshe Shelley**. Shelley spent less than six months as an undergraduate at Univ, having been expelled in 1811 for his joint authorship of a pamphlet on *The Necessity of Atheism*. Some 80 years later, in 1894, Lady Shelley presented the monument to the college. Designed by Edward Onslow Ford, it was intended for the poet's grave, in

ABOVE: the chapel at Queen's College.
BELOW: Shelley's Monument in University College.

the English Cemetery in Rome, but was found to be too large. The life-sized sculpture of the naked, drowned poet (he perished off Livorno in 1822), supported by winged lions and the Muse of Poetry, is shockingly pathetic. It can be reached via a passageway in the northwest corner of the Front Quad.

Another attraction of the college is the **Chapel**. Although refurbished by Sir George Gilbert Scott in 1862, it still retains its original, finely detailed stained glass, designed by the German artist Abraham von Linge – his last known work and full of exotic details. The ante-chapel contains fine monuments by Flaxman, including that of Sir William Jones (died 1794), judge in the Calcutta High Court, who is shown compiling his digest of Hindu law.

On the north side of the High, directly opposite the gatehouse of University College's front quad, stands a lone **sycamore tree** , whose presence endows the High Street with a rural flavour. As the only landmark that can be seen from both ends, it has long been regarded as Oxford's most significant tree and has even been described as one of the most important trees in Europe.

Queen's College

Tel: 01865-279 120
Opening Hrs: access only with an official guided tour booked at the Oxford Information Centre, tel: 01865-252 200
Entrance Fee: Charge

To the right of the tree runs the beautiful Baroque facade of **Queen's College**. Facade is perhaps the wrong term, for the High Street front is no more than a screen, with a handsome domed gatehouse, containing a statue of Queen Caroline. All this work was once attributed to Nicholas Hawksmoor, but is now thought to be by the local Oxford mason William Townesend, and was completed around 1735.

Queen Caroline occupies pride of place because she donated substantial funds to the 18th-century rebuilding of the college, which swept away all the original buildings. The college is, however, named after Queen Philippa, wife of Edward III, whose chaplain,

ABOVE: Queen Caroline under her dome in the Queen's College.
BELOW LEFT: looking down on the High Street from St Mary's.

Transport on The High

Oxford's High Street was once described by the eminent architectural historian Nikolaus Pevsner as "one of the world's greatest streets". It has, however, had a protracted battle with traffic since the advent of the motor car.

Pictures from the 19th century depict a broad, elegant and largely empty thoroughfare, but archive photos from the 1950s onwards show traffic jams. The street has always been an important artery. In the age of horse-drawn transport, The High was the site of several important coaching inns, notably the Mitre, the Eastgate and the long-disappeared Angel Inn. But cars and buses brought pollution and congestion, and several schemes, including a tram system, were proposed to counter the motor car.

The 1999 Oxford Transport Strategy finally banned private cars from The High for large parts of the day, allowing buses, taxis and, of course, bicycles to continue to use the street. Local traders complained loudly that the ban had a negative impact on their business, but the City Council insisted that a traffic-free High Street (and Cornmarket) would attract more rather than fewer shoppers.

Robert of Eglesfield, founded it in 1340. Queen's still marks the memory of its founder with an ancient ceremony whereby dinner guests are presented with a needle and thread – the French for which (*aiguilles et fils*) is a pun on Eglesfield's name. The more famous Boar's Head Feast, celebrated in December, commemorates a Queen's student who is said to have killed a wild boar by thrusting a copy of Aristotle's works down its throat.

As one passes through the centre of the Front Quad, the north range ahead has the hall on the left and the chapel on the right. The latter, consecrated in 1719, reused the colourful stained-glass windows from the old chapel, designed by Abraham van Linge in 1636, and is notable for the bold and exotic foliage framing the biblical scenes.

Beyond lies the Back Quad, with its splendid library of 1696 on the left, lit by a great expanse of glass, through which the stucco frieze and ornate bookcases may just be glimpsed. A narrow passage to the left of the library passes between high

walls into a tiny rose garden known, for reasons now forgotten, as "the Nun's Garden".

Food, glorious food

Opposite Queen's, connecting The High with Merton Street, is **Logic Lane**, so called because there used to be a school of logicians at the High Street end. Cross Logic Lane and continue along the south side of The High. **No. 84**, with its elegant windows and Corinthian columns, was once the grocery shop belonging to Frank Cooper. It was here, in 1874, that Cooper began selling jars of surplus marmalade produced by his wife, Sarah Jane, from an old family recipe on her kitchen range. It proved so popular that a factory had to be constructed on Park End Street. Although the firm sold out and moved in 1974, the marmalade is still manufactured under the original label.

The premises now house the **Grand Café ❾**, a friendly, Edwardian-style café, with high ceiling, marble, mosaics and chandeliers.

Next door, at **No. 83**, are offices of the Oxford Bus Company, worth mentioning only on account of the delightful Venetian window on the first floor.

The Examination Schools

Next comes the massive block of the **Examination Schools** ⑩, built on the site of the Angel, one of Oxford's most important coaching inns (in 1831 it was operating 11 daily coach services to London and 13 others to all parts of the country). Introduced only in the late 18th century, the first written examinations were held in the Divinity School, before moving to the various rooms of the Old Schools Quadrangle. But by the second half of the 19th century a new, purpose-built edifice was required. This was built in 1882 to replace the Old Schools, now inadequate to accommodate all the students attending lectures and sitting examinations.

The building was designed by T. G. Jackson in neo-Jacobean style with classical and Gothic elements, and the result, especially the High Street

facade, has sometimes been described as heavy-handed – designed, perhaps, to intimidate the hapless exam candidates. Students can be seen entering and leaving the building in the main exam month of June, all dressed in "sub-fusc" garb without which they are not allowed to sit their exam. The end of the examination ordeal can be a messy affair as students celebrate with champagne, flour bombs and streamers.

The High Street facade of the Examination Schools building is impressive, but the most beautiful side of the building, with its fine courtyard, overlooks **Merton Street** around the corner. On the same corner stands the **Eastgate Hotel** ⑪. It was at this point, in the middle of the street, that the east gate through the medieval town wall stood until its demolition at the hands of the Paving Commission in 1772.

There has been an inn on this site since 1605, but the present hotel was built in 1899 in the style of a 17th-century town house.

Opposite, at **No. 48**, is a shoe shop which was once the bicycle repair

ABOVE: filing out of an exam.
BELOW: Examination Schools, the students' least favourite building.

ABOVE: choristers take to the top of Magdalen's Bell Tower every May Morning. **BELOW:** Muniment Tower detail.

shop of William Morris. Continue as far as the Longwall Street traffic lights, where you cross the road and proceed towards Magdalen College, whose famous tower dominates the eastern end of the High Street.

Magdalen College ⑫

Tel: 01865-276 000
Opening Hrs: Oct–June 1–6pm or dusk if earlier, July–Sept noon–6pm
Entrance Fee: Charge

Magdalen College (pronounced *maudlin*) was founded in 1458 by William Waynflete, bishop of Winchester and lord chancellor of England under King Henry VI. It was built on the site of the Hospital of St John the Baptist, some of whose buildings still survive as part of the college's High Street range. Built outside the city walls, Magdalen had lots of space in which to expand, and its grounds encompass large areas of meadow, bounded in the east by the River Cherwell.

Completed in 1505, the **Bell Tower** is famous for the Latin grace sung from the top by the choristers every May Morning. The tradition probably dates back to the tower's inauguration in 1505. Nobody is

certain whether it has continued in unbroken succession since that date, but the ceremony was in full swing in the 18th century, when spectators were pelted with eggs by undergraduates from the tower. Today, when the Magdalen College School choristers sing from the top of the tower at 6am on 1 May, the ceremony initiates a morning of revelries: bells ring out, Morris men dance, and students take their lovers off by punt for champagne breakfasts along the banks of the River Cherwell.

During the Civil War, the tower was used as a vantage post by the Royalist forces who had established themselves in the city after the Battle of Edgehill in 1642. But while Magdalen, along with the rest of the university, lent its full support to Charles I, it did not support the unpopular James II, who tried to make the college a Catholic seminary. In 1687 James briefly had his own man (Bishop Parker) installed as college president and had Mass, run by Jesuits, set up in the chapel.

With the advance of the Protestant William of Orange, however, James promptly did a U-turn and had the original fellows reinstated on 25 October 1688, an event still celebrated in Magdalen as Restoration Day. But it was too late for the unfortunate king, who soon lost his crown and spent the rest of his life in exile in France.

Enter the college via the porter's lodge on High Street and take the diagonal path across **St John's Quadrangle**. To the right, you enter the low **Muniment Tower** of 1485, which shelters the west doorway to the **Chapel**, carved with figures of St John, Edward VI, Mary Magdalene, St Swithun and William of Waynflete. Originally built in 1480, the chapel was completely redesigned in the early 19th century. But with its stone vaulting and ornamental screens, it is still worth seeing, especially by

ABOVE: the Cloister Quadrangle, Magdalen College.

candlelight at choral evensong. The ante-chapel contains some medieval stalls with carved misericords, a good selection of monuments, including that of the founder's father, Richard Patten (died 1450), and – the most interesting feature – sepia stained-glass windows.

The passageway leads through to the delightful **Cloister Quadrangle**, the 15th-century core of the college. With its vaulted passage, the quad still looks very ancient, though the north and east wings had to be rebuilt in the early 19th century after attempts were made to have the cloisters cleared to make way for the New Buildings (*see below*). The allegorical figures on the buttresses, called "hieroglyphicals", were added in 1508. One is free to speculate what they represent, for nobody really knows – though in the 1670s, Dr William Reeks produced a 60-page treatise arguing that they symbolised the virtues (sobriety and temperance) and vices (gluttony, lust and pride) of academic life.

The grotesques of the cloister walls include more dark, mysterious subjects, and several that are explicitly erotic – surprisingly, since most are the work of Victorian carvers.

Oscar Wilde at Oxford

Perhaps Magdalen College's most flamboyant old boy was Oscar Fingal O'Flahertie Wills Wilde, who was a student here between 1874 and 1878, causing controversy in almost everything he did. Already armed with a degree from Dublin, Wilde was a brilliant and precocious Classics scholar who effortlessly won a double First. The future playwright relished his time at Oxford, likening it to Athens, where "the realities of sordid life were kept at a distance". At first, he was a keen sportsman, but gradually he adopted a more mannered, aesthetic posture, pretending to be lazy but secretly working hard throughout the night. Legend has it that he provocatively asked for extra paper after only one hour of a three-hour finals exam and then walked out half an hour before the end – only to be awarded the highest marks in the entire year. But it was Oxford, too, that contributed to his downfall, as he met Lord Alfred Douglas ("Bosie") on a visit to the city. Their openly homosexual relationship led to his imprisonment in Reading Jail and his eventual exile and early death in Paris in 1900.

New Buildings

A narrow passageway in the north range of the cloister debouches into a vast expanse of green lawns, with the stately colonnaded **New Buildings** straight ahead. Completed in 1733, this was intended to be part of a huge neoclassical quadrangle. Fortunately, the money ran out and only one range was ever built.

Opposite the New Buildings turn along the path to the left, where the massive **plane tree**, planted in 1801, is a direct descendant of a hybrid that was developed by Jacob Bobart in the Botanic Garden *(see page 122)*. It is worth following this path a short way in order to look back, southwards, over the fine jumble of towers, pinnacles and Cotswold-tiled roofs of the college – Oxford's dreaming spires in miniature.

Magdalen Grove

To the north, beyond the fence, is **Magdalen Grove** ⓭, winter home of the college herd of fallow deer. The grove once looked considerably more leafy than it does at present. Massive elm trees, planted in around 1689, unfortunately succumbed to disease and were felled in 1978. The deer have been here since the early 18th century, when they were introduced to supply the college with venison. Even today surplus animals are occasionally culled and served up in the hall.

In the other direction, through the wrought-iron gates, is a bridge over a branch of the Cherwell River. Here, if you watch on a sunny day, you are quite likely to see brown trout, or even larger fish, such as perch or pike, basking in the clear, warm waters below, ready to dart back into the shadows created by the overhanging chestnut tree branches beyond if they are disturbed.

Addison's Walk

Across the bridge the narrow path turns left to follow a raised bank beside the Cherwell, with Long Meadow, summer grazing home for the Magdalen deer, to the right. The raised causeway, almost completely enclosed by a tunnel of tree foliage, was partly created out of the remains of Civil War defensive embankments.

ABOVE: Muniment Tower carving.
BELOW: Magdalen Grove's deer.

It is known as **Addison's Walk** , after Joseph Addison (1672–1719), poet and *Spectator* essayist, whose rooms in Magdalen College over-looked these meadows.

The walk was not laid out in its present form, nor named after Addison, until the 19th century, but the name is appropriate since Addison was a pioneer of naturalistic landscape design, arguing in his *Spectator* essays that the works of nature are often superior to the artificial creations of man.

Ironically, the verdant beauty of the walk was almost changed forever by one of Addison's later followers. Humphry Repton proposed, in 1801, to dam the Cherwell and create an artificial lake out of the meadows. We must be thankful that the plan was not executed, for the meadows are now famous for a far more beautiful sight than a blank sheet of water: in late April, or early May, the grass is filled with the graceful nodding flower heads of purple and white snake's head fritillaries, one of the largest colonies of these rare wild flowers in Britain. Almost picked to extinction in the 19th century, the Magdalen fritillaries have been carefully protected since 1908.

Fellows' Garden

At the northern end of Addison's Walk, there are views across to the modern buildings of St Catherine's College (not accessible from this point). The path turns to the right and, at the eastern angle, a bridge over the Cherwell provides access to Magdalen's **Fellows' Garden**. This delightfully secluded area demonstrates just how much space the college has at its disposal. It is particularly delightful in spring when the ornamental trees are in flower and the grass is covered in daffodils and anemones. To complete the circuit, return to the bridge and turn left, following the river bank to Magdalen

ABOVE: Addison's Walk

Bridge and right to return to the college grounds.

Go back to the entrance via the cloisters and then the **Chaplain's Quadrangle**. To the left the Bell Tower soars heavenwards and to its right is the oldest bit of the college, which was part of the 13th-century hospital incorporated into the High Street range.

Passing from the Chaplain's Quadrangle into St John's Quadrangle, you'll notice on the left wall an outside **pulpit**, from where a service is conducted once a year on the Feast of St John the Baptist (24 June), a tradition that dates back to the earliest days of the college.

Exit Magdalen, and on the opposite side of the street you'll see the main entrance to the Botanic Garden *(see page 122)*.

Continue along the High to **Magdalen Bridge**. The first bridge to cross the Cherwell at this point was a timber construction built in 1004. It was replaced by a stone-built structure in the 16th century, but this was demolished during the Civil War in the 1640s and replaced with

The fallow deer grazing around Addison's Walk are part of a careful management programme, introduced to the meadows to keep down the buttercups that threatened to crowd out the vulnerable fritillaries.

a drawbridge. Today's bridge dates from 1772. It has since been widened a couple of times to cope with the ever-increasing volume of traffic.

Victoria Fountain

At the other side is the triangular junction known as **The Plain** ⓯. This busy junction marks the divergence of St Clement's, Cowley and Iffley roads, fanning out to the suburbs of Oxford. Isolated in the island in the centre stands the **Victoria Fountain**, which was originally used as a drinking trough for horses. It was unfortunately constructed two years too late to commemorate Queen Victoria's Diamond Jubilee in 1897. Until its destruction at the hands of the Paving Commission in 1772, the church of St Clements had stood on this site.

Off to the right, in Cowley Place, is **Magdalen College School**, originally founded in 1480 but relocated to this new site in 1894.

St Hilda's College ⓰

Tel: 01865-276 884
Opening Hrs: daily 2–5pm
Entrance Fee: Free

ABOVE: Victoria Fountain on The Plain. **ABOVE RIGHT:** St Hilda's College. **BELOW:** the River Cherwell under Magdalen Bridge.

A little further down is **St Hilda's College**, founded in 1893 but occupying a fine 18th-century house with fine views of the Cherwell and Christ Church Meadow.

St Hilda's, Oxford's last all-women college, voted in 2006 to admit men. Its founder was the formidable principal of Cheltenham Ladies' College, Dorothea Beale, and she named the new institution after the 7th-century Abbess of Whitby, who had been the first great educator of women in England.

Miss Beale stated, in documents relating to the aims of the college, that "I want none to go for the sake of a pleasant life", and the strict chaperonage system, along with measures such as iron grilles fitted on the hall windows, were all designed to prevent encounters between ladies at the college and members of the opposite sex.

A contemporary wit penned a few immortal lines of protest on behalf of Miss Beale's charges: *Miss Buss and Miss Beale/Cupid's darts do not feel./ How different from us/Miss Beale and Miss Buss.*

St Hilda's was given an exciting new dimension in 1995 when the purpose-built Jacqueline du Pré Music Building opened after a successful £1-million appeal in memory of the late cellist. Now one of Oxford's premier music venues, the complex hosts a wide variety of events and is famed for its state-of-the-art acoustics.

Walk across Magdalen Bridge for a superb view of the High Street. ❑

BEST RESTAURANTS, CAFÉS, PUBS AND BARS

Restaurants

Café Zouk
135 High Street.
Tel: 01865-251 600.
www.cafezouk.co.uk
Open: daily. ££ **1**
p278, C4
A cut above the usual Tandoori place, this centrally located and tastefully decorated venue aims to recreate the spicy flavours of the Mughal dynasty.

Chiang Mai Kitchen
130a High Street.
Tel: 01865-202 233.
www.chiangmaikitchen.co.uk
Open: daily. ££ **2**
p278, C4
Stylish and authentic Thai cuisine served in a beautifully preserved Tudor building. Extensive vegetarian options are on offer, and the staff are extremely helpful.

Patisserie Valerie
90 High Street.
Tel: 01865-725 415.
www.patisserie-valerie.co.uk
Open: daily. £–££ **3**
p279, D4
Smart café serving breakfast all day and salads and other lighter meals from lunchtime onwards. It is the cakes

and pastries, however, that are this outfit's real speciality.

Quod Restaurant and Bar
92–94 High Street.
Tel: 01865-202 505.
www.quod.co.uk Open: daily.
££ **4** p279, D4
A very popular and bustling brasserie-style establishment, with an emphasis on Italian cooking. The atmosphere, enhanced by eye-catching paintings from young artists, is relaxed and is considered pleasantly fashionable.

Cafés

The **Grand Café** (84 High Street **1** p279, D4) is housed in the old marmalade factory and exudes a rather faded Edwardian charm. Good-value breakfasts, light meals and afternoon teas are all available, as are cocktails. The **Queen's Lane Coffee House** (40 High Street **2** p279, D4) is a veritable Oxford institution, dating back to 1654. After a welcome refurbishment it serves good snacks, light lunches and cream teas to a mostly student clientele.

Prices for a three-course dinner per person with a half-bottle of house wine:
£ = under £20
££ = £20–£30
£££ = £30–£45
££££ = more than £45

Pubs and Bars

The Mitre (17–18 High Street **3** p278, C4) has an impressive historic facade and spacious panelled interior, and is a good place for an early evening drink. Its formulaic Beefeater menu, however, is unexceptional. Across the High, **The Chequers** (131a High Street **4** p278, C4) is a well-maintained 15th-century building hidden down an alleyway. Popular with a non-student clientele, it has a pleasant courtyard area. **The**

Wheatsheaf (129a High Street **5** p278, C4) is also invisible from the High and is reached down Wheatsheaf Yard. It has a fairly predictable menu and is best known for its Tuesday evening jazz sessions. **The High Table Bar and Brasserie** (73 High Street **6** p279, D4) has developed a reputation for its cocktails, although prices are on the high side. It stays open until 2am (except Sun), after many other pubs have closed.

RIGHT: a relaxing lunch is on the cards at Quod Restaurant and Bar, popular for its brasserie vibe.

A THIRST FOR KNOWLEDGE

Oxford is a city of learning, of course, but also a city of drinking, with a huge variety of pubs ranging from medieval inns to modern theme bars

There are pubs to suit all tastes in Oxford. Pubs for students, of course, as well as establishments that cater for other inhabitants of the city – such as in George Street, now almost entirely comprised of places for eating and drinking. But there are also plenty of the more traditional and sedate pubs, some of whose names reveal their historic connection with a particular trade or profession: the Bookbinders Arms in Jericho (publishing), the Waterman's Arms on Osney Island (canal haulage), the Bullnose Morris in Cowley (named after the first vehicle produced by William Morris, founder of the motor-car industry in Oxford).

Each suburb or inner-city neighbourhood has its local, but there are some pubs that can lay claim to strong associations with the famous (and the infamous), among them some whose drinking habits were as pronounced as their literary or artistic talents. William Shakespeare, so tradition has it, used to stop off at the Crown Tavern in Cornmarket on his way from London to Stratford-upon-Avon, while hard-drinking Welsh poet Dylan Thomas used to quench his thirst in the Turf Tavern. Naturally, many other writers have followed suit.

ABOVE: LEFT: The historian Anthony Wood recounted in 1690 how one fellow of All Souls died at the Mitre after immoderate drinking.

ABOVE: glass-fronted cases festoon the walls of The Bear, displaying its collection of more than 4,500 ties (cuttings thereof) donated by customers since the 1950s in exchange for a pint.

LEFT: the brewery may be gone but the Morrell's brand lives on.

BELOW: the "Inklings", a group of literary cronies including C.S. Lewis and J.R.R. Tolkien, author of *The Lord of the Rings*, used to meet in the back bar of the Eagle and Child, an unspoiled pub on St Giles.

A GHASTLY, GHOSTLY INN

The Mitre Inn on the High Street has been a pub in continual use since 1310. It has always had strong religious connections and in the 17th century was a hotbed of Catholicism, when secret Masses were held on the premises. This affront to Protestantism led to a riot in 1688 as mobs smashed every window and went in search of other Catholics. One of the worst chapters in the city's long history of religious intolerance occurred here during Henry VIII's Dissolution of the Monasteries. A secret tunnel then linked the Mitre with buildings across the High Street and it seems that Henry's soldiers drove a group of monks underground and then bricked up both ends of the tunnel. According to local lore, the monks' screams can sometimes still be heard in the dead of night.

LEFT: the legendary Welsh actor Richard Burton often came to perform at Oxford's Playhouse, and was nicknamed "Beer Burton" for none too subtle reasons.

RIGHT: C.S. Lewis, creator of the Narnia novels, used to meet J.R.R. Tolkien for drinks at the Eastgate Hotel on High Street.

BELOW: one of the oldest pubs in Oxford, the Bear Inn, with its low-slung ceiling, dark beams and tortuously narrow staircase, dates back to 1242, although the present building is from the early 17th century.

ABOVE: the King's Arms in Broad Street counts among its famous patrons the late novelist Kingsley Amis, father of Martin and a contemporary of the poet Philip Larkin at St John's College.

SOUTH OF THE HIGH

You can visit an old tavern and some venerable colleges, including Merton, on the way to the Botanic Garden, one of Europe's finest and Britain's oldest

Main Attractions
ORIEL COLLEGE
CORPUS CHRISTI COLLEGE
MERTON COLLEGE
BOTANIC GARDEN

Maps and Listings
MAP OF SOUTH OF THE HIGH, PAGE 118
ACCOMMODATION, PAGES 256–7

This route starts at Carfax and heads east, but soon forsakes the High Street for more evocative back streets. Merton College is especially important, as many of its features provided the model for later college foundations.

From Carfax, cross over to the south side of the High Street and proceed east as far as Alfred Street. Turn right to arrive at **The Bear ❶**, one of Oxford's oldest pubs (there has been a pub on its site since 1242), and full of genuine charm. Enclosed in its tiny, panelled rooms, with their smoke-kippered ceilings, are more than 7,000 ties displayed in cabinets on the walls and rafters – from the Cheltenham College Mind Games Society to the East of Suez Golfing Club. There is excellent pub food, and in summer you can eat outside in the adjoining yard.

Oriel and Christ Church

Walk east along Bear Lane to arrive in Oriel Square, with its 18th-century houses. At the northeast corner is the Canterbury Gate of Christ Church (*see page 158*). **Oriel College ❷** (tel: 01865-276 555; not generally open to the public), founded in 1324, originally occupied a house called La Oriole, because of its prominent upper bay window (medieval Latin: *oratoriolum*).

Nothing medieval survives now, but Oriel does have a splendidly ostentatious Front Quadrangle, built from 1620 to 1642 in the Jacobean-Gothic style. This form of architecture is peculiar to Oxford and combines beautifully shaped gables with traceried windows of medieval appearance. Dominating the quad

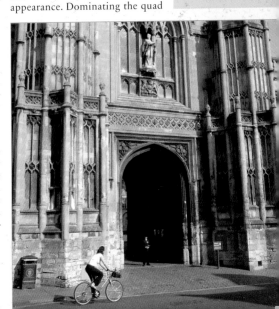

LEFT: the entrance to Oriel College, with the staircase entrance to the hall just visible.
RIGHT: Christ Church, whose northeast corner abuts Oriel.

is the staircase entrance to the hall, with its open strapwork cresting, and its inscription *Regnante Carolo* making a bold statement of Royalist support for Charles I. In the niches above are statues of Charles I and Edward II (Oriel's founder, Adam de Brome, was one of Edward's civil servants) as well as a matronly Virgin and Child.

Corpus Christi ❸

Tel: 01865-276 700
Opening Hrs: daily 2–5pm
Entrance Fee: Free

Adjacent to the Canterbury Gate, at the beginning of cobbled Merton Street, is the entrance to **Corpus Christi College**. Founded in 1512 by Richard Foxe, bishop of Winchester, this small college has always been somewhat radical. In 1963, the college took the radical step of allowing women to dine as guests in hall: they were not finally admitted as students, however, until 1979.

The intimate Front Quad of the college contains a famous **sundial** of 1581, topped by the emblem of the college, a pelican wounding her breast to feed her young, a symbol of Christ's sacrifice. The plinth below is inscribed with a perpetual calendar from 1606. A passageway on the left leads to the chapel, with its colourful Arts and Crafts window depicting St Christopher, designed by Henry Payne in 1931.

Visitors should not leave without also seeing the small college **garden** behind the Fellows Building. Dominated by a magnificent copper beech, the garden provides a fine view of Christ Church Meadow, with the Fellows Garden of Christ Church in the foreground. The view from the raised platform at the back is even better, and you can see down into the secretive Deanery Garden of Christ Church, where Lewis Carroll first got to know young Alice Liddell (*see page 71*).

ABOVE: Christ Church's dining hall.

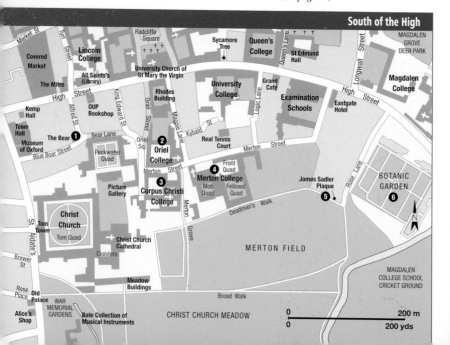

Merton College ❹

Tel: 01865-276 310
Opening Hrs: Mon–Fri 2–4pm, Sat–Sun 10am–4pm. Guided tours of the Library with the verger, for a maximum of eight people: July–Sept 2pm, 3pm, and 4pm (call ahead to check)
Entrance Fee: Free, but charge for the Library tour

Beyond Corpus Christi is the tower of Merton College Chapel. Founded in 1264 by Walter de Merton, lord chancellor of England, **Merton College** claims to be Oxford's oldest college. Two other colleges dispute this primacy: University College, on the spurious grounds that it was established by Alfred the Great, and Balliol, which was certainly in existence as a community of scholars by 1263 but was not formally endowed until 1282 *(see page 136)*. It is generally accepted, however, that the statutes of Merton served as the model for all the other colleges of Oxford and Cambridge. Like other early colleges, Merton was an exclusive institution with a privileged minority of mostly graduate fellows.

Merton Chapel, parallel to Merton Street, dates to 1290. The massive gar-

ABOVE:
Merton in winter.
BELOW LEFT: Merton College chapel.

goyles that leer from the battlements are another example of brilliant modern masonry – put up in the 1960s to replace the eroded stumps of the originals.

The statues of Walter de Merton and Henry III in the **gate-tower** are also recent, but the mysterious woodland scene carved above the arch is 15th-century. It probably depicts St John the Baptist in the wilderness – but it is a wilderness populated by numerous rabbits and bears, while the fruit-filled trees are crowded with a chorus of nesting birds. In the foreground, Walter de Merton kneels before the *Book of Seven Seals* from the Revelation of St John while a lamb and a unicorn, representing Christ, look on.

Pass through the entrance into the Front Quad, which lacks the calm regularity of some others in the city. With buildings dating from the 13th to 19th centuries, it is typical of the piecemeal development of the early colleges. Straight ahead is the Hall, the first building on the site to be completed, but virtually rebuilt in 1794 and again in 1874 when Gilbert Scott added the fine roof. The origi-

Walter de Merton (c.1200–77), a lawyer by training, made his money from property. His aim in establishing Merton College was to extend the educational benefits that the friars had established for themselves in universities. Such was his influence at court that he ran the country as Regent for two years after Henry III died in 1272 until his son, Edward I, returned from the Crusades.

nal 13th-century door, with its ornate scrollwork, has survived.

To the left of the Quad is the **Fitzjames Arch**, built by the warden (head of the college) Robert Fitzjames in 1497. He had a horoscope cast in order to find the most propitious date on which to begin building, and his astrological interests are reflected in the signs of the zodiac carved in the vault of this arch. It leads through to the 17th-century **Fellows' Quadrangle**.

Merton has some special features that provided models for later foundations. Principal among these is the **Mob Quad**, reached by going through the arch to the right of the Hall and turning right. Enclosed by 14th-century buildings, this is the oldest quad in Oxford. The origin of the name is not known, but members of Merton like to think that the characteristic form of the Oxford and Cambridge enclosed quadrangle owes its origin to this group of buildings.

Its form is probably based on that of a medieval inn. The north and east ranges (for accommodation) were completed first, in 1311, followed by

ABOVE: getting the Corpus Christi guided tour.
ABOVE RIGHT: Merton's gate-tower.

the south and west ranges, built to house, on the first floor, the **Library**, the most perfect example of a medieval library in England *(see page 119 for guided tours)*.

The entrance is in the southwest corner of the Mob Quad, where the ancient oak door is believed to have been taken from Beaumont Palace, the Royal Palace of Henry I that once stood on Beaumont Street *(see page 168)*. The library itself is up a flight of stone steps. Though its medieval structure remains intact, substantial alterations were carried out subsequent to its completion in 1379. The wooden ceiling, for example, is Tudor, while the panelling and plasterwork date from the late 16th and early 17th centuries. The library still has an original 14th-century reading stall, with chains to protect the valuable manuscripts from theft.

The west wing is adjoined by the **Max Beerbohm Room**, full of drawings by the famous caricaturist (1872–1956), who studied at Merton and wrote *Zuleika Dobson* (1911), a satire on Oxford undergraduate life.

To the north of Mob Quad is Merton's splendid 13th-century **Chapel**. Again, the plan of the chapel, consisting of an ante-chapel, screen and choir, set the pattern for all the other colleges – although this form evolved by accident: Walter de Merton intended a massive building, with an extensive nave, that was never built,

Anyone for Real Tennis?

In Merton Street, opposite Merton College's porter's lodge, stands one of England's 25 Real Tennis courts. Real Tennis has been played on this site since the late 16th century, and the present court dates from the late 18th century. The word Real is probably derived from Royal, but now mainly emphasises the sport's difference from more conventional lawn tennis. Its roots go back to medieval monastery life, when monks would play a sort of handball. Known in French as the Jeu de Paume (literally "the palm game"), the sport evolved into a more intricate affair involving rackets, a net and a complicated set of rules. What differentiates Real Tennis from the better-known lawn variety is that it must be played

inside. Players deliberately use the walls for particular shots, as in squash, while at the same time hitting the ball over a net. The ball is solid rather than pneumatic, made of tightly bound tape, and is rather like a soft cricket ball. Rackets are asymmetrical and heavier than those that are used for lawn tennis.

Visitors are welcome between 9am and 6pm on weekdays (tel: 01865-244 212; charge).

probably because of lack of funds and space. Even so, the choir alone is huge and lofty. The magnificent east window, with seven lancets, meeting to form a wheel with 12 spokes at the apex, is one of the finest in Europe.

Nearly all the windows retain original late 13th-century glass, representing apostles and saints in gorgeous colours. The choir screen is made up of pieces salvaged from one designed by Christopher Wren, sadly broken up in 1851. Of the many monuments to fellows and benefactors, the finest is to Thomas Bodley (died 1613) on the west wall; the founder of the Bodleian Library is surrounded by allegorical figures representing the arts and sciences.

As one re-emerges into cobbled Merton Street, there is a good view of Magdalen College tower to the east. On the left is **Logic Lane**, leading through to the High Street.

Recommended walks

Exit Merton and retrace your steps to the left as far as the wrought-iron gateway (daily until 7pm) leading along the attractive **Merton Grove** between Merton and Corpus Christi. A turnstile at the end provides access to the broad expanse of Christ Church Meadow. Immediately on the left is **Deadman's Walk**, following the old city wall to the east. It was along this path that funerals once processed to the old Jewish cemetery, now the Botanic Garden. It's possible to turn left here, but for better views continue south, past Christ Church Fellows' Garden, to the **Broad Walk**. To the right is the enormous neo-Gothic Christ Church, from where the delightful tree-lined **New Walk** provides a detour past Christ Church Meadow to the Thames and the College Boathouses. The main route goes left along Broad Walk, a wide avenue once planted with elm trees. The stump of one giant remains, but old age and Dutch elm disease killed them off in 1976; plane trees have been planted in their place.

When you get to Rose Lane, turn back a little along Deadman's Walk. In a wall on the right, a **plaque ❺** commemorates James Sadler, who was born in 1753 *(see page 150)*, as the "first English aeronaut who in a fire ballon made a successful ascent from

Logic Lane, a former bridleway known as Horseman Lane, acquired its new name in the 17th century when a school of logicians established itself there. Gates at each end of the lane are kept locked between dusk and dawn.

BELOW: the leafy stretch of New Walk.

ABOVE LEFT AND RIGHT: vistas of the Botanic Garden.

near this place on 4 October 1784 to land near Woodeaton".

The Botanic Garden ❻

Tel: 01865-286 690
Opening Hrs: daily May–Aug 9am–6pm, Mar, Apr, Sept, Oct 9am–5pm, Nov–Feb 9am–4.30pm
Entrance Fee: Charge except on weekdays Nov–Feb

On the right is the side entrance to the **Botanic Garden**, incorporating the fine archway paid for by the founder, the Earl of Danby, which contains his statue as well as that of Charles II (right-hand niche) and Charles I (left).

At around 5 acres (2 hectares), the garden is small but packed with interest. It was founded in 1621 by Henry Danvers, Earl of Danby, and is the oldest physic garden in Britain. The first head gardener was a retired German soldier and publican called Jacob Bobart, but he knew how to create a good growing environment. He ordered 4,000 loads of "mucke and donge" to be spread on the origi-

nal 3-acre (1.2-hectare) site to raise it above the Cherwell floodwaters, and built the 14ft (4.3-metre) high wall that still encloses the garden.

The fourth side is enclosed by laboratory buildings and the massive stone triumphal arch designed by Nicholas Stone as the main entrance in 1632 (the statues of Charles I, Charles II and the Earl of Danby were added later).

Within this sheltered, well-drained and fertilised plot, Bobart laid out a series of rectangular beds, each one devoted to one of the principal plant families. This arrangement, designed to serve the scientific objectives of the garden, has survived, although the regularity is softened by many fine specimen trees.

At the far end of the central path, on the right, is a huge yew tree, sole survivor of an avenue of yews planted in 1650 by Bobart. Beyond, the triangular New Garden, enclosed in 1944, contains a lily pond, bog garden and two rockeries for lime-loving plants. Another part of this garden is planted with roses illustrating the development of hybrid varieties in the 19th and 20th centuries.

From the central pond, the **view** through the arch to Magdalen Tower is magnificent. ❏

WHERE

The gardens can look bleak in winter, but the massive glasshouses (daily 10am–4pm) provide an instant change of climate as well as the sight of luxuriant palms and lotuses, ferns and alpines, and a number of carnivorous plants. A stroll along the Cherwell here is delightful, the river crowded with people in punts in the summer.

Elusive Gardens

Gardens and open spaces abound in Oxford, and a few of those sequestered behind college walls may still reflect the idiosyncracies of a fellow or head gardener.

Few cities in the world contain, within so few square miles, so many gardens and open spaces. There are two explanations. First, the colleges jealously guard their individual gardens and refuse to build on them; second, the rivers Cherwell and Isis almost encircle the city and have provided along their banks a ring of flood meadows that also form an effective barrier to building.

In contrast to the Botanic Garden and University Parks, it is not always possible to see the gardens sequestered behind college walls. However, most colleges do have set opening times and further restrictions are usually only applied during exam times or vacations.

The gardens are run almost as eccentrically as the university itself. In each college a fellow or group of fellows directs the college gardeners. Traditionally each fellow had some particular enthusiasm.

For example, the "Keeper of the Groves" at St John's, who favoured rhododendrons and their allies that sulk in Oxford's alkaline soil, had a huge pit dug, lined with concrete blocks and then filled with peaty soil to keep these plants happy. A fellow of Wadham has a liking for rare Chinese trees. The garden committee at Christ Church, under the influence of one member, banned yellow flowers. The gardener at All Souls once found himself planting a particular plant in one bed under the direction of one committee member, then having to replant it elsewhere at the whim of another, and so on...

Picking gardeners

The gardeners are a mixed bunch. Some are attracted to Oxford by the variety, the supposed prestige, and the general ambience of the place. Others hope to escape to a world where their distracted dreams are rarely interrupted. But a new drive for efficiency is encouraging many colleges to get rid of their aged retainers in favour of contract gardeners who drive from college to college – smart and tidy, perhaps, but without the personal touch.

The gardens of St John's, the richest college, are probably the grandest. The path meanders between shrubberies and groves of trees, providing a wonderful blend of formal and natural.

Another fine garden is at New College. It has probably the longest old-fashioned herbaceous border, and is dominated by the Mount, an avenue of clipped trees and elaborate parterres of box.

One feature that unites all college gardens is the lawn. There are two types: those you can walk on and those displaying the command KEEP OFF THE GRASS. It is on the informal lawns that the outdoor life of the college takes place: tea in the afternoon, Greek tragedies on summer evenings, croquet, bowls and frisbee-throwing. Essays are attempted, discarded and made into paper darts skimming over the grass. After the exams, elegantly attired students stroll across the lawns on their way to summer balls. ❑

LEFT: the herbaceous border at New College.

CORNMARKET AND CARFAX

This is the bustling commercial heart of modern Oxford, with a trading history dating back to Saxon times. Old coaching inns and the Covered Market are echoes of the past, and St Michael-at-the-Northgate is the city's oldest surviving building

After the beauty of the High Street, Cornmarket, Oxford's main shopping street, may come to many as something of an aesthetic anticlimax. Its timber-framed or stone medieval buildings were almost entirely demolished and replaced by commercial and office accommodation in the late 19th and 20th centuries in a process that the aesthete William Morris described as "the fury of the thriving shop". Several inns and traditional grocers gave way to larger department stores, creating today's shopping hub.

The street's mostly modern architecture and youth-oriented retailing may still not appeal to the city's many conservationists, but it is normally busy with shoppers and at weekends is the focal point for many of Oxford's younger citizens. While most of Cornmarket's shops and cafés are branches of predictable high street chains, it is worth straying a few yards from the main thoroughfare to explore some truly original outlets. The street's remaining historical buildings and landmarks are also worth exploring.

Carfax

The busy crossroads at the southern end is known as **Carfax**, after the Norman *Quatre Vois* (Four Ways). This is the ancient heart of Saxon Oxford, where the four roads from north, south, east and west met. The prime attraction is **Carfax Tower ❶**, all that remains of the 13th-century St Martin's Church which was pulled down as part of a road widening scheme in 1896 and was itself built on the site of an earlier, late-Saxon church. The east side of the tower, which can be climbed for fine views of the city (daily Apr–Sept 10am–5.30pm, Nov–Feb 10am–3.30pm,

LEFT: the Carfax quarterboys.
RIGHT: the view from the Carfax Tower.

Oct and Mar 10am–4.30pm; charge) is embellished with quarterboys, which strike the bell every 15 minutes (replicas of those taken from the original church), as well as the original church clock. Note above the gateway to the right of the tower the sculpture of St Martin giving his cloak to a beggar. Beggars were long a feature of Carfax.

As well as beggars, Carfax was historically a place of trading. As early as the 11th century the crossroads was crammed with market stalls,

offering all manner of goods, and over the next seven centuries the district remained a noisy and no doubt smelly jumble of stalls, with fish, meat and vegetables on offer. It was only in 1774 that the creation of an official market rid Carfax of its commercial clutter.

Also on Carfax stood the Swindlestock Tavern, where, on St Scholastica's Day (10 February) 1355, an argument between scholars and the landlord developed into a full-blown riot, resulting in the deaths of many scholars. The site of the tavern is indicated by a plaque attached

ABOVE:
Traditional sales technique at Carfax.

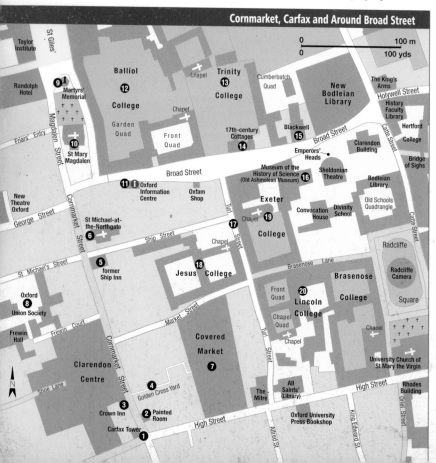

Cornmarket, Carfax and Around Broad Street

to the wall of the Santander Bank.

It takes an effort of the imagination to picture Carfax in 1610 when a large and elaborate stone conduit was built in the middle of the cross-roads in order to distribute the water that was piped from springs on distant Hinksey Hill into the centre of the city. In a revealing example of the Town and Gown divisions of those days, the water pouring from one part of the conduit was for the use of the colleges, while the townspeople had to make do with a separate supply.

The structure, featuring "a wealth of images" and "exquisite carving", also apparently had a carved ox's penis, from which water – or on special occasions – wine could flow. The conduit was pulled down in 1789 in a road-widening project.

On rare occasions, perhaps early on Sunday morning, you can stand beneath Carfax Tower and enjoy an uninterrupted view of the beautiful High Street, or alternatively look down St Aldate's to the great pepper-pot tower of Christ Church (see page 162).

Cornmarket

Cornmarket, which runs from Carfax to the former North Gate and St Michael's Church, is nowadays mostly lined with unexceptional retailers and refreshment venues, but in its day it was a vibrant mix of independent traders and bustling inns. It is estimated that in the 16th century one-third of all establishments on the street were pubs and inns. As its name implies, the street was once also a locale for the buying and selling of corn, and in 1536 an open-sided building with pillars was erected to shelter the grain from bad weather. The corn market was demolished in the course of the Civil War, when the occupying Royalist troops melted down the lead roof in order to manufacture bullets.

Shakespeare's godson, William Davenant (himself a playwright), was christened in St Michael's Church in 1606, and Shakespeare is known to have stayed regularly with Davenant's father, landlord of the Crown Tavern. This building, just across the street from Carfax Tower (No. 3 Cornmarket), was changed almost beyond

SHOP

Preoccupied window shoppers should take special care at either end of Cornmarket. It's all too easy for the unwary to step out into the path of an oncoming bus.

BELOW: Cornmarket, thronged with shoppers.

Coaching inns grew up to service the needs of the stagecoach, which forged a vital transport link between the town and London in the 1660s. Initially the journey took two days but by 1669 the "Flying Coach" had reduced this to one day, leaving the Mitre Inn in Oxford at 6am and, barring accidents, reaching London at 7pm.

recognition in 1744 when Cornmarket was widened and the tavern, then renamed the Bull Inn, had its frontage removed. Further "improvements" in the 1920s, led to the discovery by E.W. Attwood, a gentleman's outfitter, of 16th-century wall paintings, concealed behind oak panelling.

The so-called **Painted Room ❷** is thought to have been a guest's bedroom, owned by one John Tatleton of the Bull Inn, and features a design of flowers in barbed quatrefoils on a terracotta background. The room is now part of a private office but the design can be viewed by appointment through the Oxford Preservation Trust (tel: 01865-242 918).

The Crown Inn

Another historic inn stands across the road at No. 59a, hidden behind unpromising modern shop frontages. The **Crown Inn ❸** (not to be confused with the long-disappeared Crown Tavern) dates back to the 11th century and by 1490 was known as

Drapery Hall, then the King's Head and by 1625 the Crown Inn. The establishment's heyday was the 18th century when it developed into an important coaching inn. The pub that still survives was then probably the stables and outhouses of a much grander building, the site of which is now, ironically, occupied by McDonald's. Inside, it retains a somewhat Elizabethan atmosphere, although claims that Shakespeare was a regular are wide of the mark.

The third of Cornmarket's historic inn sights is **Golden Cross Yard ❹**, an enclosed courtyard surrounded by timber-framed ranges dating from the 16th to 19th centuries. The buildings were meticulously restored in 1987 to create a stylish precinct. The courtyard was originally formed in the Middle Ages for the Cross Inn; indeed, an inn may have existed on this site as early as 1193. In the 16th century the inn was used by travelling companies of players and it is said that Shakespeare stayed there on occasion. The bishops Latimer and Ridley were cross-examined here in 1555 while imprisoned at the nearby Bocardo. The first floor of the Pizza Express occupies the former bedroom accommodation of the inn and contains the major fragments of two painted rooms, the Crown Chamber and the Prince's Chamber.

The Ship Inn

Continue walking down Cornmarket until you get to the corner of Ship Street. Here is the former **Ship Inn** ❺, one of Oxford's finest timber-framed buildings. Originally built in 1389 as the New Inn, it was recently restored by Jesus College to its 18th-century appearance, and now houses shops.

Oxford's oldest building

At the other side of Ship Street stands the **tower** of the church of **St Michael-at-the-Northgate** ❻ (daily 10.30am–5pm; charge). Built as a look-out against the Danes, this sturdy tower is Oxford's oldest surviving building and dates to around 1050, exhibiting characteristic late Saxon features.

The tower was built up against the north gate of the city walls, part of the fortifications of Edward the Elder's original Saxon town. The gate (dismantled by the Paving Commission in the late 18th century) was enlarged in 1293 to create a prison known as the Bocardo. Scholars debate whether Bocardo simply means "boggard", a privy, or whether it derives from the medieval logician's term for a syllogism, implying a difficult trap from which to escape.

The Oxford Martyrs Cranmer, Latimer and Ridley were all imprisoned here before being taken outside the city wall in 1555 to be executed (*see page 98*). Their cell door is in the tower.

St Michael's Church was substantially restored after a fire in 1953 but some fine 15th-century glass has survived, including a window showing Christ crucified on a lily flower

ABOVE: the Covered Market.
BELOW: Carfax Tower, all that remains of St Martin's Church.

(symbolising purity). The medallions in the window above the altar are the oldest examples of stained glass in Oxford, dating from 1290. The font is late 14th century. The treasury in the tower is used to display a beautiful silver chalice of 1562, a lustful sheela-na-gig (a late 11th-century erotic stone carving) and a charter of 1612 bearing the great seal of King James I. In the cellar of an adjacent building a shop specialises in fair-trade produce from around the world.

The Covered Market

Only a minute down Market Street from the chain-store culture of Cornmarket is the cornucopian **Covered Market** ❼ where no quarter is given to the sensibilities of vegetarians, who will find haunches of meat, plump turkeys and blood-dripping game of every kind, hung in great quantities outside the butchers' stalls in true Edwardian style. This is particularly the case around Christmas, when the market becomes a spectacular tribute to gastronomic excess.

The market was originally built in 1774 as part of the Paving Commission scheme to rid Oxford of its untidy and often foul-smelling street markets. Fish and meat sellers, later to be joined by butter and fruit retailers, were brought into one place under the supervision of a beadle.

ABOVE: Turl Street epitomises the architecture of old Oxford.

The present structure dates largely from the 1890s when the market was rebuilt and roofed over. It retains its turn-of-the-century atmosphere, and you can buy a great range of locally produced "poor man's meats" – haggis, brawns, faggots, raised pies, black puddings and Oxford sausages – not to mention fresh fruit and fish, cheeses and pastries. There's also a high-class delicatessen and a pasta shop, as well as cake shops and tea shops all vying for custom alongside smart boutiques and florists. The market wouldn't be the same without its traditional "greasy spoon" café, but there are several more up-market eateries too. This is also the place for practical everyday services, such as shoe repair or a shop specialising in pet supplies. The market is open from 9am to 5.30pm Mon–Sat and from 10am to 4pm on Sunday.

Side streets

A couple of alleys and side streets take you away from the bustle of Cornmarket into a quieter sort of urban environment. Ship Street, between St Michael's Church and the former Ship Inn, steers the visitor towards the gentler atmosphere of Turl Street and has a couple of pleasant cafés. Opposite, St Michael's Street is a peaceful lane that leads to New Inn Hall Street and contains some attractive shops as well as the popular Nosebag café and the Three Goats' Heads pub.

Here is the main entrance to the red-brick Gothic premises of the **Oxford Union Society** ❽ (closed to the public), built in 1857 as a permanent home for the debating club founded in 1823. Harold Macmillan, Britain's prime minister from 1957 until 1963 and later chancellor of the University, called it "an unrivalled training ground for debates in the Parliamentary style". The list of past Union Society presidents reads like a *Who's Who* of the political and journalistic world *(see opposite page)*. ❑

CAFÉS AND PUBS

Cafés

Situated directly under Carfax Tower, **Sofi 2** (❼ p278, C4) is an offspring of the successful French-owned Sofi de France in the Covered Market. It has the same successful formula of good sandwiches, panini and pastries together with excellent coffee.

Georgina's (❽ p278 C4), in the Covered Market, caters to a youthful health-conscious crowd, serving organic and mostly vegetarian food and delicious cakes in a cosy upstairs retreat that tends to fill up quickly at lunchtime.

Brown's Café (❾ p278, C4), also in the Covered Market, is the polar opposite in terms of style and nutrition. If you want a classic cholesterol-loaded breakfast or lunchtime fry-up, this is the place, with its unreconstructed post-war ambience. Once there were three such greasy-spoon establishments in the market; this is the last.

The **News Café** (1 Ship Street ❿ p278, C3), as its name implies, aims to keep its visitors up to date with the news as well as refreshed. Newspapers and a plethora of TV sets should satisfy the most avid news junkie, while the menu, which ranges from big breakfasts to pasta and salads, is top quality.

Across Cornmarket, the **Nosebag** (6–8 St Michael's Street ⓫ p278, B3) is a long-standing student favourite, housed in a beautiful 15th-century building. It cultivates an unashamedly 1970s feel, with the emphasis firmly on quiches, salads and irresistible cakes.

Pubs

The **Crown Inn** (59A Cornmarket ⓬ p278, C4) is a rare reminder of what the street might once have looked like. Tucked away behind modern buildings, this Elizabethan-era pub, with a good-value menu, is a quiet and civilised place for lunch or an early evening drink.

The **Three Goats' Heads** (3A St Michael's Street ⓭ p278, B3/4) is a surprisingly ornate confection of wood and plasterwork, serving an impressive range of beers and less impressive food to a youthful clientele. Excellent for escaping the shopping frenzy outdoors.

The Oxford Union

It's a student body, but one whose weekly showpiece debates have constituted a political training ground for many a leading public figure, Richard Nixon among them.

"Again and again in its history, the young speakers who catch the president's eye have gone on to catch the eye of the country, even the eye of the world," wrote political journalist David Walter in his book *The Oxford Union*. It's a fair claim: the Oxford Union Society, founded in 1823, is the most famous student-run body in Britain, possibly in the world, and seven of its officers have become prime ministers.

Like most such student organisations, the Oxford Union runs discos and jazz evenings and operates a cheap bar. But what sets it apart are its weekly (during term-time) showpiece debates. Modelled on Westminster's parliamentary procedure, these constitute a top-notch political training ground, a chance for students not only to hear leading public figures defend their views but also to hone their own debating skills in preparation for the day when they themselves will be leading public figures.

Illustrious speakers

Richard Nixon and Jimmy Carter have both spoken here. British cabinet ministers regularly make the journey from London. Playwrights, actors and comedians have all pitted their wits against the unusually discerning and frequently rowdy audience. Even Hitler was given false hope in 1935 when the Oxford Union carried the controversial motion that "This House would not fight for King and Country".

The Union's training for the rough and tumble of real politics is ruthlessly practical. To become president of the union a student must clamber up the proverbial greasy pole by winning various elections, perhaps becoming initially a committee member and later secretary, treasurer or librarian. Just to make things more interesting, the society's celebrated Rule 33 forbids a candidate from informing anyone, except "close personal friends", that he or she is running for office.

This awkward handicap spurs candidates to find ingenious ways of circumventing the rule. They are thus liable to buy drinks for total strangers, casually letting slip in the conversation that they might be standing for election this term. Known as "hacking", this practice is scorned by non-political students.

Once elected, the president assumes significant responsibilities. Four speakers have to be found for each of the eight debates held every term, and the union, with a staff of 30 and a turnover of around £500,000 a year, has to be managed profitably.

It is no small task. In the mid-1980s, the union's fine Victorian buildings, including a library with pre-Raphaelite murals, were in serious disrepair and bankruptcy seemed a possibility. But sponsorship of debates and events and a Japanese bank donation of £1 million helped towards restoration. The resulting new-found vitality boosted university membership to 7,000 and there are now around 65,000 members worldwide. Dues are £178 for lifetime membership. ❏

RIGHT: the Oxford Union Society building.

TOWN AND GOWN THROUGH THE YEAR

The rhythms of university life have little impact on the city – but once a year, on a May morning, an event to mark the coming of summer is shared

With its three-term calendar and time-honoured diary of events and ceremonies, the university has an annual rhythm all of its own.

Each term witnesses the ritualistic conferring of degrees on successful students, the various gatherings of gowned academic notables and the occasional feast days celebrated by individual colleges.

For rowing enthusiasts, highlights of the year are the inter-college races known as Torpids (seventh week of Hilary Term) and Eights Week (fifth week of Trinity Term).

Events in the town

The city has its own annual fun events: the Lord Mayor's Parade over the Easter weekend, and St Giles' Fair in early September. A more recent innovation is the City Council's series of Fun in the Parks days, with fairs, music and multicultural activities around the city. They usually take place on Bank Holidays in spring and summer and are well attended by the non-student population.

The Cowley Road Carnival has also become an established fixture since its first outing in 2001. Taking place in either late June or early July each year, this celebration of community relations takes the form of a day-long street party (although in 2009 it was held in South Park instead) that welcomes up to 25,000 revellers.

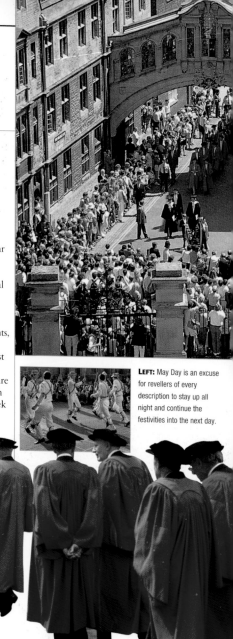

LEFT: May Day is an excuse for revellers of every description to stay up all night and continue the festivities into the next day.

RIGHT: led by the university's chancellor, dignitaries to be awarded degrees proceed, dressed in academic regalia.

YOU *SHALL* GO TO THE BALL

Most colleges hold a lavish party at least every other year at the end of Trinity Term. Officially known as "Commemoration Balls", these extravagant events celebrate the end of exams and the prospect of a lengthy summer vacation.

The dress code for undergraduates and their guests is traditional and rigorously enforced: dinner jackets and black bow ties for men, ball gowns for women. Tickets are very expensive (£100 plus for a double), and the richer colleges compete as to who can organise the most luxurious food and the best entertainment. Big-name bands often appear, paid for by the inflated ticket prices, while champagne and good food are *de rigueur*.

Understandably, security is tight, as gate-crashers attempt to scale college walls to join in the fun. Those with stamina carry on until dawn, when champagne breakfast is served, and some even set off on punting expeditions.

While undoubtedly enjoyed by those involved, college balls do not find favour with all Oxford residents, some of whom object to the noise and the ostentatious extravagance of the students.

ABOVE: Encaenia is the university's most colourful academic ceremony. In June visiting dignitaries from politics and the arts are presented with honorary degrees.

ABOVE: the 18th-century St Giles' Fair was a toy and craft fair, but today the two-day event offers hair-raising rollercoaster rides, garish prizes and sticky candyfloss.

RIGHT: happy faces at matriculation, the ceremony whereby new students are entered into the university register.

RIGHT: Eights Week, lasting four days in late May, has been around since 1815 and allows rival college rowing teams (eights) to compete against one another. It is around this time, before students depart for the long summer break, that the university lets its hair down with May Balls and parties.

AROUND BROAD STREET

This area combines peaceful college quads with the bustle of shopping streets and some of Oxford's favourite tourist attractions

The route begins at the southern end of broad St Giles', at the neo-Gothic **Martyrs' Memorial 9**. Erected by public subscription, to the designs of Sir George Gilbert Scott from 1841 to 1843, it contains statues of the martyrs Latimer, Ridley and Cranmer, and an inscription stating that they died for maintaining sacred truths "against the errors of the Church of Rome".

The Oxford Martyrs were burned at the stake in the town's north ditch, now Broad Street, just around the corner, where a cross in the road opposite Balliol College marks the site of their execution. Latimer and Ridley went to the stake first, in 1555. Latimer offered the following words of comfort to his desperate colleague before both were consumed by the flames: "Be of good comfort, Master Ridley, and play the man. We shall this day light such a candle, by God's grace, in England, as I trust shall never be put out."

Charles I's church

Immediately to the south of the Martyrs' Memorial the road splits into two and the **Church of St Mary Magdalen 10** occupies the island in the middle. Usually locked, this church is a centre of Anglo-Catholicism, and the congregation remains loyal to the memory of Charles I, celebrating the Feast of King Charles the Martyr on 30 January. The north aisle, funded out of money left over from the building of the Martyrs' Memorial, is an interesting early example of Gothic Revival architecture, and was designed by Gilbert Scott in 1842. Scott was a keen supporter of the Oxford Society for the Study of Gothic Architecture, founded in

WHERE

It is well worth investigating the range of walking tours organised by the Oxford Information Centre. As well as the more conventional history and architecture walks around the city and university, there are also pub tours, garden tours, ghost tours, and even tours of sites associated with fictional characters Harry Potter and Inspector Morse, and author J.R.R. Tolkien.

1839, whose members believed that this medieval style was morally better than the pagan classical.

Broad Street

Broad Street is aptly named, though it was originally known as Horse-mongers Street after a horse fair held here from 1235. Narrow at each end and wide in the middle, it has a feeling of spaciousness, emphasised by the grounds of Trinity College on the north side, which are separated from the street by a wrought-iron gate. The far end is dominated by the Sheldonian Theatre and Clarendon Building and much of the south side is distinctive for its colourful facades above some interesting shops including **Oxfam** (Oxford Committee for Famine Relief), the first permanent shop to be opened by the charity in 1948 *(see panel)*.

Also located on the south side, at Nos 15–16, is the **Oxford Information Centre** ⓫ (Mon–Sat 9.30am–5pm, Sun 10am–1pm and 1.30–3.30pm). The centre offers advice on accommodation, events and special attractions and is one of the

Oxfam

The Oxfam shop in Broad Street was the UK's first permanent charity shop. Today the Oxford-based aid agency has a network of more than 700 retail outlets, an annual income of some £300 million and a staff of 1,300 (plus 30,000 volunteers) in the UK. It works in 70 countries and lobbies for an end to unfair trade and the debt crisis in the developing world.

The Oxfam story began in 1942 when the Allies blockaded Greece, then occupied by the Nazis. As Greeks began to die of hunger and disease for lack of food and medicines, the Oxford Committee for Famine Relief was established to send supplies. A week of fund-raising netted £12,700.

best places to find a qualified guide for walking tours of the university.

Balliol College ⓬
Tel: 01865-277 777
Opening Hrs: daily 2–5pm
Entrance Fee: Charge

BELOW LEFT: taking in the hustle and bustle of Broad Street.
BELOW RIGHT: Balliol welcomes visitors.

merit in the result. William Morris, who watched the demolition of the medieval Balliol buildings with dismay, later founded the Society for the Protection of Ancient Buildings, with the avowed aim of seeking means to repair and protect old buildings rather than replacing them.

The fellows of Balliol, however, thought the buildings too decayed to be rescued. They had stood for a long time: Balliol claims to be the oldest Oxford college (also a claim made by University College and Merton) on the grounds that John Balliol founded it in 1263, as penance for insulting the bishop of Durham; the statutes, drawn up under the patronage of Balliol's widow, Dervorguilla, date to 1282.

The college was never very wealthy, however, until some ancient estates in Northumberland were discovered to be a rich source of coal. Three major Victorian architects were employed in the rebuilding that resulted – Salvin, Butterfield and Waterhouse – yet all produced second-rate work.

The Front Quad, entered from Broad Street, contains the former

At the other side of the street is **Balliol College**, a college that has produced a greater number of eminent men – in particular statesmen and politicians – than any other. These include Lord Jenkins of Hillhead, and prime ministers Harold Macmillan and Edward Heath.

The liberal traditions and academic strengths of the college in its heyday were due to the reforming measures of Benjamin Jowett (master 1870–93), who believed that his students should not merely be filled with facts but educated for life. His self-proclaimed mission was to "innoculate England with Balliol" – which he sought to do by encouraging his charges to devote their lives to public service. But Jowett wasn't the first Balliol Master to espouse progressive ideas: back in 1361 the religious reformer John Wycliffe spoke out against corruption and worldliness within the established church. His teachings resonated throughout Europe.

Jowett also supervised the near-total rebuilding of the college and, sadly, it is difficult to find much of

ABOVE LEFT: ghost tours setting off from Broad Street.
ABOVE RIGHT: Blackwell's exterior.
BELOW: Oxford-based charity chain, Oxfam.

WHERE

Outside Trinity College is one of the most popular stops for open-top bus tours of Oxford. Various touts also congregate here to sell tourist trinkets and college tours.

hall, now the library, and one of the few surviving pre-Victorian buildings, last remodelled in the 18th century. The chapel, Butterfield's work of 1856–7, was once lavishly decorated with Gothic furnishings – too ornate for the taste of Balliol dons who had them removed in 1937. The silver-gilt altar frontal commemorates college members who died in World War I.

The chapel exterior, partly clad in ivy and Virginia creeper, is built in alternating bands of buff and red stone and is best appreciated from the Garden Quad. Here things begin to improve slightly: a group of trees and rose beds softens the appearance of the ill-harmonised buildings, and the steep flight of stone steps up to the porch of the dining hall – the work of Waterhouse, 1876 – makes a dramatic statement.

Trinity College ⑬

Tel: 01865-279 900
Opening Hrs: daily 10.30am–noon, 2–5pm
Entrance Fee: Charge

ABOVE: Trinity College's dining room.
BELOW: the open approach to Trinity College.

Adjacent to Balliol is **Trinity College**. Unlike in most other Oxford colleges, the Front Quad is not closed off, and its tree-filled lawn almost invites visitors to enter, which they do through a small entrance between the wrought-iron gates and a row of humble **17th-century cottages** ⑭, which were rebuilt in 1969.

A path leads northwards across the lawn to Durham Quad, so called because it occupies the site of the

original Durham College, founded in 1286 by the monks of Durham Abbey. When the monasteries were dissolved by Henry VIII, the property was purchased by Sir Thomas Pope, a wealthy Treasury civil servant, and he refounded the college in 1555.

Durham Quad is fronted by the elegant Baroque chapel – so much like Wren's City of London churches that the design has been attributed to him, although any college records that could prove or disprove this theory are missing. Certainly the chapel, which attracts the highest eulogies from architectural historians, was the first in Oxford to break away from the Gothic style. Completed in 1694, the tower is carved with fruit and flowers, and the pinnacles consist of allegorical figures representing Theology, Medicine, Geometry and Astronomy.

Inside, the panelling, stalls and screen, carved with figures of the Evangelists, are principally of juniper wood, with walnut veneer. The beautiful reredos, all cherubs and foliage, is certainly good enough to

be the work of the great 17th-century master of wood carving, Grinling Gibbons. The centrepiece of the plaster ceiling is painted with an Ascension by the Huguenot artist Pierre Berchet.

A passageway on the north side of Durham Quad leads through to the peaceful Garden Quad. Here, the north range, of 1668, is known to be Wren's work, but 19th-century alterations have obscured his design beyond recognition.

Four handsome lead urns form a prelude to the college garden to the right, entered through a wrought-iron gateway, made as a World War II memorial. The expansive gardens stretch all the way to Parks Road, creating a fine vista that is closed at the far end by 18th-century wrought-iron railings.

The heart of publishing

Blackwell ⑮ (Mon–Sat 9am–6pm, Tue 9.30am–6pm, Sun 11am–5pm),

ABOVE: the Baroque chapel at Trinity.
BELOW LEFT: Trinity's gardens.
BELOW RIGHT: inside Blackwell bookshop.

ABOVE: Persian astrolabes at the Museum of the History of Science.
BELOW: more exhibits at the Museum of the History of Science.

on Broad Street, was opened in 1879 by Benjamin Henry Blackwell. The original shop was tiny, and even today the initial impression is of an average-sized provincial bookshop. Downstairs, however, is the underground **Norrington Room**, an enormous space stacked with shelves devoted to every topic under the sun. The pre-eminence of Blackwell in Oxford is reflected not only here in its flagship shop, but in other premises in the city, including the Music Shop at 23 Broad Street and the Art Shop, just across the street. (*See profile of Blackwell, page 145.*)

Old Ashmolean Museum

Before leaving Broad Street, go back to the Emperors' Heads (*see page 87*). Just to the right is the **Old Ashmolean Museum**, built between 1678 and 1683 to house the "cabinet of natural curiosities" inherited by Elias Ashmole from the Tradescants (*see page 166*). Designed, perhaps, by Thomas Wood, it picks up motifs and

ideas from Wren's building alongside, and is equally ornate.

Museum of the History of Science ⑯

Tel: 01865-277 280
Opening Hrs: Tue–Fri noon–5pm, Sat 10am–5pm, Sun 2–5pm
Entrance Fee: Free

The contents of the Old Ashmolean Museum were transferred to the newly built Ashmolean in Beaumont Street in the late 19th century and the building now houses the **Museum of the History of Science**, a comprehensive collection of early instruments. The museum may seem daunting, with its cases packed with complex astrolabes, quadrants and armillary spheres, but there is much to enjoy, even for non-scientists.

The ground floor has a collection of very early photographs, dating from the experimental period of the 1840s; they include one of John Ruskin's views of Venice, used as reference material by the artist for his own hand-drawn illustrations for his pioneering work on Renaissance architecture, *The Stones of Venice*. There are also some novelties among the exhibits: George III's ornate silver microscope and an extraordinarily elaborate machine turning handwriting into minuscule engravings, which can be seen only under a microscope.

In the former chemistry laboratory in the basement, a blackboard covered with Einstein's neatly chalked theorems is carefully preserved, a memento of his first Oxford lecture on the Theory of Relativity, given on 16 May 1931. It is partnered by an assortment of gruesome medical and dental instruments, early radios, gramophones and phonographs, and a display on the wartime work of Oxford scientists racing against time to prepare penicillin for large-scale production, using improvised materials such as milk churns and tin baths.

Turl Street

Between Blackwell Art Shop and the Music Shop on the other corner, **Turl Street** ⓱ marks a boundary of sorts between Town and Gown, for most of the colleges lie to the east and the shops and markets to the west. The street is thought to be named after a pedestrian turnstile or twirling gate that stood in the city wall at the Broad Street end. Looking south, you can see how the street gradually narrows to its original medieval width.

Jesus College ⓲

Tel: 01865-279 700
Opening Hrs: daily 2–4.30pm
Entrance Fee: Free

Down Turl Street, on the right, is **Jesus College**. It is said that college porters hate being on duty on Christmas Day because of the constant stream of telephone calls from pranksters ringing to ask "Is that Jesus?" – to which, if the answer is yes, the caller responds by singing "Happy Birthday to you".

Jesus is also known as the Welsh college because it was founded, in 1571, by Brecon-born Hugh Price,

and took many of its students from the grammar schools of Wales until 1882. T.E. Lawrence ("Lawrence of Arabia") was one of the non-Welsh alumni, admitted in 1907, although he resided only a term in college and spent most of his time studying medieval military architecture in a summer house built for him by his parents in the garden of their North Oxford home (2 Polstead Road). There is a bust of Lawrence in Jesus College Chapel.

The chapel itself, consecrated in 1621, contains a High Victorian altar reredos so out of keeping with the surviving 17th-century woodwork that it is usually curtained off from view. In the same north range of the first quad, the Principal's Lodging has a delicate shell hood dating from 1700 over the doorway.

ABOVE: Jesus College.
BELOW: the dining hall at Jesus.

ABOVE:
gardens in bloom at
Jesus College.

Exeter College ⑲

Tel: 01865-279 600
Opening Hrs: daily 2–5pm
Entrance Fee: Free

Exeter College, opposite Jesus, was

Tolkien's Turning-Point

John Ronald Ruel Tolkien was born in 1892 in Bloemfontein, South Africa, but was brought up in Birmingham, England. Both his father and mother died when he was young, and he and his brother came under the care of a stern aunt and a local parish priest.

A natural linguist, Tolkien had studied Greek and Latin and was interested in lesser-known languages such as Finnish even before he went to Exeter College in 1911. There he specialised in Old English and also developed his childhood habit of inventing private languages. After World War I, a spell working on the *Oxford English Dictionary* and a teaching job at Leeds, Tolkien returned to Oxford as professor of Anglo-Saxon. A turning-point came when he met the young writer C.S. Lewis, who encouraged him to publish what he had thought was unpublishable: *The Hobbit* (1937). The huge success of this book was followed in 1954 by *The Lord of the Rings* trilogy.

But such was Tolkien's following and so insistent were his fans, especially in the psychedelic days of the 1960s, that he was forced to escape Oxford for the anonymity of Bournemouth. He eventually returned to rooms in Merton College, where he died in 1973.

founded in 1314 by the bishop of Exeter, Walter de Stapledon. Much of the college now looks Victorian, owing to rebuilding, and the first quadrangle is dominated by the over-large chapel. This was built from 1854 to 1860 to the design of Sir George Gilbert Scott, and the resemblance to a miniature French cathedral is no accident – Scott borrowed freely from the Sainte-Chapelle in Paris.

The interior is bathed in the rich colours of stained glass, even on a dull day, and the sense of opulence is enhanced by the mosaic work of the apse. On the right of the altar, the large tapestry of the *Adoration of the Magi* was made in 1890 by the firm founded by William Morris, and designed by Burne-Jones. The two artists met in 1853 as fellow students at Exeter College, and their shared interest in the ideas of Ruskin and the pre-Raphaelites led them to devote their lives to the revival of medieval arts and crafts.

Another Exeter man was J.R.R.

Tolkien, author of *The Lord of the Rings*, who much enjoyed the magnificent chestnut trees of the Fellows' Garden, beyond and to the rear of the front quad.

The vast tree, "Bishop Heber's chestnut", seems as ancient as the college itself, and members of the Exeter boat club watch its growth in spring with interest. It is said that if the foliage of the branches, arching over the garden wall, succeed in touching Brasenose College opposite, Exeter will beat its neighbour in the Bumping Races.

The magnificent **view** from the top of the garden wall (accessible by stone steps and a walkway) provides a fresh perspective of Radcliffe Square (*see page 98*).

Lincoln College ⑳

Tel: 01865-279 800
Opening Hrs: Mon–Sat 2–5pm, Sun 11am–5pm
Entrance Fee: Free

Lincoln is the last of the colleges fronting on to Turl Street. It was founded in 1427 by the bishop of Lincoln, Richard Fleming, but he died four years later, leaving the college with little income and few endowments. Because it remained relatively poor,

ABOVE:
Exeter College's front quad.
BELOW LEFT:
stained-glass window in Exeter Chapel.
BELOW: the richly decorated organ in Exeter Chapel.

ABOVE:
Lincoln's library.

carved woodwork inside is much more typical of its age. Richly coloured stained glass shows prophets, apostles and biblical scenes.

One of the ironies of Lincoln College is that, founded during an age of heresy specifically to train priests in orthodox church teachings, it nevertheless elected John Wesley (who is largely credited with founding the Methodist movement) to a fellowship in 1726. Members of the Holy Club – nicknamed "the Bible moths" and "Methodists" because of their regular and methodical devotions – used to meet in his rooms, in Chapel Quadrangle. Another room in the Front Quad, erroneously thought to have been Wesley's, was restored as a memorial by American Methodists in 1925.

Brasenose Lane, shaded by the chestnuts of Exeter, has a leafy, rural feel and the cobbled gulley down the middle marks the line of the original open sewer. Undergraduates use the lane as an unofficial cycle path.

many of the original 15th-century buildings escaped "improvement", and much of the charm of the Front Quad is in its unspoiled character.

The Chapel Quad, to the south, was added in the 17th century. The chapel exterior (1629) is conservatively built in the Perpendicular style of the previous century, but the fine

The lane ends on Radcliffe Square with the Radcliffe Camera and Brasenose College *(see page 95)*. Opposite Brasenose Lane, Market Street leads west to arrive at the north entrance of the Covered Market *(see page 129)*. ❑

CAFÉS AND PUBS

Cafés

The Campus Buttery (11 Broad St ⑭ p278, B3) is housed in what used to be the legendary second-hand Thornton's Bookshop and offers above-average sandwiches and snacks as well as delicious teas.

Similar fare is to be found at **Morton's** (22 Broad Street ⑮ p278, C3), one of a local chain of sandwich shops. This café has a pleasant upstairs room in its 18th-century premises, where you can where you can take a perch and look out on to Balliol College. It is worth remembering that there are very attractive cafés and snack bars in **Blackwell** (⑯ p263, C3), and **Waterstone's** (⑰ p278, B3), on the corner of Broad Street and Cornmarket. All pro-

vide a comfortable place to enjoy a coffee and sandwich while browsing on the written word.

Pubs

The White Horse (52 Broad Street ⑱ p279, C3) is squeezed between two Blackwells' buildings in a much-restored 16th-century building. The pub is small, intimate and friendly, with a very good lunchtime menu. Several real ales are available, and Inspector Morse enthusiasts will recognise the front bar from the popular TV series.

The Turl Bar (Turl Street ⑲ p278, C4) is actually connected to the Mitre on the High, but operates as a separate venue. Catering to a rather youthful crowd, it has a decent menu and an outdoor courtyard, but it has lost some of its former appeal.

Blackwell

It was legendary customer service that made Blackwell, once a tiny family firm thought of as off-the-beaten-track, into one of the most famous bookshops in the world.

Blackwell first opened in October 1879 and is situated at the end of Broad Street, in one of the most beautiful parts of the city, surrounded by Trinity, Balliol, Exeter, Hertford and Wadham colleges and opposite Wren's Sheldonian Theatre.

Benjamin Henry Blackwell's original shop was just 12ft (3.6 metres) square and was criticised by many for its situation – furthest from the city centre and with two well-established bookshops opposite. Frederick Macmillan, proprietor of the publishing house of Macmillan and forebear of Harold Macmillan (prime minister and chancellor of Oxford University), said: "Well, Mr Blackwell, we shall be pleased to open an account with you but I fear you have chosen the wrong side of the street to be successful."

This pessimism was soon disproved. Blackwell's devotion to books – he characterised bookselling as "the infinite capacity for taking pains" – quickly became legendary. Professors, dons and undergraduates hastened to his door. The shop was originally so small that, when more than three customers came in, the apprentice had to be sent outside.

Right from the start the tradition was established that customers should be allowed to browse among the books, undisturbed by the staff. The custom has continued until the present day.

Naturally enough, famous literary figures have always been among the customers and the shop itself has been the subject of many writings. In *Summoned by Bells*, John Betjeman wrote: *I wandered into Blackwell's, where my bill / Was so enormous that it wasn't paid / Till ten years later, from the small estate / My father left.*

RIGHT: food for thought at Blackwell.

Other well-known customers have included Hilaire Belloc, A.E. Houseman, Oscar Wilde, George Bernard Shaw and Lewis Carroll.

Blackwell gradually expanded in order to meet the steadily increasing business and took over more space behind the shop. After World War II some departments were moved to nearby premises. The most notable part of the expansion was the development of a vast underground room, the Norrington Room (opened 1966), extending under Trinity College and named after its president.

Publishing credentials

Still a family firm, Blackwell is also a publisher in its own right. Benjamin Henry Blackwell began publishing poetry in the 1880s, and this was continued by his son, Basil, publishing early works by many writers who subsequently became famous, among them Tolkien and Robert Graves.

From these small beginnings, two major publishing companies have grown: Blackwell Publishers, which specialises in humanities, and Blackwell Scientific Publications, which concentrates on scientific and medical titles. Sir Basil Blackwell, known to all as "the Gaffer", was awarded a knighthood in 1956 for his services to bookselling.

Today, Blackwell has three bookshops in town, as well as one at Oxford Brookes University and another in the academic centre of the John Radcliffe Infirmary. ❏

AROUND NEW COLLEGE

Span the entire history of Oxford by taking in the site of a pagan well, a Norman crypt, the medieval town walls and the birthplace of Morris Motors

On the east of Catte Street, linking the two halves of **Hertford College**, is the ornate aerial corridor known as the Bridge of Sighs, after the famous Ponte dei Sospiri in Venice. Although it is now a much-photographed landmark, the bridge's erection was strongly opposed when it was built by Sir Thomas Jackson in 1913–14. The other buildings of the college are Jackson's design, too, put up after 1887 and remarkably varied in their use of Italian, French and English Renaissance motifs.

Hertford College ❶

Tel: 01865-279 400
Opening Hrs: daily 10am–5pm
Entrance Fee: Free

Hertford (pronounced *hartford*) is a college that only just survived to see the 21st century. The original Hart Hall, named after Elias de Hertford, dates from the late 13th century. For centuries it was embroiled in disputes with its predatory neighbour, Magdalen Hall, which wanted room to expand, and took every opportunity to take control of the impoverished Hart Hall. Magdalen achieved its objective in 1813 – only to be destroyed itself by a fire in 1820. It

was then decided to refound the college, calling it Hertford and combining the properties of Magdalen and Hart Halls with funds donated by the banker Thomas Charles Baring in 1874. The principal buildings, with their neo-Palladian details, lie on the south side of New College Lane.

The Bridge of Sighs

The site on the north side, linked by the **Bridge of Sighs** ❷, was acquired in 1898 and is interrupted on the Broad Street frontage by the History

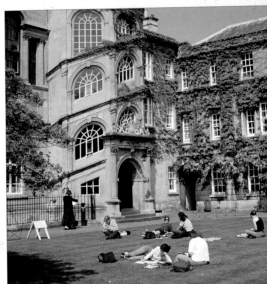

LEFT: the Bridge of Sighs.
RIGHT: the lawn at Hertford College.

ABOVE:
Hertford College Choir.

Faculty Library, originally built as the Indian Institute by Basil Champneys, beginning in 1883. Hindu deities and tiger heads carved in stone on the facade, and the elephant weather vane, mark its original use.

Ghostly lane

Pass under the Bridge of Sighs and into the dark, narrow and traffic-free **New College Lane**. This lane is the result of the replanning of the northeast quarter of town in the late 14th century, when many early medieval dwellings were replaced by residential colleges. The original street pattern was obliterated, leaving New College Lane to wind its way between the high walls of the college.

Immediately on the left, a narrow opening between two houses, St Helen's Passage (formerly Hell Passage), leads through to the **Turf Tavern** *(see page 153)*.

Further along on the left, a plaque on a house wall indicates the home of astronomer **Edmund Halley** (1656–1742). Having calculated the orbit of the comet that now bears his name, and carried out many scientific investigations, Halley was appointed Savilian professor at Oxford in 1703.

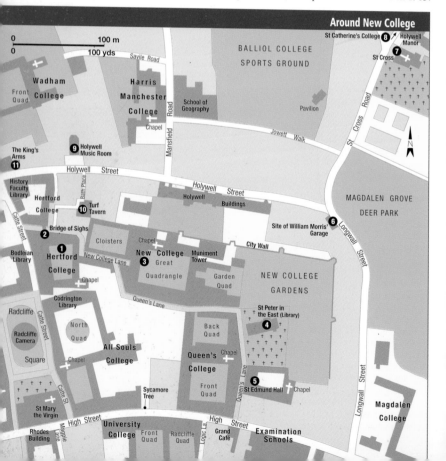

Around New College

He built an observatory at his home, still visible on the roof.

New College ❸

Tel: 01865-279 555
Opening Hrs: Easter–mid-Oct daily 11am–5pm, winter months (access only via gate on Holywell Street) daily 2–4pm
Entrance Fee: Charge, but free during winter months

The lane turns sharp right, between the cloister walls of New College on the left and the New College warden's barn on the right. Round another bend and straight ahead stands the gate-tower of **New College**. The narrow gate-tower, with statues of the Virgin, an angel and the founder, William of Wykeham, belies the spaciousness and grandeur of what lies beyond.

Wykeham, bishop of Winchester, founded the college in 1379, having acquired land in the northeast corner of the city wall, which, according to contemporary accounts, was "full of filth, desolate and unoccupied". Building work proceeded speedily – in part because Wykeham was a very wealthy man.

The range of buildings surrounding the Great Quadrangle was largely completed by the time of Wykeham's death in 1404. What is more, most

of it has survived intact, although a third storey was added to the accommodation range in 1674.

On the left of the gate-tower is the spacious chapel, a fine example of Perpendicular architecture. A dramatic stone figure of Lazarus, struggling to break free of his funeral bonds, dominates the antechapel and was carved by Sir Jacob Epstein in 1951. It stands beneath a controversial window designed by Sir Joshua Reynolds and painted by Thomas Jervais between 1778 and 1785 (the two artists appear as shepherds in the Nativity scene).

Sir Horace Walpole called it "washy" and Lord Torrington described the figures of the Virtues as "half-dressed languishing harlots". As models, Reynolds used society beauties of the day, including Mrs Sheridan, wife of the playwright; she appears as the Virgin.

There is no glass in the east end of the chapel. Instead, a great 19th-century stone reredos rises from floor to ceiling, filled with life-sized statues of apostles, saints and martyrs. The hammerbeam roof is also Victorian,

During the Civil War of 1642–9, New College Lane was the assembly point for a Royalist force preparing to ride out from the city and confront the Parliamentarians. Ghost experts maintain that their psychic energy lives on in those high walls. This and other spooky places are included on Ghost Tours (details from Oxford Information Centre, tel: 01865-726 871).

ABOVE LEFT:
New College.
BELOW: part of the old city wall, within the New College gardens.

One of the yews in St Peter in the East's churchyard was planted to commemorate James Sadler, the "first English aeronaut", whose inaugural balloon flight took off from Christ Church Meadow on 4 October 1784.

by Sir George Gilbert Scott, as is the stone sedilia (group of three seats) to the left of the altar; one is used to display the founder's gilt and enamelled episcopal staff.

Scott also designed the woodwork of the choir stalls, but incorporated original armrests and 38 misericords that provide a glimpse of 14th-century life, with bishops preaching, acrobats tumbling and monsters with multiple heads.

On the left, as you emerge from the chapel, is the cloister, dominated by a vast and ancient holm oak tree, that evokes medieval Oxford with its original 14th-century wagon roof and atmosphere of tranquillity.

At the northeast corner of the Great Quad is the **Muniment Tower**, again with statues of the Virgin and Wykeham. The steep staircase within leads to the hall, lined with 16th-century linenfold panelling under Scott's 1877 roof. The wall above the high table is hung with portraits of benefactors and wardens (heads of college).

An archway in the Great Quad east range leads through to the Garden Quad, lined with 17th-century neo-Palladian buildings and separated from the gardens beyond by a curvaceous wrought-iron screen – a replica of the original designed by Thomas Robinson in 1711.

The gardens contain a substantial stretch of Oxford's medieval town wall, dating from 1226 when the original timber defensive walls of the town were rebuilt. The college was made responsible for maintaining it under the terms of the original

BELOW: detail of the New College gardens gate.

William Spooner

William Spooner (1844–1930), elected as warden of New College in 1903, was famed for his habit of transposing the initial letters of words to create "Spoonerisms". Many of these lapses – known to academics as metathesis – are thought to be apocryphal, made up subsequently to nurture the myth. There is no evidence, for example, that he once proposed a toast to "our queer Dean". It is also said that he expelled one undergraduate with the words "Sir, you have tasted two whole worms, you have hissed my mystery lectures and you were found fighting a liar in the quad: you will leave at once by the town drain."

land purchase; as a result it is one of England's best-preserved examples of a town wall.

The tree-covered Mound, in the northeastern angle of the wall, looks like a Norman castle motte but was created in the 16th century as a prospect from which to view the gardens.

Saxon church

Exit the college via the New College Lane gatehouse, and turn left under the archway and round another bend into **Queen's Lane**. Traffic-free, the walk along Queen's Lane is enlivened by Michael Groser's series of corbels on the New College buildings to the left, carved in the 1960s with harvest mice, beetles, frogs, lizards and other zoological subjects.

Beyond the sharp right-hand bend in the lane is the church of **St Peter in the East** ❹, whose 11th-century tower is one of the oldest in Oxford. Originally dating from Saxon times, the present church is now the library of neighbouring St Edmund Hall, but visitors can gain access to the cavernous 11th-century **crypt**, one of the finest in Oxford, by asking for the key at St Edmund's porter's lodge.

During the war local residents used the crypt as an air-raid shelter, though Oxford was never actually bombed. A torch is useful for those who want to study the details: the capitals are carved with dragon-like beasts. In summer, St Edmund Hall students study beneath the yews in the churchyard.

St Edmund Hall ❺

Tel: 01865-279 000
Opening Hrs: daily 10.30am–3pm, college functions permitting
Entrance Fee: Free

Noted for its small, flower-filled quads, **St Edmund Hall** achieved independent status as late as 1957. Before that, it had been controlled by Queen's College, next door. It is, however, the only surviving example in Oxford of the medieval halls that pre-dated the foundation of the colleges. By tradition, it dates to the 1190s, when St Edmund of Abingdon taught here, and therefore has every right to be considered Oxford's oldest educational establishment.

Everything about St Edmund Hall is built on a diminutive scale, includ-ing the chapel, on the east side of the Front Quad. Note that the pillars supporting the 1682 door pediment are carved to resemble a stack of leather-bound books. Fans of pre-Raphaelite artists William Morris and Edward Burne-Jones should check with the lodge for permission to see some of their stained-glass work in the chapel, together with original cartoon drawings. There is also a bold modern altar painting of *Christ at Emmaeus* (1958) by Ceri Richards.

Morris Oxford's birthplace

The narrow confines of Queen's Lane finish as it emerges on the High Street. Immediately to the right is Queen's College *(see page 105)*, while on the corner on the left you can rest your legs at Queen's Lane Coffee House.

Turn left here and continue for a short stretch along The High towards the traffic lights at Longwall Street. At No. 48 is a shoe shop, once the bicycle repair shop of William Morris, where the famous mechanic began his career.

To follow Morris's career further, turn left again into **Longwall Street**.

ABOVE:
Morris memorabilia – a 1951 advertisement for the Nuffield Organization.
BELOW: St Edmund Hall.

Just around the first corner on the left is the building that housed the **garage**  in which Morris built the prototype of the "bullnose" Morris Oxford in 1912, a project that was to launch him on the road to fame and fortune and launch Oxford into the industrial era. Though the garage was converted to residential accommodation in 1981, there is an information window with further details on the career of Morris, later Lord Nuffield (*see pages 46–8*).

Church of St Cross

Adjacent is Holywell Street, but first continue north along the main road to the **Church of St Cross** ❼ on the right. The present church was founded in the 11th century on the site of an ancient chapel of St Peter in the East, which was established beside a pagan Saxon holy well (hence "Holywell"), and became an important place of pilgrimage.

The only surviving Norman part of the church is the chancel, but the 13th-century tower has a fascinating feature, namely the **sundial clock**. The grave of Kenneth Grahame,

author of *Wind in the Willows*, is in the churchyard. The key to the church is available from the porter of the neighbouring Holywell Manor; sadly, the ancient holy well is no longer there.

St Catherine's College

Opposite the church are the huge brick cubes of the **Law Library** (1964), while a turn right into Manor Road brings you to a classic example of 1960s architecture, **St Catherine's College** ❽ (usually closed to the public, but enquire at the porter's lodge), designed by Danish architect Arne Jacobsen and completed in 1964.

While modern architects rave over its pioneering "functional" style, most find the plain yellow-brick buildings dull. However, the landscaping, also planned by Jacobsen, is now mature and does much to compensate – especially the long vista between the Cherwell and the water gardens, backed by the splendid trees of Magdalen College meadows.

Linacre College

On the corner of South Parks Road is another "new" college, **Linacre** (tel: 01865-271 650; enquire at the porter's lodge for admission). It was founded in 1962 for students studying for higher degrees, notably gradu-

ABOVE: sign outside the Turf Tavern.
ABOVE RIGHT: Church of St Cross.
BELOW: St Catherine's College.

ates of universities other than Oxford. Thomas Linacre (1460–1524) was an Oxford medical scientist and classicist whose multidisciplinary approach the college seeks to emulate.

Back towards the centre, **Holywell Street** is one of Oxford's quietest and most charming streets, closed to traffic and lined with pastel-painted, timber-framed houses and Cotswold-stone vernacular; most are now student lodgings. New College's imposing Holywell Buildings, with the college's main entrance, are also here, on the left.

Music and mead

On the other side of the street is the **Holywell Music Room ❾** (tickets from the Playhouse box office; tel: 01865-305 305), opened in 1748 and reputedly the world's oldest surviving concert hall. Restored in 1959–60, it can seat 250 and has acoustics that do particular justice to solo recitals and chamber concerts.

In Holywell Street, too, you can see how effectively the town wall marked the limits of the city, for, apart from the 17th- and 18th-century houses of

Holywell Street itself, everything to the north belongs to another age, part of the 19th-century expansion of the city.

Near the western end of Holywell Street, on the left, is **Bath Place**, a narrow, cobbled alley with many right-angled bends, leading past ramshackle houses – former slums but now picturesque leaning cottages backing up against the town wall. Follow it through to the rambling **Turf Tavern ❿**. Recently renovated, the Turf is a splendid, low-beamed English tavern. Its foundations date to the 13th century, though most of the present building is 16th-century. At the back is an attractive beer garden, and along the alleyway is another terraced area, tucked up against the exterior wall of New College cloisters.

Another venerable Oxford watering hole is at the end of Holywell Street on the right: **The King's Arms ⓫** is a pub much frequented by students, particularly when exams are over. ❏

ABOVE: recital at the Holywell Music Room.

RESTAURANTS AND PUBS

Alternative Tuck Shop

24 Holywell Street.
Tel: 01865-792 054.
Open: Mon–Sat. £ ❺ p279, D3

Catering to the area's student population, this café serves up some of central Oxford's best sandwiches as well as pies and pastries. Queues can be long at the peak lunchtime period.

Edamame

15 Holywell Street. Tel: 01865-246 916. L Wed–Sun, D Thur–Sat, closed during Sept. £ ❻ p279, D3

In the rather unlikely setting of pastel-painted medieval Holywell Street, Edamame takes the diner (or, more likely, luncher) into an entirely different cultural eating experience. The atmosphere is authentically Japanese, as is the food, which tends to be limited in choice but of high quality. Canteen-style service and reasonable prices means long queues at lunchtime, but on weekend evenings there is more time and

space to enjoy sushi and such Japanese delicacies as squid pieces in soy and ginger.

The Rose

51 High Street. Tel: 01865-244 429. Open: daily. £ ❼ p279, D4

A restaurant/tearoom serving good traditional English food, ranging from cooked breakfasts to delicious afternoon teas. The restaurant closes at 6pm.

• • • • • • • • •

Price for a three-corse meal with half-bottle of house wine.
££ = £20–30,
£ = under £20.

Pubs

The Turf Tavern (Bath Place ⓴ p279, D3) is an Oxford legend. Atmospheric gardens surrounded by medieval buildings and city walls, and a snug interior are the setting for good food and drinks including (in winter) hot rum punch.
The King's Arms (40 Holywell Street ㉑ p279, C3) is also almost part of the university. Its solid Georgian exterior, a local landmark, promises good beer, an extensive menu and a busy atmosphere.

CHRIST CHURCH AND BEYOND

Here can be found the origins of the city, the only college with a cathedral, recurring echoes of *Alice in Wonderland* and alternative art

The road heading south from Carfax is called St Aldate's. It was here, down towards the river, that the first Oxford settlement is thought to have been established, beside the Abbey of St Frideswide. St Frideswide's Abbey provided the core of the massive college of Christ Church, part of whose rich folklore includes the tales told by one of its dons, Charles Dodgson (writing as Lewis Carroll).

Heading down St Aldate's, you pass the **Town Hall** ❶ on the left, a fine neo-Jacobean building, opened in 1897, with Queen Victoria seated in the apex of the central pediment. It was built to the greater glory of the City Council, reflecting Oxford's newly found status and self-confidence after it was declared a county borough in 1889. Above, the three-tiered belvedere on the roof is topped by a weather vane in the shape of a horned ox – for Oxford was originally called Oxenford.

Tea dances are still regularly held in the Town Hall Main Hall and sometimes in the adjoining Assembly Room, beneath a large and incongruous painting of the *Rape of the Sabines* by Pietro da Cortona (1596–1669) and portraits of former mayors and members of parliament. The Town Hall contains the city archives, and as Oxford was never bombed or burned the records are particularly complete.

Museum of Oxford ❷

Tel: 01865-252 761
Opening Hrs: Tue–Fri 10am–5pm, Sat–Sun noon–5pm
Entrance Fee: Charge

Round the corner, in Blue Boar Street, is the entrance to the former library, built at the same time as the Town Hall and now housing the **Museum of Oxford**. The museum has an easy-

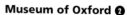

LEFT: Saxon exhibit at the Museum of Oxford.

to-digest history of the city's development. Displays highlight its history from prehistoric times to the industrial age, with exhibits ranging from reconstructions of Roman kilns to the legend of St Frideswide, and from the origins of the university to the development of car production at Cowley. Best of all are the reconstructions of Oxford houses, contrasting the working-class district of Jericho (*see page 171*) with the stylish drawing-rooms of North Oxford's villas, decorated with the latest William Morris textiles, and the reconstruction of a 1930s living room in the newly built Morris Motors suburb of Cowley. Other highlights are the Keble College Barge, an example of one of the ornate floating boathouses of the late 19th century from which spectators watched river races during Eights Week. The most macabre exhibit is the skeleton of Giles Covington, an Oxford Freeman who was convicted of murder and executed in 1791.

The Town Hall building enlivens an otherwise dull stretch – the 1879 **post office** on the right is of interest only for the brass-bound wooden posting box in front. **Pembroke Street**, the first turning on the right, provides a better flavour of old Oxford, before Victorian improvers and modern developers set to work – lined as it is with jettied and pastel-coloured bay-windowed houses.

Modern Art Oxford (MAO) ❸

Tel: 01865-722 733
Opening Hrs: Tue–Sat 10am–5pm, Sun noon–5pm
Entrance Fee: Free

Down Pembroke Street, **Modern Art Oxford** (**MAO**), at No.30, occupies an old brewery warehouse on the right-hand side of the road. MAO mounts highly regarded exhibitions of contemporary work. The **café**, in the basement, is a good place to rest the legs.

On the other side of St Ebbe's Street, in **Pennyfarthing Place**, is the **Church of St Ebbe's ❹**, dedicated to a 7th-century Northumbrian abbess. The church was demolished and rebuilt in 1816, but the 12th-century west doorway, ornamented with beakheads, has survived.

ABOVE: sign for the Museum of Oxford.
BELOW: Modern Art Oxford.

Back now to St Aldate's, where the eponymous evangelical church stands back from the main road, in leafy Pembroke Square: **St Aldate's Church** was virtually rebuilt in 1832, and is the centre of the city's lively young evangelical congregation – services are noisy affairs, at which hymns are sung with much *joie de vivre* and to the accompaniment of guitars and tambourines.

Pembroke College ❺

Tel: 01865-276 444
Opening Hrs: enquire at the porter's lodge for access

Entrance Fee: Free

The square also provides access, on its southern side, to **Pembroke College**. The college was founded in 1624 by King James I, and his statue occupies a niche in the tower of the Hall, which is situated on the right-hand side of the Chapel Quad and is reached by means of a steep, stone staircase.

The hammerbeam roof and tall Perpendicular windows all look convincingly 15th-century, but the hall was actually built in 1848 by John Hayward. The chapel, on the opposite side of the quad, was completed in 1732.

ABOVE: architectural finesse at Pembroke College.

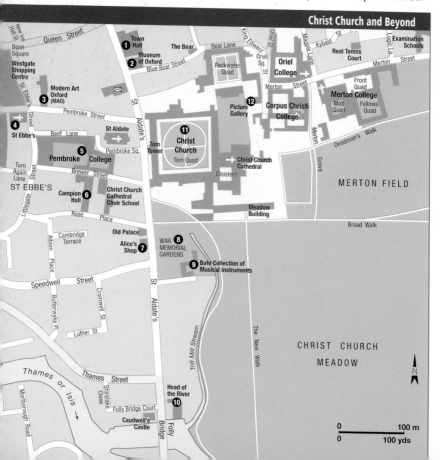

ABOVE: tutorial at Pembroke College.

Opposite Pembroke Square looms the magnificent **Tom Tower** of Christ Church, by Wren. To the north are the first-floor rooms in which Charles Dodgson, creator of *Alice's Adventures in Wonderland*, last resided while at Christ Church. Dodgson, a mathematics don at the college, made friends with Alice, the daughter of the dean, while taking photographs of the cathedral from the Deanery garden, and together they plunged into their own fantasy world *(see page 71)*.

Because there is often no public access to Christ Church through the entrance under Tom Tower, continue for the moment down the right-hand side of St Aldate's. For another diversion, turn right into Brewer Street.

The buildings on the left house **Christ Church Cathedral Choir School**, and the delightful music of boys rehearsing for evensong is often carried on the breeze.

Further down, on the left, is **Campion Hall** ❻, a rather austere building of 1935 and Oxford's only example of Sir Edwin Lutyens' architecture. Campion Hall was set up in 1895 as a place of study for Roman Catholic priests. The chapel has a striking set of Stations of the Cross painted by Frank Brangwyn.

The friendlier-looking garden wing of Campion Hall, built in Cotswold vernacular style, can be seen by turning left into Littlegate and left again into Rose Place. At the end of Rose Place, on the right, is the **Old Palace**, built for the first bishop of Oxford in the 16th century. The oriel windows, supported by carved wooden grotesques, are dated 1628.

Alice's Wonderland

Back in St Aldate's, the little shop on the right (No. 83) is **Alice's Shop** ❼ (daily 11am–5pm). It is here that Alice Liddell used to buy her favourite barley sugar, before setting out on river trips with Charles Dodgson. In *Through the Looking Glass*, Alice visits the shop and is served by a

The lexicographer Samuel Johnson was a student at Pembroke. He didn't complete his degree there, but was later awarded an honorary degree in recognition of his achievements in compiling the first English dictionary.

ABOVE: Alice's Shop, for souvenirs relating to Lewis Carroll's *Alice in Wonderland*, and (BELOW) the shop sign.

Gardens, a gateway leads to the University Music Faculty, with a sign indicating the **Bate Collection of Musical Instruments**. Established from a donation by Philip Bate in 1963, the collection is an unrivalled survey of woodwind instruments, added to by many donations of brass instruments, pianos and harpsichords, as well as a fine gamelan from Indonesia.

Further down, with the redeveloped district of St Ebbe's on the right, lies **Folly Bridge**, thought to be on the site of the first crossing point ("oxen-ford") over the Thames, created in the 8th century to serve the expanding Saxon community. The present bridge dates from 1827.

From Folly Bridge, visitors can enter through the turnstile gate behind the **Head of the River** pub ❿ and walk along the Thames to the **College Boathouses** *(see page 204)*. On the other side of the bridge stands Cauldwell's Castle, also known as Isis House, an ornate red-brick folly decorated with white classical statues that was once rumoured to be a house of ill repute.

Nearby is the Aziz Pandesia restaurant, fusing Indian, Bangladeshi and Thai influences and offering great views over the river.

Christ Church ⓫

Tel: 01865-276 150
Opening Hrs: college and cathedral Mon–Sat 9am–5pm, Sun 2–5pm; entry through Meadow Building; guided tours available
Entrance Fee: Charge

Christ Church was founded as Cardinal College in 1525 by Thomas Wolsey, Henry VIII's all-powerful lord chancellor, on the site of a priory thought to have been founded by St Frideswide as long ago as 730 *(see margin note)*.

The earliest Oxford settlement may have been a lay community serving St Frideswide's; Saxon tools, artefacts and items of clothing have

bad-tempered sheep – indeed it was illustrated in that book by Sir John Tenniel as "the Old Sheep Shop".

Directly opposite is Christ Church Cathedral rising beyond the **War Memorial Gardens** ❽. Laid out in 1926, the colourful raised perennial beds provide access to the public entrance to the college, through the **Meadow Building**.

Because of the way the official route round Christ Church is organised, starting at the Meadow Building and finishing in Merton Lane, before entering visitors may first want to continue down St Aldate's towards the Thames.

Bate Collection of Musical Instruments ❾

Tel: 01865-276 139
Opening Hrs: Mon–Fri 2–5pm, also Sat 10am–noon during term-time; guided tours by arrangement
Entrance Fee: Charge

On the left-hand side, south of the

been found during excavations in St Aldate's. But the first truly historical reference comes in a royal charter of Ethelred the Unready, compensating the community for the burning down of its church by the Danes in 1002. A new Augustinian priory, dedicated to the saint, was re-established here by the 12th century, and had been greatly extended by Wolsey's time.

Wolsey dissolved it, using the endowments to found his new college, originally called Cardinal College. But his grand scheme came to an end in 1529 when he fell from grace after failing to secure the speedy annulment of Henry VIII's marriage to Catherine of Aragon. Henry rescued the church and took over the college, refounding it as King Henry VIII's College in 1532. Ten years later, Oxford was made a diocese and the priory was elevated to a cathedral, which Henry then combined with the college, renaming it Christ Church in 1546. Thus the church is unique in being both a college chapel and a cathedral.

Tour of the college

Having entered Christ Church, follow the visitors' trail to the **Cloister**, which dates from the 15th century. Wolsey destroyed the west and south sides of the cloister, as well as three bays of the priory church, to make way for Tom Quad *(see page 161)*.

ABOVE: Christ Church College's Meadow Building.
BELOW LEFT: "Blue Button" guides are noted for their expertise.

According to 12th-century accounts of her life, St Frideswide, Oxford's patron saint, refused to marry the king of Mercia and fled to Binsey, where she hid for three years in the woods, working as a servant to a swineherd. When the king tried to take Frideswide by force, he was, it is said, struck and blinded by a lightning bolt.

Follow the cloister round to the left, arriving, just before the opening to Tom Quad, at the foot of the **staircase** to the Hall. Designed by James Wyatt in 1829, the stairs were built under the splendid fan-vaulted ceiling that had been created in 1640 by Dean Samuel Fell. The best view of the ceiling, and the single slender pillar supporting it, is from the top of the stairs.

Across the landing is the entrance to the **Hall**. With its magnificent hammerbeam roof, this is easily the largest old hall in Oxford, representing the full splendour of the Tudor court. The walls are adorned with portraits of some of the college's alumni, including William Gladstone and Anthony Eden (two of the 13 prime ministers produced by Christ Church) as well as John Locke, the great philosopher, and William Penn, the founder of Pennsylvania. The portrait just inside the door is that of Charles Dodgson.

The cloisters, the staircase and the Hall itself will be familiar to the millions who have enjoyed the film versions of the *Harry Potter* novels. The

BELOW: Christ Church's dining hall.

Hall was used as the inspiration for Hogwarts Hall, with its magically moving portraits, while the staircase featured in the scene in which first-year Hogwarts students are greeted by Professor McGonagall.

The Cathedral

Exit the hall and return to the top of the stairs for a view over the enormous Tom Quad; then go out into the quad and turn right into the **Cathedral**.

Begun towards the end of the 12th century, when Norman architecture was giving way to the new Early English style, the old priory church part of the cathedral is rather disappointing from an architectural point of view. The aisles are too squat when compared to the size of the columns, and the small pairs of rounded arches fit too awkwardly into the main ones.

By contrast, the 15th-century **Choir** with its lierne-vaulted ceiling – similar to that of the Divinity School – is magnificent. To the north of the choir is the reconstructed canopy from St Frideswide's tomb.

In the **Latin Chapel**, to the north, is a Burne-Jones window of 1858, depicting the life of the saint, including a depiction of St Margaret's Well at Binsey – the "Treacle Well" from *Alice's Adventures in Wonderland (see page 209)*. This is one of Burne-Jones's earliest works, and the crowded scenes are full of dramatic detail, though the calamine-lotion colour of the faces is less successful.

In 1877, Burne-Jones also designed the **St Catherine Window** next to the altar, depicting Edith Liddell, sister of Lewis Carroll's Alice, as the saint. Nearby is a monument to Robert Burton (died 1640), author of *The Anatomy of Melancholy*. There is more excellent stained glass around the cathedral, much of it designed by William Morris and Edward Burne-Jones.

St Lucy's Chapel

Further west, **St Lucy's Chapel** contains a wealth of early 14th-century glass, including a scene showing the martyrdom of St Thomas Becket, the archbishop of Canterbury brutally murdered by King Henry II's henchmen in 1170. He keeps company with a number of lewd and grotesque beasts that inhabit the tracery lights.

Exit the cathedral by the south door, turning left to re-enter the cloister. Through a doorway, the Old Chapter House, with its Norman doorway and tall Early English lancet windows, now houses a souvenir shop as well as a collection of cathedral and college treasures. Continue clockwise around the cloister, arriving back at the opening to Tom Quad.

Tom Quad

Measuring 264ft by 261ft (roughly 80 metres square), **Tom Quad**, the college's Great Quadrangle, is by far the largest quadrangle in the city. While considering its size, it is also worth stopping to consider the history of the college and its architecture. Wolsey intended everything about his foundation to be built on the grandest scale. However, all that was completed when he fell from grace in 1529 was the hall, the kitchens behind, and three sides of the Great Quad, including the lower stage of the gate-tower.

The college remained in this half-finished state for more than a century. Building work began again around 1640, when Samuel Fell commissioned the splendid fan vault under which we now stand. Shortly afterwards, Charles I made Christ Church his residence and work stopped during the Civil War.

After the monarchy was restored, the autocratic John Fell (Samuel's son) was appointed dean. He completed the fourth side of the Great Quad, adding the north range, copying Wolsey's

work exactly, even right down to the truncated pillars and arches that had been intended to support a vaulted cloister all around the perimeter.

At the western side of the quad – and intended to be its focal point – Fell commissioned Christopher Wren to finish the great gate-tower (**Tom Tower**), which he did in adventurous style, adding the bulky octagonal tower with its lead-covered cupola in 1681. Inside the tower, weighing more than seven tons, is the **Great Tom** bell. Recast before being installed, the original bell came from the enormous Osney Abbey to the west of the town, which was completely destroyed at the Dissolution in 1536.

The bell is named not as some people think after Thomas Wolsey, but after Thomas Becket, whose martyrdom gave him a considerable cult following.

The central fountain, dug originally to supply water to the college, is also contemporary with this work. A statue of Mercury was put up in 1695

ABOVE: Tom Quad.
BELOW: the ornate ceiling of Christ Church Cathedral.

ABOVE:
Peckwater Quad.
BELOW:
Canterbury Quad.

but was removed in 1817 after being damaged. The current statue, a copy of Giovanni da Bologna's *Mercury*, was donated in 1928 and is sometimes to be seen clothed in sports kit or academic dress when students play their pranks in the relaxed post-exam weeks of summer.

Follow the eastern range of the quad to the northeastern corner and the **Deanery**. It was here, during the Civil War, that Charles I resided when in the city. The Deanery Garden is just over the other side.

The **Fell Tower**, the castellated tower facing on to the quad, was built in 1876–9, with its statue of John Fell who, for all that he did to improve Christ Church, was a strict disciplinarian and far from popular.

Peckwater Quad

Passing beneath Fell Tower, you pass **Killcanon** on the left, built in 1669 and so called because of the icy winds that blow around the block in winter, and enter **Peckwater Quad**, named after a medieval inn that stood on the site until these grand classical buildings were constructed in 1713. The three enclosed sides of the quad

(containing student accommodation) are perfectly proportioned according to all the classical rules.

Opposite stands the college **Library**, built in 1716 and originally designed with the ground floor as an open loggia. Its giant Corinthian columns lend weight and splendour to this side of the quadrangle. The library is not open to the public but you can, with discretion, peer through the windows at the ceiling-high bookstacks, leather-bound volumes and fine stucco ceiling.

Christ Church Picture Gallery ⓬

Tel: 01865-276 172
Opening Hrs: May–Sept Mon–Sat 10.30am–5pm, Sun 2–5pm, Oct–Apr Mon–Sat 10.30am–1pm and 2–4.30pm, Sun 2–4.30pm
Entrance Fee: Charge

From Peckwater Quad, proceed to Canterbury Quad; on the right is the entrance to the **Picture Gallery**. It contains a small but important collection of Old Masters, including works by Tintoretto, Veronese and Van Dyck, as well as a famous Holbein portrait of Henry VIII. ❑

BEST RESTAURANTS, CAFÉS, PUBS AND BARS

Restaurants

Shanghai 30s
82 St Aldate's.
Tel: 01865-242 230.
Open: daily ££–£££ **❽**
p280, C2
A far cry from the normal Chinese take-away, this is an up-market and sophisticated place, housed in the premises of the former and legendary Elizabeth Restaurant. The emphasis is on seafood, but many other classics, including a large vegetarian menu, are available in a restaurant that succeeds in being both elegant and friendly.

Cafés

Café Loco (85 St Aldate's **㉒** p280, C2) is a cheerfully busy café, serving a good range of sandwiches, salads and daily specials. Open every day, it provides good breakfasts and afternoon teas, even if the drinks can seem rather over-priced.

The café in the basement of **Modern Art**

Prices for a three-course dinner per person with a half-bottle of house wine:
£ = under £20
££ = £20–£30
£££ = £30–£45
££££ = more than £45

Oxford (Tue–Sat 10am–5pm, Sun noon–5pm **㉓** p280, B1), housed in a building which first saw the light of day as a brewery warehouse, is a pleasantly relaxed spot where you can enjoy a wholesome lunch of salads or afternoon tea and cakes. Child-friendly and welcoming, it offers a good alternative to central Oxford's more predictable eateries.

Another good option is **George & Danver's** (1 Pembroke Street **㉔** p280, C2), a hospitable café/sandwich bar that specialises in its own brand of ice cream (there is a sister outlet, George & Davis, in Little Clarendon Street).

Further down St Aldate's you will find **Reservoir Books** (84 St Aldate's **㉕** p280, C2), something of an intellectual centre, with second-hand books and an exhibition space as well as a well-run café with excellent coffee and cakes. The café's mission is not only to cater for peckish bookworms but also to preserve the wonderful yet dilapidated 16th-century building in which it is housed.

RIGHT: the Head of the River, by the water's edge.

Pubs and Bars

Next to MAO, the **Royal Blenheim** pub (13 St Ebbe's Street **㉖** p280, B1) is a quiet inner-city local, with none of the youth-oriented atmosphere of nearby competitors. It serves a good range of pub lunches.
The St Aldate's Tavern (108 St Aldate's **㉗** p280, C1) is a spacious, high-ceilinged establishment, with a good mix of Town and Gown custom and an above-average range of real ales.
The Old Tom (101 St Aldate's **㉘** p280, C1),

named after Christ Church's Tom Tower opposite, is a real Oxford institution, but is worth visiting only for the small beer garden.
The enormously popular **Head of the River** (Folly Bridge **㉙** p280, C3) draws big crowds in the summer on account of its attractive riverside terrace. Housed in an imaginatively restored warehouse, the pub is a reliable, if pricey, place for lunch, but the views of the river compensate. It has guest rooms that overlook the river.

NORTHWEST OF THE CENTRE

After exploring the Ashmolean, discover the city's
publishing heritage in the district of Jericho
and round off with a drink in a pub
linked to the literary set

Looking across from the Martyrs' Memorial, the entrance to Beaumont Street is dominated on the left by the famous, yellow-brick **Randolph Hotel** ❶, a splendid Victorian-Gothic edifice dating from 1863. The Randolph is Oxford's most famous hotel. It is a popular venue for conferences, and at the beginning of the academic year in October you can often see nervous Freshers eating in the restaurant with their parents – a last meal before a new life begins. The lounge contains paintings by Sir Osbert Lancaster, commissioned to illustrate Max Beerbohm's 1911 satire on Oxford life, *Zuleika Dobson*.

The Taylor Institute

Facing all this Gothicry is the **Taylor Institute** and, beyond, the Ashmolean Museum. Built between 1841 and 1845 and a rare example in Oxford of neo-Grecian architecture, the forceful design of the two linked buildings is freely based on the Temple of Apollo at Bassae which the architect, Charles Robert Cockerell, had studied. The four statues standing on top of the columns of the Taylor Institute – that is the east wing, facing St Giles – represent France, Italy, Germany and Spain, for the institution was founded, under the will of Sir Robert Taylor, mainly for the study of the languages of these countries. The building now houses lecture theatres and the Taylorian Library, devoted to books published in the principal European languages.

The Ashmolean ❷

Tel: 01865-278 000
Opening Hrs: Tue–Sat 10am–5pm, Sun noon–5pm, June–Aug until 7pm
Entrance Fee: Donation

LEFT: medieval cottages in Worcester College.
RIGHT: Oxford's most famous hotel.

Fronting on to Beaumont Street, and surmounted by a statue of Apollo, is the pillared portico of the **Ashmolean Museum**. Containing the University of Oxford's collections of art and antiquities, the building was originally known as the University Galleries, housing a sculpture collection donated by Francis Randolph.

The name "Ashmolean" was first applied when extensions were built in 1899 to house the collections of the antiquary and scholar Elias Ashmole. These had hitherto been housed in purpose-built premises on Broad Street (now the Museum of the History of Science, *see page 140*), established by Ashmole in 1683. Regarded as one of the oldest museum collections in the country, its origins go back to before Ashmole's day, and not to Oxford, but to Lambeth, London. There, in a pub called The Ark, the early 17th-century naturalist and royal gardener John Tradescant

displayed his extensive collection of rarities and curiosities either gathered by himself on his trips to Europe or given to him by sea captains. After his death in 1638, Tradescant's son, also called John, infused the collection with items from Virginia, to which he travelled on several occasions. Meanwhile, Ashmole had befriended the Tradescants and persuaded them that he would be a suitable curator for their curiosities after their deaths. The younger Tradescant left a contradictory will bequeathing the collection to both Oxford and Cambridge, which his widow and Ashmole challenged. Ashmole won, in time, and in return for an honorary degree, he passed it to Oxford.

Items from the original "Ark" are still displayed in the museum, in room 8 on the lower ground floor. It is a wonderfully eccentric and eclectic group of objects, including Guy Fawkes' lantern, Oliver Cromwell's death mask and a piece of the stake

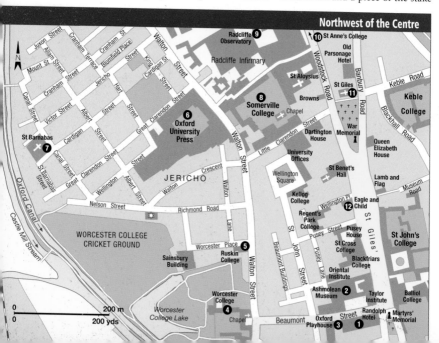

at which Bishop Latimer was burned, as well as a rhinoceros-horn cup from China, Henry VIII's stirrups and hawking gear, and, as the star attraction, **Powhattan's Mantle**. Powhattan was the king of Virginia, and as any child will tell you, the father of Pocahontas.

Since moving to Beaumont Street, the Ashmolean has developed into one of the world's great museums, hugely enriched by archaeological material, given by such notable excavators as Sir Flinders Petrie, the late 19th-century Egyptologist, and Sir Arthur Evans, who discovered the great palace complex of Knossos on Crete. In 2009, the museum reopened after a £60-million redevelopment. Behind the original 1845 Cockerell Building, a brand new gallery space has been created. This has doubled the capacity, with 39 more galleries plus an education centre and rooftop restaurant. The stunning design, by architect Rick Mather, also features interlinking glass-enclosed walkways and airy stairwells ranging over five floors.

The museum has completely reorganised its exhibits, bringing the interaction of civilisations and cultures to the fore. Thus, on the Ancient World (ground) floor, objects dating from pre-history to 700 AD plot the emergence and flowering of ancient cultures from Egypt and the Near East, through Greece and Rome, to India and China, a theme continued on the next floor with coverage of the Silk Road. Art occupies the upper levels. Don't miss the drawings by Michelangelo and Raphael, as well as *The Hunt in the Forest*, painted by the Florentine Paolo Uccello in 1466. There are also more recent works by pre-Raphaelite and Impressionist artists.

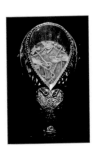

The Alfred Jewel

Back down on the lower ground floor, the museum's superb coin collection is now housed in room 7, next to the Ark. But it is on the second floor (room 41, England 400–1600) that the museum's most famous artefact is to be found. Unearthed in Somerset in 1693, the **Alfred Jewel** is regarded as the finest piece of Saxon art ever discovered. Consisting of an enamel seated figure set under a rock crystal in a gold frame bear-

ABOVE: the Alfred Jewel, one of the stars of the Ashmolean. **BELOW:** the Ashmolean Museum.

ABOVE: entertainment at the Oxford Playhouse.
BELOW RIGHT: Worcester College chapel.

WHERE

Just round the corner from the Oxford Playhouse, in Gloucester Street, is the Burton Taylor Studio. A 50-seat theatre at the top of two flights of stairs, it showcases student productions during term and, out of term, hosts touring companies or community theatre groups. Tel: 01865-305 305. www.oxford playhouse.com.

ing the inscription *Aelfred mec heht gewyrcan* ("Alfred had me made"), it isn't in fact an item of personal jewellery but would have been affixed to a pointer for following the text in a manuscript. Such pointers are known to have been given as gifts by Alfred (849–99), along with copies of his translation of Gregory the Great's *Pastoral Care*.

To the theatre

Opposite the Ashmolean and adjacent to the Beaumont Street side of the Randolph is the **Oxford Playhouse** ❸ (tel: 01865-305 305). Opened in 1923, the original Playhouse, opposite Somerville, was known as the "Red Barn" and in 1938 it moved to the present building on Beaumont Street. It has often struggled with financial problems and in 1987 was forced to close after the imposition of new fire regulations and funding cuts. But in 1991 the Playhouse reopened and in 1996 underwent a major refurbishment project costing £4 million, £2.5

million of which was provided by the Arts Council Lottery Fund.

Early members of the Playhouse company included Dame Flora Robson and Sir John Gielgud, but perhaps its most celebrated supporters were Richard Burton and Elizabeth Taylor, who in 1966 performed *Doctor Faustus* free of charge, earning the theatre enough extra revenue to afford an extension, the Burton Taylor Studio *(see margin tip)*. Burton, who had first acted while in Oxford during World War II, retained a strong allegiance to the city and was a generous donor to the Playhouse, and also to St Peter's College and the student newspaper, *Isis*.

Today, the Playhouse offers a broad programme of work that includes drama, dance, opera, musical theatre, popular music and jazz. It has a fledgling youth and education community scheme, plus an attractive bar and coffee shop.

The rest of **Beaumont Street** consists of Regency terraces, several with delicate cast-iron fanlights, verandahs and balconies, built between 1822 and 1833. Slightly humbler town houses of the same date line **St John Street** to the right. For anyone wanting to live in Oxford, this is about as close to the city centre as you can get.

Most of the houses serve as college lodgings, or the premises of solicitors, doctors and dentists – but occasionally one does come up for sale.

The western end of Beaumont Street was once occupied by Beaumont Palace, built in the early 12th century by Henry I as his royal residence in Oxford, and the birthplace of his sons Richard (the Lionheart) and John. Though the palace represented the town's rise in importance during the early Middle Ages, it did not remain here for long; the original door was used by Merton's founders as their library entrance, where it can still be seen (see page 120).

Worcester College ④

Tel: 01865-278 300
Opening Hrs: daily 2–5pm
Entrance Fee: Free

At the end of Beaumont Street, cross the road to enter **Worcester College**. Worcester is different from most other colleges in that it has no intimate, enclosed quadrangles. But this in no way detracts from the appeal of the place, for as well as some fine architecture, the college has some of the most beautiful gardens.

Founded in the early 18th century, the origins of the college go back to Gloucester Hall, established on the site for Benedictine monks in 1283, but dissolved in about 1539. After the Dissolution, Gloucester continued as an academic hall, despite several Benedictine changes of ownership, but slid into debt and decline. The doorheads of the west range bear the coats of arms, carved in stone, of the principal abbeys connected with the college: Glastonbury, Malmesbury, Canterbury and Pershore.

Revival only came at the end of the 17th century with funds provided by Sir Thomas Cookes, a Worcestershire baronet. The new Worcester College received its statutes in 1714, but the 18th-century building programme was financed by another man, George Clarke, who is remembered by the college as *tantum nos Fundator*

ABOVE: the original Gloucester Hall medieval cottages.
BELOW: the crest of one of Worcester College's founding abbeys.

Worcester's library contains many of the drawings of Inigo Jones (1573–1652), the first great English architect, whose masterpiece was the Banqueting Hall in London's Whitehall.

("almost our Founder"). Despite this infusion of money, Worcester was never very wealthy, and the original Gloucester Hall **medieval cottages** owe their survival to the fact that the college could only afford the two neoclassical ranges we see today. Of these, the front or west range is the most interesting, for it contains the **Library** (above the cloister), the **Hall** and the **Chapel** (in the two wings).

Designed by Nicholas Hawksmoor, the library was founded on a substantial collection of books and manuscripts donated by George Clarke and includes a large proportion of the surviving drawings of Inigo Jones. The hall and chapel were completed by James Wyatt in the 1770s. Both were transformed internally by William Burges, in the latter half of the 19th century. The hall was, controversially, restored to its 18th-century appearance in 1966, but the chapel remains as a splendid example of Burges's highly unusual style. Sadly, the gloom created by

the dark stained glass prevents a full appreciation of the lavish interior, with its Roman-style floor mosaics, Raphaelesque frescoes and gilded ceiling. Evangelists fill the niches at each corner of the chapel, and the pew ends are carved with a menagerie of animals and birds.

Worcester is sited on a slope, the land dropping away to the west. A tunnel at the end of the Gloucester Hall cottages leads through to the **gardens**, which are as beautiful as any in Oxford, a fact endorsed by Lewis Carroll in *Alice's Adventures in Wonderland* (1865) when he describes the tunnel "not much larger than a rathole" leading "to the loveliest garden you ever saw".

Landscaped like a small park, the gardens are planted with magnificent trees and shrubs and include a lovely willow-fringed lake, where Alice used to feed the ducks. The lake was reclaimed from the water meadows when the park-like gardens were laid out in the early 19th century, and is now topped up by the overflow from the Oxford Canal, which forms the western boundary of Worcester's grounds. A walk around the lake is recommended.

Looking back through the trees there are glimpses of the Palladian facade of the **Provost's House**, while at the northern end of the lake is

the **Sainsbury Building**. Regarded as one of the best pieces of modern architecture in Oxford, its carefully juxtaposed roof lines and walls descend to a delightful lakeside terrace. Worcester College's playing fields stretch away to the north.

Ruskin College

Exit Worcester and walk north along **Walton Street**. On the corner of Worcester Place stands **Ruskin College ⑤**. Not strictly part of the university, this is one of several institutions founded in memory of the art and social critic John Ruskin, for the education of working men and women. The college has strong links with the trades union movement and the Workers' Educational Association.

Ruskin is appropriately sited on the edge of the former working-class suburb of **Jericho** *(see page 173)*, occupying the block between Walton Street and the Oxford Canal. Some say that the name derives from the

insubstantial nature of the jerry-built terraced houses, a few of which date to the 1830s. There was, however, a pub called the Jericho House here as early as 1688, and the name was used in the 17th century for any remote place, by analogy with the biblical town in Palestine.

The area was developed to house the increasing numbers of workers in this part of the city after the arrival of the Oxford Canal in 1790. When the Oxford University Press moved here from the Clarendon Building in 1830, further houses were built to accommodate the print workers.

Around the first corner from Ruskin, also on the west side of Walton Street, the huge, neoclassical **Oxford University Press** building ⑥ takes up most of the block between Walton Crescent and Great Clarendon Street. The south wing (left) was originally devoted to Bible printing, the north to learned books. To learn more about the history of this world-famous publishing house,

ABOVE: the OUP building on Clarendon Street. **BELOW:** the OUP has a major presence in the city.

St Giles' Fair

Once a religious event, by Victorian times St Giles' Fair had become a whirl of bright lights, freak shows and wondrous inventions – and the thrills are still there for the taking.

The Fair (as it is always called) is one of Oxford's most cherished annual events. Of course, there are those hard-headed citizens who complain that it disrupts trade and traffic, but most people would spring to the defence of an occasion enjoyed by the vast majority.

St Giles' Fair was originally a parish wake, a religious event dating from 1624. The association with St Giles, the patron saint of beggars and cripples, fixed both the date of The Fair (Monday and Tuesday following the first Sunday in September) and the location, the splendidly wide St Giles Street. By the 18th century, the occasion had become a time for feasting, sporting events, and the selling of "small wares".

The Fair came into its own in Victorian times, when "wonders of art and nature" were added. Menageries and freak shows brought an elephant, the Bear Lady and the Double-bodied Hindoo Boy as regular visitors.

New inventions were a big draw: the photographer with his three-for-a-shilling portraits; the miniature railway; the Chairoplane rides. In the late 19th century, the Fair was a dazzling event, with traction engines providing brilliant illuminations. Taylor's Bioscope Show glittered with 4,000 coloured lights, while Jacob Studt's entertainment was approached through Corinthian pillars and graced by troupes of women dancers. More surprisingly, female wrestlers also appeared at The Fair, wearing corsets and black tights.

Little wonder, with such attractions on offer, that The Fair became, by 1900, the major holiday not only for Oxford city, but the county beyond. The huge caravan of wagons and engines gathered in Woodstock Road – then open country – on Sunday, and at 5am on Monday morning, the procession moved into the city.

A brush with the law

The Fair had its problems, of course. In 1838, the mayor of Oxford issued an order excluding gypsies from the site because of pickpocketing. Horseplay was firmly dealt with in 1898, when the mayor decreed a penalty of two months' imprisonment or a £5 fine for anyone found assaulting another with "a Squirt, Scratch-back, Cracker, Whip, or Brush".

In many ways, The Fair today looks much as it did in Edwardian times. The traction engines still provide power, and a splendid roundabout always occupies pride of place by the Martyrs' Memorial. But much more elaborate and terrifying rides now take the place of the freaks and theatre shows. ❏

ABOVE: all the fun of the fair.
LEFT: carousel at St Giles' Fair.

Life in Jericho

Featured as the cholera-ridden slum of Beersheba in Thomas Hardy's *Jude the Obscure* (1895), Jericho's working-class credentials have long expired, for its prime location at the threshold to the city has made it a desirable area to live, particularly for wealthy students and young professionals. House prices have soared and Walton Street is now lined with craft shops, boutiques, delicatessens and restaurants.

Much of Jericho is terraced housing built by speculators and St John's College for the workers of the university, OUP, an iron foundry and the canal. A reputation for seediness in the 1960s led to calls for its demolition.

make an appointment to visit the OUP Museum *(see page 49)*.

It was the print workers who made up the majority of the congregation of the massive **Church of St Barnabas ❼**, which was built by the canal in 1868. You can get to the church and take in some of the atmosphere of old Jericho by taking a stroll down Great Clarendon Street. The church is distinctive for its tall, Italian-Romanesque style tower.

Opposite the Press building is the neo-Grecian facade of the old St Paul's Church, built in 1936. It no longer serves as a church today but as **Freuds**, an unusual wine bar and restaurant with live-music programmes specialising in jazz.

If you continue along Walton Street, you will notice away to the north the distinctive octagonal tower of the Radcliffe Observatory *(see page 174)*. Passing the **Phoenix Picture House**, which shows foreign and non-mainstream films, and Raymond Blanc's brasserie, **Le Petit Blanc** (an affordable offshoot of the great French chef's Le Manoir aux Quat'Saisons),

both on the left, you'll get to Walton Well Road, which leads over the canal and railway line to Port Meadow.

Otherwise, retrace your steps to **Little Clarendon Street**, which links Walton Street with St Giles. Among the various modern administrative buildings of the university are bars, brasseries, cafés, boutiques and gift shops.

Little Clarendon Street emerges at the Woodstock Road end of St Giles. Immediately on the left is **Maison Blanc**, a wonderful patisserie, and adjacent to that is **Browns**, a long-established restaurant popular with families.

Somerville College ❽

Tel: 01865-270 600
Opening Hrs: daily 2–5pm
Entrance Fee: Free

Forth along Woodstock Road, just after St Aloysius Church is **Somerville College**. Founded in 1879 specifically for the education of women, it is now mixed.

ABOVE: Raymond Blanc, begetter of Le Petit Blanc.
BELOW: the Phoenix Picture House.

ABOVE RIGHT: the Radcliffe Observatory. **BELOW:** setting up the Freshers' photograph at Sommerville.

The first "ladies'" college, Lady Margaret Hall, had been established the previous year, but under the aegis of the Anglican Church. A group of breakaway liberal nonconformists founded Somerville, named after the scientist and suffragette Mary Somerville (1780–1872), to take women of all religious persuasions – or none.

Women at Oxford were at first patronised rather than welcomed. They were not allowed to attend lectures; instead, tuition was provided by the AEW, the Association for Promoting the Higher Education of Women. They were not allowed to take degrees until 1920, and Somerville, along with the other four women's halls founded in the late 19th century, was not recognised as a college until 1959.

Despite this, its students include an extraordinary number of public figures, not least Indira Gandhi and Margaret Thatcher. Although Mrs Thatcher may have had her differences with the university, she was loyal to Somerville, making a large donation to the £4-million Margaret Thatcher Centre.

The buildings of Somerville are small and homely in scale, some built in the "Queen Anne" style of the late 19th century, others in 1930s neo-Georgian.

Radcliffe Observatory

Further up Woodstock Road is the **Radcliffe Infirmary**, built from the estates of John Radcliffe, the 18th-century physician, but now surrounded by an accretion of later hospital buildings. The adjacent **Radcliffe Observatory ❾**, completed in 1794, has now been swallowed up by the graduate-only **Green Templeton College** – Oxford's newest college, formed from the merger of two preexisting colleges in 2008.

The Observatory, mostly designed by James Wyatt, does not have the expected dome; instead, it is topped by an elongated octagon, carved with personifications of the four winds and modelled on the ancient Greek Tower of the Winds in Athens. Unfortunately there is no public access to the observatory except for one day a year, the college's open day (tel: 01865-274 770 for information).

St Anne's College

St Anne's College ❿, opposite, traces its origins to the Society of

Oxford Home Students, an organisation formed in 1879 to provide higher education for the daughters and wives of dons and students from the local girls' high schools. Because they lived at home, rather than in one of the two women's halls of residence (Somerville and Lady Margaret), they were known as "unattached students", and opponents of women's education were fond of referring to the society as "Soc. mul. Ox. priv. stud". (abbreviated from the Latin name *Societas mulieram Oxoniae Privatum Studentium*).

The Home Students were taught and supervised in the houses of sympathetic Oxford dons and their friends until, in the 1930s, their number became so great that more permanent arrangements were needed, and so the library and lecture rooms were added to the existing Victorian houses on the current site. Designed by Sir Giles Gilbert Scott, son of the Victorian Gothicist Sir George, they were completed in 1937.

During World War II, so many Oxford families were involved in war work that it became increasingly difficult to accommodate students at home and find suitable "hostesses" or chaperones. Hostels were built and by 1942 St Anne's had been transformed into a residential institution like any other, achieving full college status in 1959.

A number of buildings were added after the war, notably the **Founder's Gatehouse** (1966), a building in the Modernist idiom reflecting medieval precedents in its polygonal turrets, and the **Dining Hall** (1958–60), with its glass walls and rooftop lantern.

Church of St Giles

Heading back towards Oxford city centre, the **Church of St Giles** ⓫ sits at the apex of the fork where Woodstock and Banbury roads take their separate ways. The church is largely 13th-century and sits in an island of green, facing down the wide, tree-lined thoroughfare, best seen in early September when the traffic is excluded for the annual

ABOVE LEFT: the Church of St Giles.
ABOVE RIGHT: St Anne's College.
BELOW: Somerville College student.

St Giles' Fair *(see page 172)*. These days the ancient fair is no different from any of those that are held up and down the country, except for the poignant contrast between the flashing lights, candy floss and bingo stalls set against the sedate and ancient college buildings.

The west (right-hand) side of St Giles' Street is lined with a pleasing mixture of mainly 17th- and 18th-century buildings, many of them owned by religious bodies who, in this century at least, seem to co-exist in neighbourly harmony. They include the Christian Scientists at Nos 34–6, **St Benet's Hall** for Benedictine monks at No. 38, and the Quakers at No. 43.

Beyond Pusey Street is **St Cross College**, a graduates-only college founded in 1965. It has around 220 students and prides itself on its friendliness and the quality of its food.

The Eagle and Child

Perhaps the most interesting building on this side of St Giles' is the **Eagle and Child** pub , on the corner of Wellington Place, always very popular among students. Its name supposedly relates to the legend of a noble-born baby being found in an eagle's nest, but its fame derives from the fact that, from the 1930s to the 1960s, it was the meeting place of the informal literary group known as the "Inklings". Led by C. S. Lewis (described by his pupil John Betjeman as "breezy, tweedy, beer-drinking and jolly"), the Inklings included such luminaries as Charles Williams, Nevill Coghill and J. R. R. Tolkien *(see page 142)*.

It was here, in these cosy, fireside surroundings, that Tolkien began discussing his saga *The Lord of the Rings* with the assembled company – little realising that it would become such a success that he would be forced, by a torrent of letters, phone calls and visits from fans, to exchange the comforts of Oxford for a life of seclusion in Bournemouth.

Eventually, after his wife died in 1971, he returned to Oxford's womb, taking rooms in Merton and becoming an honorary fellow. He died in 1973 and lies buried in Wolvercote Cemetery, just beyond the ring road to the north of the city.

Continuing this literary tradition, the Eagle and Child was a regular watering-hole for Colin Dexter, creator of Inspector Morse. ❑

ABOVE: the pannelled interior of the Eagle and Child pub, an inn since 1650, and (**BELOW RIGHT**) its exterior. **BELOW:** Worcester College gate.

BEST RESTAURANTS, CAFÉS, PUBS AND BARS

Restaurants

The Big Bang
124 Walton Street. Tel: 01865-511 411. www.thebig bangoxford.co.uk Open: daily. £ ⑨ p278, A2
A new initiative, this cheerful restaurant appeals to aficionados of bangers and mash, offering a range of sausages including the famous and eponymous Oxford Sausage. If you don't like sausages, there are various pies, and vegetarians will be relieved to learn that there are several suitable sausage options. A good-value and up-beat establishment, it draws a big student crowd.

Branca
111 Walton Street. Tel: 01865-556 111. www.branca-restaurants.co.uk Open: daily. ££ ⑩ p278, A1
The Italian alternative to Raymond Blanc's French cuisine, Branca is a well-established yet refreshingly modern place specialising in authentic Italian cooking, with a strong emphasis on fresh local produce and attractive presentation. The interior is spacious and welcoming, and the staff helpful.

Prices for a three-course dinner per person with a half-bottle of house wine:
£ = under £20
££ = £20–£30
£££ = £30–£45
££££ = more than £45

Browns Restaurant and Bar
5–11 Woodstock Road. Tel: 01865-511 955. Open: daily. ££ ⑪ p278, B1
The first of Oxford brasserie-style venues, Browns maintains its combination of good simple food and attentive service. It offers everything from a drink to a three-course dinner, with traditional classics such as steak and Guinness pie. At weekends the queues can be long.

Le Petit Blanc
71–2 Walton Street. Tel: 01865-510 999. www.lepetit blanc.co.uk Open: daily ££ ⑫ p278, A1
Oxford's less expensive sister of the acclaimed Quat'Saisons also offers elegant French cuisine, but in the more palatable form of good-value *prix fixe* menus as well as à la carte. The food is a beautifully prepared blend of French regional dishes, served in a pleasantly stripped-down ambience of modern furniture and wooden floors. Booking is highly recommended.

Randolph Hotel Restaurant
Beaumont Street. Tel: 0844-879 9132. www.macdonald hotels.co.uk/randolph Open: daily £££ ⑬ p278, B3
This award-winning restaurant is one of Oxford's finest. Traditional dishes such as braised oxtail, Highland venison and seabass, and the grandest of cheese trolleys make a meal here an occasion to remember. The service is excellent, the wine list impressive, and the surroundings – wooden panelling, fine paintings and coats of arms around the architrave – make you feel you're in a stately home.

Cafés

The smart café in the **Ashmolean Museum** (⑳ p278, B3) provides drinks, snacks, excellent tea and cakes and a range of hot meals at lunchtime.

The **St Giles'** (52 St Giles ㉛ p278, B3) is an above-average "greasy spoon" establishment, with big cooked breakfasts and other fried treats.

Pubs and Bars

The **Morse Bar** in the Randolph Hotel (㉜ p278, B3) is a civilised place for an early evening drink, while the hotel's Drawing Room is the perfect venue for afternoon tea – with cucumber sandwiches, strawberries, and perhaps even champagne – and a good way to sample the old Oxford Victorian elegance.

The **Eagle and Child** (㉝ p278, B2) is a literary landmark in its own right and a good old-fashioned pub serving traditional dishes such as fish and chips or sausage and mash.

Freuds (119 Walton Street ㉞ p278, A2), housed in a converted church, is one of several trendy cocktail bars in the area; it specialises in jazz and student social life.

Raoul's (32 Walton Street ㉟ p278, A2) is another fashionable watering-hole with an impressive cocktail list and an emphatically cool clientele.

The **Duke of Cambridge** (5–6 Little Clarendon Street ㉞ p278, B1) stands out as the most stylish establishment in this stylish street. Prices reflect the status of its up-market clientele.

RIGHT: St Giles' Café.

ST JOHN'S AND THE NORTH

Apart from St John's College, this area was developed after the great university reforms in the mid-19th century, and includes two remarkable museums

Starting in St Giles, follow the east side along the long Balliol facade to the point where it meets the considerably more varied frontage of **St John's College**.

St John's College ❶

Tel: 01865-277 300
Opening Hrs: daily 1–5pm
Entrance Fee: Free

This college, one of the richest in Oxford, was originally founded by Archbishop Chichele, in 1437, for Cistercian monks and named after St Bernard. After the Dissolution of the monasteries, it was refounded, in 1555, by Sir Thomas White, a wealthy member of the Merchant Taylors' Guild. A statue of St Bernard, flanked by the two founders, occupies a niche on the gate-tower. The niche on the inner side contains Eric Gill's splendid *St John the Baptist* (1936).

The Baylie Chapel

The buildings of the Front Quad survive from the original St Bernard College. The hall, though, was remodelled in the 18th century and given its stone screen, designed by James Gibbs, in 1742. The chapel, on the left, was comprehensively spoiled, internally, in the 19th century. More interesting is the **Baylie Chapel** to the north, with its plaster fan-vault. This was built in 1662 and houses the monument to Richard Baylie (died 1667), the Royalist president (head) of St John's, who was forcibly ejected from the college by Parliamentary troops during the 17th-century Civil War but was reinstated at the Restoration.

In remaining staunchly loyal to Charles I, Baylie was following the example of his predecessor, Archbishop Laud, who was president

LEFT: symbol of the college's patron saint, St John the Baptist, the lamb and flag carved on the new organ case in St John's chapel.

from 1611 to 1621 and chancellor of the University from 1629. During his time as chancellor, Laud drew up a long list of rules governing the behaviour of Oxford scholars, which, for all that Laud was strongly opposed to the Calvinist doctrines of his day, could have been written by a staunch Puritan.

Under the Laudian Code, as it is known, professional actors were forbidden to enter the university and scholars were forbidden to hunt, gamble, smoke, drink or wear their hair long or in curls – these rules remained the basis of university discipline until 1854.

Canterbury Quad

It is all the more remarkable, therefore, that Laud also financed the construction of the **Canterbury Quad** at St John's – a group of buildings unmatched in Oxford for their showy exuberance. The passage linking Front Quad and Canterbury Quad is fan-vaulted, a last touch of late Gothic before the Baroque splendours beyond.

We emerge to face a bold, two-storey portal containing a bronze statue of Charles I (by Le Sueur)

under the royal coat of arms. To either side, the delicate arcade, carried on slender Tuscan columns, has medallion busts of female figures (by Anthony Gore), representing the Virtues and the Liberal Arts, beneath a running frieze of foliage. Crossing the quad and turning round, we find that the opposite range is similar but with a statue of Queen Henrietta Maria, wife of Charles I, in the niche. For long the design was attributed to Inigo Jones or Nicholas Stone, two of the greatest architects of their day, but now the credit goes to Adam Browne, a craftsman-architect so obscure that you will search in vain for his name in architectural reference books.

When the quad was completed in 1636, Charles I and his queen were invited to view the buildings and watch a play in the hall (despite the Laudian Code). It is said that the king's entertainment nearly cost more than the buildings.

Posthumous move

The library on the south side of Canterbury Quad (not open) contains memorabilia of both Laud and the

ABOVE LEFT: Charles I in Canterbury Quad, St John's College.
ABOVE: carved detail, St John's.
BELOW: St John's College.

ABOVE: the monument to Richard Baylie, in St John's Baylie Chapel.

monarch, both of whom died on the scaffold – Charles, famously, in 1649 and Laud in 1645, accused by the Long Parliament of high treason. Originally buried in Barking, his bones were quietly re-interred in St John's chapel in 1663.

The east side of Canterbury Quad leads out to the college gardens. Like neighbouring Trinity College (see page 138), St John's was built outside the city walls and so the gardens are very spacious. The path around the lawn twists and turns between carefully tended shrubs and groves of trees that were first planted in 1712,

providing a wonderful blend of the formal and the naturalistic.

Visitors can extend their walk by taking a side path to the north, past rockeries and shady lawns, catching glimpses of more modern college buildings to the north. These include "The Beehive", built in 1958 and so called because its plan is based on clusters of interlocking octagons; and the Sir Thomas White Building of 1975.

Through to Keble

From St John's turn right, up St Giles, and look for a passageway on the right, by the **Lamb and Flag** ❷

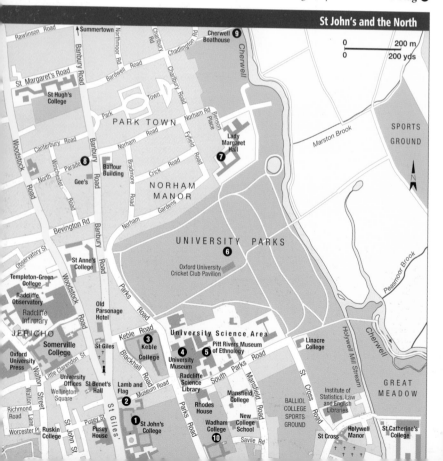

St John's and the North

– a tavern that opened in 1695 and takes its name from the St John's College coat of arms. The passage takes you, in a matter of a few yards, from medieval Oxford straight into the 19th century, leading as it does to Museum Road, lined with 1870s villas, and out into Parks Road, first laid out in the 1830s.

Directly opposite stands the mighty neo-Gothic facade of the University Museum *(see page 182)*. Before crossing the road, turn left to arrive at the unmissable bulk of Keble.

Keble College ❸

Tel: 01865-272 727
Opening Hrs: daily 2–5pm
Entrance Fee: Free

At a time when the other Oxford colleges were becoming more liberal and preparing to abolish ancient rules that excluded all non-Anglicans from membership, **Keble College** set out to be assertively different. Committed to turning out clergymen formed in the strict High Church mould, Keble demanded that its students lead an almost monastic life of poverty and obedience.

Fortunately for the students, this objective, the antithesis to intellectual freedom, was soon modified and, while remaining primarily a theological college, Keble adopted more progressive attitudes – accepting, for example, that Darwin's evolutionary theories were not necessarily incompatible with Christian teaching.

The Tractarian founders of the college chose one of their own, William Butterfield, as the architect, who proceeded to produce a riot of Victorian Gothic on a scale hitherto unseen. Contentious from the very start, Keble continues to attract its fair share of criticism. It was built not of Oxford stone, but brick, and in addition to the dominant red, Butterfield used different colours to create his hallmark polychromatic patterning.

Nowhere are the aspirations of the college's creators more evident than in the enormous **Chapel**. But the interior here could only appeal to connoisseurs of kitsch, for the stained glass is lifeless and the mosaics of biblical scenes around the walls (inspired by Giotto's great fresco cycle at Assisi) are sickly sweet, like

The student unrest of the early 1970s didn't impinge on Tony Blair, one of St John's law students at the time. The future prime minister, then more interested in forming a rock band, didn't even join the Labour club. "I went through all the bit about reading Trotsky and attempting a Marxist analysis," he said later. "But it never went very deep."

BELOW: Keble College.

illustrations from a child's *Life of Jesus*.

A small side chapel to the south was added in 1892, specifically to house Holman Hunt's famous painting *The Light of the World*. Butterfield refused to allow the picture to be hung in the main chapel on the grounds that it is "a place of worship, not a gallery". Holman Hunt, on the other hand, was so angry when he learned that the college was charging visitors to see the picture that he painted another and gave it to St Paul's Cathedral in London. The side chapel also contains a painting by William Keys, *The Dead Christ Mourned by His Mother*.

Brick remains the preferred building material at Keble. Though much derided by Keble critics, the new Arco building along Keble Road, both blends in with its brick surroundings and sets new dynamic accents of its own.

University Museum ❹

Tel: 01865-272 950
Opening Hrs: daily 10am–5pm
Entrance Fee: Free

Opposite Keble is another assertive Victorian building, a cross between a French château and London's St Pancras railway station, that houses the **University Museum**. This, however, is in an entirely different class, a delightful and innovative building with many ingenious, half-humorous, half-serious details.

The museum was begun in 1855 at a time when Oxford was beginning to teach experimental science.

The mixed voice choir of Keble College not only sings in the chapel at services on Wednesday and Sunday evening but also tours in Britain, Europe and the US, and has recorded several CDs.

ABOVE RIGHT:
University Museum.
BELOW:
University Museum's
dinosaur collection.

Unlike the old humanities, which could be taught in a room, or even while strolling around the river meadows, science teaching required laboratories, and the block of land to the east of Parks Road was set aside for this purpose.

The museum was the first building to be erected, together with the Inorganic Chemistry Laboratory alongside – curiously enough designed to resemble the medieval Abbot's Kitchen at Glastonbury Abbey. The aim of the museum was didactic and all-embracing: to tell the history of life on earth. Its construction was supported by numerous progressive thinkers of the age, including John Ruskin.

Such an objective was bound to be controversial in an age that still clung to biblical ideas of Creation – and when the building was completed in 1860, it was inaugurated by the now-famous debate between the bishop of Oxford, Samuel Wilberforce and Professor Thomas Huxley on Darwin's evolutionary theories.

The bishop, according to contemporary accounts, thought that he had won the day when he asked Huxley "was it through his grandfather or his grandmother that he claimed his descent from a monkey?". At least one lady fainted and the meeting degenerated into a near-riot when Huxley said that he was "not ashamed to have a monkey for his ancestor, but he would be ashamed to be connected with a man who used great gifts to obscure the truth".

Controversies of a different nature surrounded the building itself. Critics called the design "indecent" and "detestable", because to them the Gothic architectural style should be reserved for religious buildings, not one devoted to a secular purpose. The Dublin firm of builders employed to erect the museum hired as stonemasons two brothers who have passed into Oxford legend.

The brothers O'Shea, who carved all the animals and birds of the corbels and window surrounds, were not only renowned for their fondness for drink but also for their irascibility. Dons who continually interfered with the brothers' work, objecting to the subjects portrayed, were likely to find themselves featured in unflattering caricature in stone. Sadly, the brothers were ordered to destroy this work.

The interior of the museum is lit by a glass roof, supported by slender columns and a wrought-iron vault that makes you feel as if you are inside the rib cage of one of the great dinosaurs displayed on the floor below. Slender iron columns, ornamented with representations of trees and shrubs, divide the hall into three bays; the arcade columns around the perimeter of the main hall are each hewn from a different British rock, all clearly labelled.

Statues of eminent scientists line the walls, looking down on cases of stuffed animals and skeletons of crea-

ABOVE: prehistoric reconstruction.
BELOW: kids can get to grips with dinosaur teeth and bones on University Museum science days.

Dead as a Dodo

John Savery's remarkable painting of the dodo in the University Museum is now considered to be something of an exaggeration, for experts agree that the ill-fated bird was not nearly as grotesque as the depiction might suggest. What is beyond dispute, however, is that the dodo was the unfortunate victim not only of hungry sailors, who were easily able to capture the flightless creature, but of evolution itself.

First sighted around 1600 on the Indian Ocean island of Mauritius, the dodo *(Raphus cucullatus)*, a close relative of the pigeon, was a large bird with a heavy, ungainly body and short, useless wings. Because it could not escape, it rapidly fell prey to the Dutch sailors who first visited the area and to imported cats, rats and pigs, which destroyed its nests. The destruction of the island's forest – and hence the dodo's food supply – was another factor in its rapid extinction. The last living bird was sighted in 1681.

Today, scientists believe that the dodo actually evolved from a bird capable of flight into a flightless one. Having discovered in Mauritius a habitat with plenty of food and no natural predators, the dodo did not need to fly and over the course of the generations, lost the ability to do so.

ABOVE RIGHT: detail from John Savery's painting of the ill-fated dodo.
BELOW: the O'Shea brothers at work on the University Museum in 1906.

tures living and extinct. At the centre of the hall are the Oxford dinosaurs – not reactionary dons, but fossil skeletons found in the Jurassic rocks of the Oxford area as the city began to expand in the 19th century. The focal point is the fine skeleton of an iguanodon.

Apart from the dinosaurs, a famous attraction of the museum is the painting by John Savery of the Dodo in the northwest corner of the building *(see above)*. The bird in question, described as an over-sized flightless dove with a hooked beak, was brought to England in 1638 and formed part of the Tradescant and subsequently Ashmolean collections. This same painting inspired Lewis Carroll's famous character in *Alice in Wonderland*.

It is also worth visiting the upper gallery for its collections of insects, butterflies and birds. There are great views across the main hall; notice the scale model of the sun, moon and earth attached to the balustrade.

Pitt Rivers Museum of Ethnology ❺

Tel: 01865-270 927
Opening Hrs: Mon noon–4.30pm, Tue–Sun 10am–4.30pm
Entrance Fee: Free

If you're impressed by the University Museum, then you'll be staggered by what lies through the doors to its rear. The **Pitt Rivers Museum of Ethnology** was built in 1885 to house the collection of Lieutenant-General Augustus Henry Lane Fox Pitt-Rivers (1827–1900), acquired during his service in exotic lands with the Grenadier Guards.

Pitt-Rivers pioneered a sociological approach in archaeology and ethnology and emphasised the instructional value of common artefacts. His original collection consisted of some 15,000 objects, but since then the number has swelled to well over half a million, of which some 400,000 are on permanent display. The museum is literally packed with case after case of splen-

did objects from all corners of the earth – scary demons, potent fertility figures, colourful totem poles and exotic masks – as well as practical objects such as boats, tents, saddles and snowshoes.

A remarkable theme of the museum is the continuity and similarities that exist between cultures; illuminating parallels are drawn between the use of magical charms among the tribes of Asia and similar practices among Christians in "civilised" Europe. To help achieve this, and in accordance with Pitt-Rivers' wishes, the objects are displayed not by region but by type, so model Chinese junks are to be found next to African dug-out canoes, and so on. The museum's extraordinarily eclectic range of exhibits stresses themes of everyday problem-solving gleaned from every conceivable culture. With plenty of outlandish objects to examine, children will be fascinated by items such as the witch in a bottle.

Flanking the south side of the lawn in front of the museum is the **Radcliffe Science Library**, the science department of the Bodleian, which receives free copies of all British scientific publications (including popular and children's publications). Access to the library – an unmatched resource for any kind of scientific research – is possible with a Bodleian Library reader's ticket.

University Parks

Just to the north of the museum, bright summer days in particular attract locals and visitors alike to the huge expanse of the **University Parks ❻**. Dotted with magnificent trees and shrubs and bordered on its eastern side by the River Cherwell, the park is a wonderful place for a stroll. It is also the home of the **Oxford University Cricket Club**, and this is one of only two places in England where first-class matches can be watched free of charge. If you're not there for the Australians

ABOVE LEFT: tribal exhibit at the Pitt Rivers Museum.
ABOVE RIGHT: the Pitt Rivers Museum of Ethnology puts on a show.

KIDS

Parents with bored children can ask one of the obliging attendants at the Pitt Rivers Museum to point out some of the more bizarre exhibits. These include shrunken heads, a witch in a bottle, and drawers full of giant toads.

A Cyclist's City

With 20 percent of journeys within the city made by bike, cycling is part of the fabric of everyday life in Oxford – as, unfortunately, is cycle theft.

Cycling has always played an important part in Oxford's transport system. William Morris, the car magnate, began his career building and racing bicycles, and in 1922 Morrell's Brewery produced a *Hunting and Cycling Road Map of Oxford and District*, overprinted with a list of hotels and inns representing distances from Oxford. Today, as the authorities seek to reduce car use, 20 percent of short journeys in the city are made by bike, compared with 4 percent nationally. Racing is also popular and there are three local clubs for national and international races. The Oxford University Cycling Club is Britain's oldest surviving cycling club.

But thieves like bikes too, and some of the theft is on an industrial scale. Forty cycles can be fitted into a large van and smuggled out of the city by night. Thames Valley Police assigned three full-time officers solely to bike theft and began fitting tracking devices to decoy bikes in order to trap thieves. Oxford City Council, one of the first local authorities to provide for the needs of the urban cyclist, installed hundreds of "Sheffield" stands. These steel hoops are impossible to break, and together with the increased use of U-bolt steel locks, they helped bring about a decline in the number of reported thefts, down by a third in the past 15 years to around 3,000 a year. About a third of bikes are recovered.

Cycle security has been studied so intensively that you almost expect it to be part of a degree course. A normal bike chain can be cut with a bolt cropper in less than five seconds and even a steel shackle can be hacksawed in a couple of minutes. Many thieves prefer the wheel swap trick: they remove the front wheel from a bike whose rear wheel is secured and fit it to an adjacent bike as a replacement for a front wheel that has been chained or padlocked. Few people bother to secure both wheels.

Keeping track of theft

To counter theft, the Police Cycle Department, attached to the Central Police Station, keeps records of all bikes and can produce serial numbers, colours, decoration, modifications and accessories for almost every model. Bikes are kept in two cycle stores, each cleverly designed to hold 200–300 cycles: one for the "found" and "miscellaneous" and the other for "crime" bikes (pending court cases). The "found" bikes are kept for at least six weeks, the unclaimed auctioned.

The university also launched a cycle registration scheme, encouraging students and staff to attach hologram security stickers (part of a 50p security kit) to their bikes and use an ultra-violet pen to mark a registration number on them. The police routinely give all recovered cycles a UV scan.❑

ABOVE AND LEFT: objects of desire that need to be secured.

or the Pakistanis, there may be a county fixture going on.

Detour to North Oxford

The University Museum was part of the 19th-century expansion of the university, particularly in the field of science. Since that time, the area around it has developed into the University Science Area, consisting of a not always harmonious jumble of buildings ranging from 1930s functionalism (clearly visible in the Inorganic Chemistry faculty building from University Parks) to 1960s concrete and glass structures, each housing different faculties, ranging from Mathematics to Applied Physics to Microbiology.

As the university grew beyond its old medieval core, new accommodation was required for increasing numbers of professors and their families, as well as wealthy merchants and traders. This demand helped spawn the development of the affluent district known as North Oxford, which begins just north of the University Parks and extends out along the Banbury and Woodstock roads.

Just to the north of University Parks, **Norham Gardens** was laid out from 1860, and although Italianate villas feature in early plans, neo-Gothic was all the rage by the time the estate came to be developed (*see margin note*).

Lady Margaret Hall ❼

Tel: 01865-274 300
Opening Hrs: enquire at the porter's lodge for access
Entrance Fee: Free

At the end of Norham Gardens (also reached via an alley from University Parks) is **Lady Margaret Hall**, founded in 1878 as a women's hall of residence (it is now mixed) and itself occupying one of the newly built villas. Strong connections with the Church of England distinguished this college, named after Lady Margaret Beaufort, the scholarly mother of Henry VII, from its contemporary, Somerville.

The original villa, Old Hall, is the undistinguished yellow-grey brick building to the right of the entrance. Better by far is the Queen Anne-style red-brick extension, designed by Basil Champneys and similar to the fine work he did at Newnham College, Cambridge.

For the chapel, yet another style was employed – Byzantine – with an external octagon that forms a dome inside. It was designed by Sir Giles Gilbert Scott in 1931. The beautiful

Built of brick, with high gables, ornate stone dressings sculpted with fruits and flowers and the occasional turret, Norham Gardens' houses were praised by Ruskin as "human and progressive". But the Rev. W. Tuckwell complained that professors, tutors and fellows now lived family lives in the "interminable streets of villadom", rather than residing in college "celibate and pastoral".

ABOVE LEFT: University Parks.
BELOW: springtime blossom out in force.

Public executions used to be carried out not only in Oxford's prison (which has now been turned into the luxurious Malmaison Hotel and Restaurant) but also close to Park Town. When the university ran the town, it would carry out executions in St Margaret's Road.

North and South Parades

One of Oxford's many eccentricities in the realm of street names is that North Parade lies to the south of South Parade. Officially called North Parade Avenue, its name is believed to hark back to the English Civil War when Oxford was periodically besieged by Parliamentarians. North Parade, it is said, was the north patrolling ground of the defending Royalists, while South Parade (a mile or so further north along Banbury Road), was the south patrolling ground of the Parliamentarians. Christopher Hibbert's *Encyclopedia of Oxford* dismisses this as a myth.

triptych was painted by Burne-Jones around 1863. The Hall is also blessed with gardens that stretch to the River Cherwell, where remnants of old water meadows are carpeted with daffodils, cowslips, fritillaries and primroses in spring.

Opposite the Balfour Building on Banbury Road (now no longer open to visitors) is the glass-covered conservatory of **Gee's** restaurant, and immediately north of that is **North Parade ❽**, which offers a variety of good restaurants, and has a definite "villagey" atmosphere in comparison to all the grand neo-Gothic residences round about. There are two good pubs in North Parade, the Gardeners' Arms and the Rose and Crown. The latter was built in 1867 on the site of a small market garden, evidence of the area's semi-rural character at the time.

Park Town

Further north, entered from the east side of Banbury Road, is the elegant residential enclave known as **Park Town**, interesting from an architectural point of view because its houses are much admired examples of late Regency style – so late (built from 1853 to 1855) that they might almost be called neo-Regency. Built around crescents, these stucco-fronted houses, with attractive iron railings, remind us more of Cheltenham than of Oxford.

The next street on the right beyond Park Town is Bardwell Road. Just around the corner beyond the famous Dragon School, where Bardwell Road merges with Chadlington Road, a path on the right leads down to the River Cherwell and the **Cherwell Boathouse ❾**. This is a popular base for punting (*see page 206*) as well as home to the Cherwell Boathouse restaurant, a small, intimate and elegant place, with river views, good food and local artists' work displayed on the walls.

Continuing up Banbury Road, one reaches the suburban shopping area

of **Summertown**, home to Oxfam before the charity's move to the new business park in East Oxford. Here is a handful of good restaurants, especially on fashionable South Parade, and some traditional and not so traditional shops catering to North Oxford's well-heeled residents.

The heart of Oxford is easily reached again by returning down Parks Road towards Broad Street, stopping first to admire the 18th-century gates, on the right, that separate the road from the long vista of Trinity College Gardens.

Wadham College ⑩

Tel: 01865-277 900
Opening Hrs: daily 1–4.15pm
Entrance Fee: Free

Wadham College is regarded as the youngest of the "old" (pre-Victorian) foundations. Nicholas Wadham, a retiring and obscure Somerset landowner, left his considerable wealth for the foundation of a college at his death in 1609. Wadham's widow, Dorothy, proved an energetic executor, despite being over 75 years old, and by 1613, less than five years later, the college was virtually complete. Thus Wadham is the only ancient college to have been built in one go, and it has scarcely changed.

The buildings are strictly symmetrical and were designed by the West Country builder William Arnold,

ABOVE: combine punting and a bite to eat at Cherwell Boathouse.
BELOW LEFT: a leafy residential area in North Oxford.
BELOW: Wadham College chapel.

who borrowed motifs from other Oxford Jacobean-Gothic buildings, but put them together in a highly accomplished manner. The Front Quad is entered through the fan-vaulted gate-tower.

The chapel is entered by the passageway on the far left (northeast) corner of the quad, and has some of Oxford's finest 17th-century stained glass. The east window, depicting the Passion and Resurrection, is the only one in Oxford painted by Bernard van Linge (dated 1622), brother of the more prolific Abraham, whose work is found in several college chapels. The other significant object is the fine screen of 1613, with its strapwork, slender columns and cresting.

Fellows' Garden

To the left of the chapel is the **Fellows' Garden**, filled with rare and ancient trees, including a striking copper beech, planted in 1796. The garden completely surrounds the chapel, and the **Cloister Garden**, to the rear, contains a modernistic bronze statue of Sir Maurice Bowra by John Doubleday. Bowra, a literary

scholar who presided over Wadham as warden from 1938 to 1970, was renowned for his ascerbic and often bawdy wit. ("Awful shit, never met him" is one of his renowned judgements. Of the Master of Balliol, he once remarked: "He has been ill but unfortunately is getting better. Otherwise deaths have been poor for the time of year.")

Famous alumni include the architect Christopher Wren and chemist Robert Boyle, who, having finished their studies, went on to pursue their careers in London and to found the Royal Society.

The southeast side of Wadham's Front Quad is an exact match of the northeast, with the hall a mirror of the chapel but with a splendid hammerbeam roof. The garden of the adjacent Back Quad contains a giant lime tree of considerable, though unknown, age. The heady scent of its summer flowers is not only irresistible to bees but spreads to fill the air as far as the city centre, which, for all that it seems a long way off in Wadham's quiet precincts, is only a few steps away. ❑

ABOVE: Nicholas and Dorothy Wadham, founders of the college that bears their name.
BELOW: Wadham College.

BEST RESTAURANTS, CAFÉS, PUBS AND BARS

Restaurants

The Cherwell Boathouse

Bardwell Road. Tel: 01865-552 746. www.cherwellboathouse.co.uk Open: daily. £££ (Off map)

One of Oxford's most enviable locations, right on the banks of the Cherwell and next door to a punt-hiring station. The food is "modern English" with a strong Italian accent, set lunchtime menus represent very good value, and you can eat outside in summer. Unusually varied wine list.

Chez Gaston

6 North Parade. Tel: 01865-311 608. Open: daily. £ (Off map)

Chez Gaston stands out for its exuberant decor as well as its irresistible crêpes, savoury and sweet. Other dishes – snacks, pasta, French plats du jour – are on offer in a relaxed and rather Bohemian atmosphere.

Cibo Restaurant and Café

4 South Parade. Tel: 01865-292 321. www.ilovecibo.co.uk Open: daily. £ (Off map)

One of a cluster of more or less trendy restaurants on South Parade, with an authentically Italian menu highlighting pasta, risotto and salads alongside meat and fish dishes. Bright modern decor and friendly staff, but food quality can vary.

Gee's

61 Banbury Road. Tel: 01865-553 540. www.gees-restaurant.co.uk Open: daily. ££–£££ (Off map)

Housed in a former florist's conservatory, this restaurant is beautifully light during the day, cosy in the evening. The food is simple and features a good deal of delicious fish as well as Italian-influenced salads and meat dishes.

Luna Caprese

4 North Parade. Tel: 01865-554 812. Open: daily. ££ (Off map)

This old Italian restaurant is impervious to fads, and rightly so given the consistent quality of the food. The walls are decked with fishing nets and shells, the pasta is always freshly made, and if it is your birthday the Italian waiters may even sing for you.

The Old Parsonage Hotel

1 Banbury Road. Tel: 01865-310 210. www.oldparsonage-hotel.co.uk Open: daily. ££–£££ ⑭ p278, B1

A rural feel reigns within this beautifully restored ancient building, where the food ranges from English breakfasts to elegant post-theatre dinners, and

---

Prices for a three-course dinner per person with a half-bottle of house wine:

£ = under £20
££ = £20–£30
£££ = £30–£45
££££ = more than £45

Pubs and Bars

There are several good pubs in North Oxford. The **Lamb & Flag** (12 St Giles' ㉗ p278, B2), next to St John's, is an atmospheric old inn that serves robust lunches and good beers. The **Rose & Crown** (North Parade; off map) is a charmingly traditional pub, full of nooks and crannies, and serving generous bar lunches to a regular clientele.

There is a pleasant outside seating area. The **Gardeners' Arms** (North Parade; off map), almost opposite, is another old-fashioned hostelry, frequented by North Oxford locals. The **Dewdrop Inn** (258 Banbury Road; off map) is Summertown's most popular pub, attracting a mainly young crowd and serving above-average lunches.

---

the emphasis is on good, unfussy cooking using local ingredients. The private-club atmosphere draws an older crowd

Spice Lounge ·

193 Banbury Road. Tel: 01865-510 071. www.spiceloungeoxford.co.uk Open: daily except Friday lunchtime. £–££ (Off map)

Excellent Indian cuisine in smart, contemporary setting. Buffet lunch Sunday.

RIGHT: Chez Gaston.

WEST TO THE CANAL

In medieval times the western part of the city was crowded with wharves unloading cargo from the Upper Thames. Today it gives an insight into Oxford's industrial past

Main Attractions

BONN SQUARE
NUFFIELD COLLEGE
OXFORD CASTLE
CANAL WALK
GLOUCESTER GREEN SHOPS
ST PETER'S COLLEGE
FREWIN HALL

Maps and Listings

MAP OF WEST TO THE CANAL, PAGE 194
RESTAURANTS AND PUBS, PAGE 199
ACCOMMODATION, PAGES 256–7

This route includes a journey into Oxford's industrial past. When the canal arrived from the Midlands in 1790, the area around Castle Mill Stream became a bustling inland port. Activity declined with the arrival of the railway in 1844, but the brewing industry was to continue until the closure of Morrell's Brewery in 1998.

From Carfax walk along **Queen Street**, lined by chain stores and every bit as busy as Cornmarket Street, but perhaps more chaotic, with buses nudging nose to tail through the crowds of shoppers.

In the summer, some light relief is provided by **Bonn Square ❶**, named after Oxford's twin city in Germany, and a popular meeting place; it is also the site of a memorial to men of the Oxfordshire Regiment who died in various campaigns on India's northwest frontier. There is often live music in the form of buskers playing on or near the square.

Nuffield College

On the opposite side of Queen Street is the sprawling Westgate Shopping Centre, one of numerous ugly modern buildings erected in this part of

the city centre during the 1970s. The Westgate is scheduled to be revamped and extended over the next few years, though the developers' uninspired designs are raising local opposition.

Continue on into **New Road**, whose construction across the castle bailey in 1769 marked the beginning of local road improvements, which were formalised by the creation of the Paving Commission two years later. On the left you'll see an imposing, fortress-like building. Formerly the prison entrance, this is now part

---

LEFT: Oxford's canal is the key to its industrial past.
RIGHT: Nuffield College.

RIGHT:
signposted it may be, but little remains of the original castle.

of **County Hall**. Down the hill on the right is the unmistakable sturdy tower of **Nuffield College ②**.

The site and funds for the college were donated to the university in 1937 by Lord Nuffield, alias William Morris, who began life repairing bicycles in the High Street (see page 46), progressed to designing the "Bullnose" Morris in Longwall Street and ended up by establishing the first ever mass-production line for cheap cars at Cowley (whose successor continues to thrive, albeit under BMW ownership).

Having achieved his manufacturing goals, Nuffield was determined to use part of his vast fortune for good causes, including hospitals and charities. As far as the university was concerned, he had originally envisaged establishing a college specialising in the practical skills of engineering and accountancy, but was persuaded instead to fund a postgraduate college devoted to the study of social,

economic and political problems.

Formal agreement was reached in 1937, but progress was slow because Nuffield disliked the original "un-English" designs for the college, and, by the time new designs were completed, war had been declared. In the event, work did not begin until 1949, and this Lutyens-inspired, Cotswold-style college, very much a product of 1930s architectural thinking, was not completed until 1960. Nuffield had devoted the best part of his wealth to the project, but still referred to it as "that bloody Kremlin, where left-wingers study at my expense". Committed to providing a bridge between the academic and the non-academic worlds, Nuff-

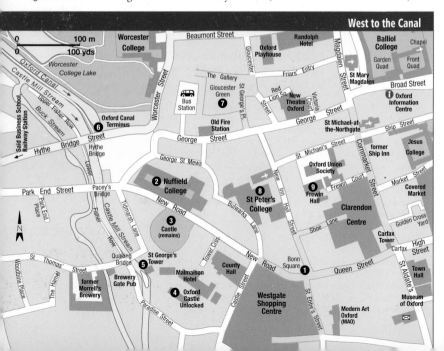

West to the Canal

ield College has been the source of some major research developments in British social science.

Attractive to some, plain ugly to others, the Stalinesque **tower** houses the library, which contains 70,000 books on its 10 floors. It was intended to be part of a large college chapel, but this plan was altered as a consequence of the delays and financial problems surrounding the whole project. Except for the tower, Nuffield is much like a Cotswold country house on a large scale, with two courtyards in the pattern of traditional colleges, linked by steps, surrounding lily ponds and rose beds.

The chapel of Nuffield, scaled down from its original grand proportions because of escalating costs, is now no more than a room on the top floor of "L" staircase, entered from the lower quad. John Piper, the artist, designed the glass and simple wooden box pews, modelled on those of Ivychurch in Kent's Romney Marsh.

Oxford Castle

The green mound on the other side of the road is what remains of the **Castle ❸**, built by Robert d'Oilly, Oxford's Norman governor, in 1071. The mound was originally topped with a wooden keep (later rebuilt in stone), and the outer bailey was surrounded by a moat with water from one of the branches of the Thames used to power the castle mills – hence Castle Mill Stream.

Many historic figures are associated with the castle. In 1142, Matilda (the Empress Maud) was holed up here for three months while battling to gain the English throne from King Stephen after the death of her father, Henry I, in 1135. She escaped in the depths of winter down the frozen Thames, camouflaged against the snow in nothing but a white sheet. She never became queen. From the mid-12th century, the castle was used to house prison-

ers, and although the fortifications were torn down after the Civil War, it remained the site of a prison.

The present forbidding structure was built in the 19th century. The last public execution took place here in 1863, and the last prisoner moved out in 1993.

The role of the prison was dramatically transformed in 2005 with the long-awaited opening of the 94-room **Malmaison Hotel** (tel: 01865-268 400; www.malmaison-oxford.com). The exterior of the Grade I listed building was largely preserved and the interior was entirely refurbished to create an unusual and elegant ambience. The hotel's rooms are essentially the former cells, but in most cases three have been combined to form spacious en suite accommodation. The prison project was the first of its sort in Britain. The complex also includes a range of restaurants and bars in addition to Malmaison's own excellent brasserie.

ABOVE: Oxford Castle, the 19th-century incarnation.
BELOW: prison bed at Oxford Castle Unlocked.

In 1142 King Stephen laid siege to Oxford Castle, where Henry I's daughter Matilda, a claimant to the throne, was holed up.

St George, which he founded within the walls. It was the Secular Canons of St George who established here what is regarded as the first learning establishment in Oxford.

Follow the road round to the right, across Quaking Bridge and into St Thomas Street. On the opposite side of the road stands the former **Morrell's Brewery**, which closed in 1998. An independent, family-run concern that had belonged to the Morrell family since 1792, this was the last brewery in Oxford. At one time no fewer than 14 breweries thrived in this part of the city, drawing their water from wells deep beneath the Thames and using the river and the canal for transport. The first brewery here in Tidmarsh Lane was established in 1452 by the monks of neighbouring Osney Abbey. The Morrell's premises have been sold, but the adjoining **Brewery Gate** pub remains open.

Canalside

Return to the Quaking Bridge. On the corner of **Lower Fisher Row** is the house lived in by Edward Tawney, who ran the brewery prior to its takeover by the Morrell family in 1792. Follow the attractive Fisher Row, which leads north along the Castle Mill Stream. The original fishermen's and canal bargees' cottages have gone, but it remains a pretty spot, overhung by willows and often frequented by swans.

Emerging at the end, cross Park End Street to Hythe Bridge Street and the present-day terminus of the **Oxford Canal ❻** on **Upper Fisher Row**, where a sign headed **Oxford Canal Walk** indicates the distances to towns further up the waterway. While visitors might find the 83 miles (134km) to Coventry somewhat ambitious, a short walk along the canal towpath, lined with colourful narrowboats, is worthwhile. The canal runs along the back of Worcester College (*see page 169*), past the district of Jericho and then the former site of Lucy's Eagle

ABOVE: footbridge over the canal.
BELOW: canal boats provide a restful holiday.

Oxford Castle Unlocked ❹

Tel: 01865-260 666
Opening Hrs: daily 10am–5.30pm, last tour 4.20pm
Entrance Fee: Charge

The recently opened heritage centre, **Oxford Castle Unlocked**, explains the history of the castle and its absorption into the former prison. The centre gives access to the castle mound, the crypt of St George's Church and the forbidding-looking Debtors' Tower as well as St George's Tower (*see below*). With more than £5 million of public funding, the project was the realisation of a 60-year dream for the Oxford Preservation Trust, which back in the 1940s had pressed for the rescue of the city's medieval heritage as the prison faced closure and possibly demolition.

Continue along New Road until the next turning on the left, into Tidmarsh Lane. At the very end, the view is dominated by **St George's Tower ❺**, which Robert d'Oilly built at the southern side of the castle bailey in 1074, above the chapel of

Ironworks (now a redevelopment featuring mainly apartments), where steps up to the bridge provide access to Port Meadow.

To the west along Hythe Bridge Street and Park End Street is **Oxford railway station**. Park End Street, until recently an undistinguished row of offices and shops, is now filled with bars and restaurants – a continuation of George Street. The original station was deliberately kept well out of the centre of Oxford largely because the railway was thought likely to corrupt young students – making it easy for them to travel to places of ill repute, such as Ascot racecourse. The existing station lies on the Great Western Railway line to London.

Another line, closed in 1967, terminated at the junction of Park End Road and Hythe Bridge Street: part of the old station, painted red, white and blue, stood on the site until 1999, when it was demolished to make room for a new road scheme and the new Saïd Business School, built by the university from funds donated by various businesses and benefactors, notably Wafic Saïd.

The demolition of the old railway station created considerable controversy, especially when environmental activists occupied the site in an

attempt to save a row of trees. The listed building was eventually dismantled and carted off to the nearby Quainton Railway Centre.

The **Saïd Business School** (tel: 01865-288 800; access by appointment), which specialises in MBA courses and research into business organisations, combines a classically simple symmetry with an exotic copper-clad ziggurat. Its serene gardens, lecture theatre and airy library create an atmosphere that combines modern corporate chic with a traditional monastic feel.

Beyond the railway line lies the district of **Osney** (*see page 208*).

Gloucester Green shopping

To the east, Hythe Bridge Street leads back towards the city centre. Opposite, fronting on to Worcester Street, is an adventurous brick building, with three lead-covered angle towers enclosing Gloucester Green, which is entered a little further up Worcester Street, on the right.

ABOVE: Gloucester Green street performers.
BELOW LEFT: Saïd Business School.
BELOW: taking a break from the Gloucester Green shopping.

Opened in 1989, **Gloucester Green** ❼ is a large pedestrianised shopping square. It has been a welcome addition to the Oxford townscape, tidying up an area that had served as a windswept and litter-strewn bus station ever since 1932, when the cattle market on the site was closed down. The present bus station has been integrated into the scheme.

Before you get into the main square, look out for the Old School House, once Oxford's first boarding school and now a popular pub. Continue under the arch into the square itself, which is surrounded by shops and eating places and is the scene every Wednesday of an **open-air market**, with stalls selling everything from pots and pans to brooms and door knobs. A popular **flea market** is held every Thursday.

Of the pubs that once served the thirsty cattle drovers, only the Eurobar (formerly the Welsh Pony), in George Street, now survives, though it has lost much of its character. Further up, the **Old Fire Station** has been redeveloped to house a theatre as well as a bar/restaurant which is transformed into a disco in the evenings.

Opposite, the neo-Jacobean Social Studies Faculty was originally built in 1880 as the City of Oxford High School, and numbered T. E. Lawrence among its pupils.

George Street is now lined with pubs and restaurants, ranging from the more traditional inn (The Grapes) to the Lebanese Tarbouch Restaurant.

Along New Inn Hall Street

Proceed up George Street to **New Inn Hall Street** on the right, past the cinema. This street marks the eastern boundary of the medieval city, and was once just inside the walls. The original New Inn Hall has gone but St Peter's College, halfway up on the right, now occupies part of the site.

St Peter's College ❽

Tel: 01865-278 900
Opening Hrs: enquire at porter's lodge for access
Entrance Fee: Free

St Peter's College was founded in 1929, and did not achieve college status until 1961, but the buildings are much older.

The college is entered through **Linton House**, built in 1797 as the headquarters of the Oxford Canal Company, which then moved, in 1828, to the neoclassical **Canal House**, which now serves as the Master's Lodge. The college chapel is the former church of St Peter-le-Bailey, which was built in 1874 to the design of Basil Champneys on the site of the original Norman church.

Opposite St Peter's, **Frewin Hall** ❾ is an attractive house, set well back from the street, dating to the 16th and 18th centuries, and converted into student accommodation in the 1970s. Next to the entrance, a plaque indicates a house that was the first Methodist meeting house in Oxford, used for the first time in 1783, eight years before the death of John Wesley, who had sown the seeds of Methodism while at Lincoln College. ❑

ABOVE:
Frewin Hall.
BELOW: the street that once marked the city's eastern boundary.

NEW INN HALL STREET

BEST RESTAURANTS AND PUBS

Restaurants

4500 Miles from Delhi
41 Park End Street. Tel: 01865-244 922. http://miles fromdelhi.com/oxford/index.html Open: Mon–Fri L & D, Sat–Sun D only. ££ ⑮ p278, A4
This sleek modern restaurant is not your usual Balti house, but instead aims to reinvent Indian cooking for the fine-dining crowd. The menu offers some pleasant variations from the more conventional restaurant fare and dishes are subtly flavoured. Numerous vegetarian options.

Café Opium
67–9 George Street. Tel: 01865-248 680. Open: daily. ££ ⑯ p278, B4
An airy, bustling Chinese restaurant with dramatic, stylish decor and quality food. Ideal for a quick meal or a group outing.

Chutney's
36 Michael's Street. Tel: 01865-724 241. Open: daily L & D. ££ ⑰ p278, B4
Among the Indian restaurants in the centre, Chutney's stands out. The extensive menu includes many good vegetarian dishes. The decor is sim-

ple and modern but the tables are somewhat cramped and it can get crowded at weekends. There is also a good-value lunchtime buffet.

The Living Room
1 Oxford Castle. Tel: 01865-260 210. www.thelivingroom. co.uk Open: daily. ££ ⑱ p278, B4
Part of the flagship Castle redevelopment, the Living Room belongs to an upmarket chain of bar/brasserie venues. Its interior is pleasingly retro chic, while its menu offers an elegant selection of English, French and Italian dishes. The large bar area, complete with white piano, pulls in a large, mostly image-conscious crowd.

Malmaison Brasserie
Malmaison Hotel, 3 Oxford Castle. Tel: 01865-268 400. www.malmaison-oxford.com Open: daily. £££ ⑲ p278, B4
Situated in the basement of Oxford's former prison, this stylish restaurant serves up food of a quality about as far removed as it could possibly be from the porridge once doled out to inmates. The cooking is modern European in style.

Sojo
6–9 Hythe Bridge Street. Tel: 01865-202 888. Open: daily. ££ ⑳ p278, A4
Situated in what one might, with some exag-

geration, call Oxford's Chinatown, Sojo certainly attracts a lot of Chinese diners. The atmosphere is refreshingly modern, and the food, including home-made dim sum and Shanghai local specialities, is definitely a cut above the average. The place doubles as a bar, and karaoke entertainment is available.

Jamie's Italian
24–6 George Street. Tel: 838 383. Open: daily. ££ ㉑ p278, B3
Jamie Oliver brings his well publicised love of Italian cooking to the streets of Oxford, aiming for simple, no-fuss fare, the way Italians eat back home. Freshly made pasta, seasonal ingredients, and a competitively priced wine

list – featuring organic house wine – make this laidback local a hit.

Pubs

There are countless pubs and bars in and around the George Street–Park End Street area, but many of these are blandly themed establishments, aimed principally at Oxford's youth. One of the few real exceptions is the **Far from the Madding Crowd** (㊳ p278, B3), tucked away in Friar's Entry, a small alley joining Gloucester Green to Magdalen Street. It's an eminently civilised pub that hosts art exhibitions as well as dispensing good food and beer.

Prices for a three-course dinner per person with a half-bottle of house wine:
£ = under £20
££ = £20–£30
£££ = £30–£45
££££ = more than £45

RIGHT: the Living Room.

OXFORD'S GREEN CORRIDOR

Neglected for much of its 200-year history, the Oxford Canal might easily have been lost forever after World War II. Now it enjoys renewed esteem

When the Oxford Canal was completed in 1790, it had a huge and immediate impact. After centuries of academic and religious privilege, Oxford suddenly found itself confronted by a rapidly changing industrial world. Those who welcomed this workmanlike intruder were not disappointed. Investors soon saw the demand for their principal product, coal, turned into massive profits.

Within a decade the Canal Company expanded its original city centre wharves just south of Hythe Bridge Street to encompass the site now occupied by Nuffield College. The labour for this work came from the conveniently located Oxford Castle Gaol, whose governor, Daniel Harris, also found time to grace Oxford's waterways with his skills as an engineer, surveyor and architect.

Benign neglect

Until the mid-19th century Oxford treated the canal as an honoured guest. When the railway arrived in the 1840s, however, a decline set in, and although it took another century before the company conceded the struggle to carry freight in any volume, the canal suffered a kind of benign neglect. The company withdrew from the city centre in the 1930s, and the entire canal could easily have been lost forever. But it survived thanks to the efforts of enthusiasts who foresaw the waterway's leisure potential.

ABOVE: as narrowboats are less than 7ft (2.2 metres) wide, those who call them home have little room for the material comforts of a land-bound existence – but that doesn't stop some of them!

LEFT: the canal has always defied the industrial stereotype, apart from a foundry in Jericho – from where Oxford's busy hire fleet and floating restaurant also operate.

ABOVE: in 1898 the canal was described as "an arcadian scene of pastoral beauty."

WHAT LIFE'S LIKE ON THE CANAL

A step along the Oxford Canal towpath from Hythe Bridge Street brings an instant sense of relief. The noise, pollution and traffic are forgotten as you enter a calmer, gentler world of boats, anglers and swans.

It's the boats that make the scene really special, and in Oxford there is an unusually high number that are year-round homes. Distributed along the 3 miles (5km) of canal between Wolvercote and the city, they form a single linear community, united by shared dependence on and responsibility for the same stretch of water, and by an unspoken awareness of common chores and comforts.

The canal residents have had to struggle to gain acceptance, perhaps a throwback to the prejudices against working boatmen. Today they provide interest in a quiet part of the city. They are not alone. Dotted around Britain's 2,000 miles (3,200km) of inland waterways are other pockets of residential boats. The national Residential Boat Owners' Association (RBOA) gives these "floating voters" a collective voice.

RIGHT: children and even dogs were once essential crew for the working boatman. Today a boating holiday provides all with exercise, fun and an appreciation of both history and nature.

ABOVE: people are today's cargo, sustaining the original commercial intent of the waterways.

BELOW: a rare day off for this boatman and his family, pictured around 1900. The last horse-drawn cargo boat on the canal ceased trading in the 1950s.

RIVERS, MEADOWS AND ABBEYS

The rivers Thames and Cherwell and their surrounding meadows provide a playground not only for energetic oarsmen, but also for walkers, picnickers and punters

For many towns and cities built by a river, the water is simply an obstruction to be bridged, or a convenient sewer. For Oxford, the rivers **Thames** and **Cherwell** (pronounced *charwell*) have historically played a vital role in the development of the city. Early signs of human habitation are to be found on Port Meadow, while the Thames and its various arms were also the site of some of the earliest monastic foundations in Oxford, which spawned the development of the university. They include Osney Abbey (now a Victorian terraced-house community) to the west, and Godstow Nunnery, beyond Port Meadow to the northwest of the city.

Christ Church Meadow

Less sensitive souls have often mooted plans to tame or use these "wastelands": a four-lane highway, crossing Christ Church and providing an inner-city relief road, was first proposed in 1933 and revived in 1968. W.H. Auden penned a poem in protest at the proposals ("may the Meadows be only frequented by scholars and couples and cows"). The combined efforts of Oxford's townspeople and the academics brought a halt to these plans, proving with what affection everyone in the city holds their river landscape.

Christ Church Meadow ❶ borders the River Thames to the south of the city. It is not actually possible to walk on the meadow itself because it is fenced off to contain its herd of fine cattle. However, a walk around it is very worthwhile, not only for giving the feeling of country so close to the city, but also for the magnificent views of the spires and

LEFT: Christ Church Meadow brings the countryside to the city.
RIGHT: Magdalen Bridge.

towers of the colleges to the north.

There are several ways of reaching the meadow: either through the War Memorial Gardens past the Meadow Buildings of Christ Church *(see page 158)*; from Merton Lane through to Merton Grove and on to the Broad Walk *(see page 121)*; or via the turnstile gate behind the Head of the River pub *(see page 158)*.

Approaching from the north, joining the Broad Walk just opposite the Meadow Buildings is the **New Walk ❷**, which leads along the west side of Christ Church Meadow towards the river. The New Walk is lined with tall trees planted by the head of Christ Church, Dean Liddell, in 1872, turning a muddy pathway into an avenue. The dean's daughter, Alice, came this way with Lewis Carroll in July 1862, on the way to a boat trip during which he began to tell the stories that resulted in *Alice's Adventures in Wonderland*.

The New Walk leads to a wide, straight stretch of the Thames – also called the Isis within Oxford. This Latin name was first coined in 1535 by John Leland, who seems not to

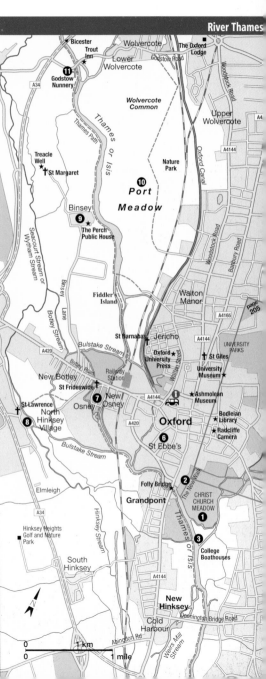

River Thames

have been at all happy with the pre-Roman Celtic name (from *tam*, meaning "broad" and *wys*, meaning "water"). Moored on the other side of the river you will see a variety of cruise boats run by Salters Bros, which ply the river between Oxford, Dorchester and Abingdon.

Transport options

If you want to explore the rivers yourself, there are punts, rowing boats, pedalboats and motorboats for hire next to the Head of the River pub (reached by turning right and through the turnstile gate).

To continue the walk, head downstream (southeast) along the river. During term-time you will probably see rowing crews training along

this stretch of the river. Activity gets particularly frenetic during the Trinity term in May, when it is the scene of Eights Week *(see page 132)* – also a lively social event, with partisan crowds either celebrating or drowning their disappointment in wine, depending on their team's success.

College Boathouses

College members and their guests watch the races from the verandahs of the bankside **College Boathouses ❸**, situated beyond the arched bridge at the confluence of the Thames and an arm of the Cherwell. The best way to see the excitement of Eights Week races is the stand on the towpath down river from the boathouses, near Donnington Bridge.

Until the turn of the century, ornate floating barges were used instead – the last of these, Keble College barge, remained in use until 1958 and part of it is now displayed in the Museum of Oxford *(see page 154)*. In his satirical novel, *Zuleika Dobson*, Max Beerbohm has the entire student population of Oxford commit mass suicide by leaping from their barges

ABOVE RIGHT: some college boathouses.
BELOW: punting along the Cherwell.

into the river, all hopelessly in love with Zuleika – not, perhaps, so far from the truth as one might think, since romantic emotions still run high as the summer term draws to a close and final-year students either cement or break their Oxford liaisons on these banks.

The path stops just beyond the boathouses, so if you want to see any more of the Thames, go back along the path, through the turnstile, and cross Folly Bridge to the south bank of the river. It is possible, from here, to follow the Thames path for some 2 miles (3km) down to the lock at **Iffley** (*see page 214*).

The Cherwell

Returning to the Thames at Christ Church Meadow, there are further possibilities for walkers. Just before the arched bridge that leads to the boathouses, take the leftward path that follows the bank of the River Cherwell from its confluence with the Thames. The Cherwell rises in Northamptonshire, to the northeast. It is narrow and shallow, used for punting rather than races, with many a tree-hung peaceful backwater, rich in birds and plants.

From the area around the confluence, the **views** across Christ Church Meadow, with the spires of Oxford in the background, are magnificent, particularly the towers of Christ Church, Merton and Magdalen. After a short stretch, the River Cherwell divides – the right-hand (southernmost) branch is the **New Cut ❹**, dug during the 1640s Civil War as part of the city defences, intended to halt Parliamentary troops approaching from the London side.

The Cherwell path eventually returns to meet Broad Walk, on the left, and Rose Lane to the right, which leads to the Botanic Garden (*see page 122*).

At the other side of Magdalen Bridge, visitors to Magdalen College

ABOVE: a boathouse on the modern side.
BELOW: strong-arm tactics.

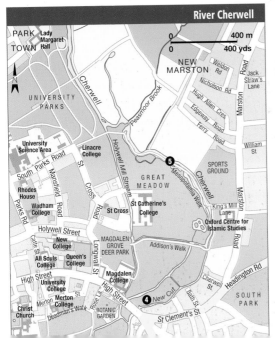

Messing About on the Rivers

Punts have come to embody the timeless romance of the privileged university world, but it is rowing that is the most popular sport among Oxford students.

Long before the first student ever skipped lectures in favour of punting up the slow-flowing Cherwell, the punt played a vital part in the lives of watermen up and down the Thames. River dredging, fishing, ferrying, transporting and delivering were all duties once carried out by this humble craft.

Decline in river transport in the mid-19th century could have led to the disappearance of the punt altogether. Fortunately, the Victorians claimed it as their leisure craft. Punts were modified from broad pontoons that could carry cattle to the slender "saloon" comprising two back rests for passengers – a design still in use today.

Increased use of power craft on rivers has resulted in a sharp decrease in punting and it has survived as a feature almost unique to Oxford and Cambridge. As a Thames craft, the punt was not introduced to Cambridge until the early Edwardian era, when it was imported from Oxford. The Oxford tradition is to punt from the slope, stern first; in Cambridge, punting from the deck end is the norm.

Some Oxford colleges have their own punting fleets and most have private hire arrangements. Punts can be hired in the summer from 10am to sunset from Folly Bridge, Magdalen Bridge and the Cherwell Boathouse. They cost £10 to £14 an hour (US$16–22) and can take up to six people, but their use is restricted to swimmers. Rowing boats can also be hired.

Newcomers might find that the Cherwell provides fewer hazards than the Thames and doesn't have rowing crews and powerboats. It is navigable by punt up to Islip. The Thames will be congested with university rowers below Iffley Lock.

Rowing for a Blue

Numerically, rowing is by far the most popular sport among students and a large proportion of rowers are women. Each college has its own rowing society and the societies are brought together under the umbrella of Oxford University Boating Club (OUBC), founded in 1939. From early morning until dusk throughout the year, Eights, Fours and Sculls can be seen accompanied by coaches who cycle or run along the towpath, megaphone in hand. On the stretch of river beyond Christ Church Meadow are the college and oubc boathouses. The two main events in the rowing calendar are Torpids and Eights Week *(see page 132)*.

By far the most glamorous event in rowing is the inter-Varsity race, first staged in 1829. Oxford "dark blues" take on Cambridge "light blues" in the annual Putney-to-Mortlake race. The prestigious Blue is awarded in rowing and other sports to those competing in a university team against Cambridge. ❑

ABOVE: rowing, the sport of choice in Oxford.
LEFT: punting is a major summer attraction.

can explore the Cherwell along Addison's Walk *(see page 111)*.

If you want to see more of the Cherwell, you don't have to reach it via Magdalen College. Exit the Botanic Garden and walk down to The Plain *(see page 112)*. The road to the left, off The Plain, forms the main street of the suburb of **St Clement's**. A few 17th-century, timber-framed buildings survive from the time when St Clement's was a village, but most now date to the early 19th century, when speculative developers laid out a network of new streets. The area now has many characterful pubs and unusual shops.

Mesopotamia Walk

Where St Clement's Street divides, take the left-hand fork into Marston Road and look for the lane that leads to the river, past the new **Oxford Centre for Islamic Studies** with its landmark minaret. This path leads to **Mesopotamia Walk** ❺; the name derives from the Greek, meaning "between the rivers", as in the ancient kingdom that lay between the Tigris and Euphrates. Here the path follows a narrow strip of land between two branches of the Cherwell, a popular stretch of the water for punting and picnics. The path crosses a number of bridges, before reaching a weir where punters have to disembark and man-handle their boats over the metal rollers to one side.

From the weir, a path to the left crosses a concrete bridge to merge with South Parks Road and Linacre College. On the right we meet again the huge expanse of **University Parks** *(see page 185)*, with its magnificent trees and shrubs and lovely walks by the river. Here it is possible to continue north along the banks of the River Cherwell, over bridges and across fields towards the northern edge of the city.

St Ebbe's

From Folly Bridge, the path along the Thames also leads west. The north side of the river at this point is occupied by recent residential developments with attractive terraces and walkways along the river. These mark the southern boundary of St Ebbe's. Once a working-class suburb of

The distinctive Oxford Centre for Islamic Studies, on King's Mill Lane, was set up by the university in 1985 to encourage the scholarly study of Islam and the Islamic world.

ABOVE: Oxford Centre for Islamic Studies.
BELOW: punting the easy way.

ABOVE: Folly Bridge.

Oxford, **St Ebbe's ⑥** was chosen as the site for the town's new gasworks in 1818, and the arrival of the railway in Oxford in 1844 further stimulated speculative building.

Not much of the original St Ebbe's remains today, most of its Victorian houses having been pulled down in the 1960s and the population rehoused at the purpose-built Blackbird Leys estate in east Oxford.

If you continue along the south bank of the river, you soon leave the residential district of Grandpont behind and once more enter a riverscape flanked by green, with the occasional used or disused bridge as a reminder of past industrial progress. **Grandpont nature park** is just a step away from the river, a popular recreation area for local residents. Look out for the wooden sculpture of a giant hand emerging from the grass.

Osney

Continue beyond the railway bridge to a long, straight section of the river,

beyond which lies Osney Lock and the suburb of **Osney ⑦**. Also reached from Botley Road over a bridge built in 1888, the main part of Osney is an island surrounded by arms of the River Thames. The district has nicely preserved 1850s terraces and characterful waterside pubs. In summer the river is usually busy with narrowboats and cruisers.

It may seem difficult to imagine today, but back in the Middle Ages the whole island was occupied by one of the largest Augustinian monasteries in England. Founded in 1129, but completely destroyed at the Dissolution in 1536, **Osney Abbey** was among the first major centres of learning in Oxford. Once the third-largest church in England, Osney Abbey housed Great Tom, the huge bell that chimes in Christ Church's Tom Tower (see page 161). Nowadays, only the remnants of a 15th-century outbuilding can be glimpsed through the gates of the Osney Marina at the end of Mill

The 270 households on Osney Island have maintained a notable community spirit, and the active Osney Sustainable Island Group makes news for its efforts to improve energy efficiency and maximise recycling. Its aim: to become the world's first 100 percent renewable energy island.

Street (second left after the railway bridge heading out of town).

From Ferry Hinksey Road there is an attractive short walk over the meadows, via a bridge over the Thames, to the village of **North Hinksey** . This village, with its thatched cottages, riding stables, Norman church of St Lawrence and pub, retains a rural feel. John Ruskin is commemorated on one of the picturesque cottages. In 1874, Ruskin organised teams of undergraduates to work on road improvements in the village – with the intention of convincing his students (who included Oscar Wilde) of the "pleasures of useful muscular work".

Binsey

Back in Osney, the church of St Frideswide on Botley Road contains a door panel, with a relief of the saint praying by the Thames, carved by Alice Liddell, herself a pupil of Ruskin's, in 1890. Other reminders of the saint as well as the heroine of *Alice's Adventures in Wonderland* can be seen in the remote church of St Margaret in **Binsey** ❾. The church is reached down Binsey Lane on the other side of Botley Road, and, once past the messy builders' yards, the suburbs give way to a patchwork of small fields surrounded by high hedges and tall trees.

Binsey itself is a tiny farming hamlet but with a renowned pub, **The Perch**, beside the Thames, a favourite lunchtime retreat for weekend walkers, with a good playground for children.

Beyond the village, a single-track road leads to the little late Norman church. Just past the west end is the **Treacle Well** that features in the story told by Lewis Carroll's Dormouse at the Mad Hatter's Tea Party. In Middle English "triacle" meant any liquid with healing or medicinal powers – only later did it come to mean a syrup.

This well is said to have sprung up at the command of St Frideswide. The king of Wessex, her enforced and self-appointed suitor, was struck blind by thunder when he tried to carry the saint away forcibly. Frideswide agreed to cure him on condition that he leave her in peace; the well appeared miraculously and its waters restored the king's sight.

Hundreds of pilgrims used to visit

ABOVE: North Hinksey's Norman church in winter.
BELOW LEFT: a narrowboat berthed at Osney.
BELOW: peeking into the Treacle Well at Binsey.

the church. Few come now and the rustic nave, lit only by oil lamps, has been colonised by bats. The simple wooden pulpit has a carving of St Margaret trampling on a dragon. Inside is another relief of St Margaret on the inner face – not by Eric Gill, as has been claimed – with clearly delineated breasts. Regarded as rather too sensual, she is condemned to face the feet of the incumbent preacher rather than risk arousing the passions of the congregation.

Port Meadow

Binsey seems remote from all the bustle of central Oxford, even though the nearest suburbs are only half a mile (1km) away. It sits just to the west of the Thames, while to the east, sandwiched between the river and the city, is the great expanse of **Port Meadow ⑩**. Used continuously for grazing ever since its first mention in the *Domesday Book* (1087), the meadow is a rare piece of Old England: it has never once been ploughed over, and is still used for grazing horses and cattle.

In winter, when the flooded

meadow freezes over, skaters come out to test the strength of the ice. The birdlife is rich at all times of the year, and in summer you can often make out the outlines of Iron Age farming enclosures and hut circles, delineated by the buttercups that grow taller over buried features such as ditches and foundation trenches.

A pleasant walk crosses the meadow and the bridge over the Thames, and follows the west bank of the river past Binsey to Godstow, where a 15th-century bridge leads to the scant remains of the medieval **Godstow Nunnery ⑪**. Founded in 1138 by Benedictine monks, the nunnery is now a romantic ruin.

Nearby, the **Trout Inn**, originally a fisherman's cottage, was rebuilt in 1737, and is famous for the peacocks that wander around the attractive riverside garden. It is a popular place on long summer evenings, and in winter has roaring log fires.

For the route back, it is possible to take the Godstow Road until it meets the Oxford Canal, and follow the towpath all the way to its end at Hythe Bridge. ❑

BELOW: geese grazing in Port Meadow.

BEST RESTAURANTS, PUBS AND BARS

Restaurants

Fishers Restaurant

36–7 St Clement's Street. Tel: 01865-243 003. Open: daily. **££**

An exuberantly colourful exterior and nautically themed interior give this adventurous fish restaurant a welcoming feel. Fresh fish, delivered daily from London's Billingsgate market, is served in generous portions. Popular in the evenings with a student-oriented clientele, it's good-value set lunch is also worth investigating.

The Fishes

North Hinksey Village. Tel: 01865-249 796. Open: daily. **££**

Now more of a restaurant than a pub, The Fishes has won plaudits for using good, locally sourced ingredients. This gastro-pub is set in a lovely, shaded streamside setting, with a tolerant attitude towards children and genuinely friendly service. Traditional Sunday roasts are complemented by more exotic dishes and an exceptional choice of desserts.

Moya

97 St Clement's Street. Tel: 01865-200 111. Open: daily. **£**

In a city full of cosmopolitan eateries this really is an original: apparently the UK's one and only Slovakian restaurant. In fact, Moya is as much a stylish cocktail bar as anything else, specialising in sophisticated but not overpriced concoctions. The food is Central European and filling: goulash, dumplings and potatoes, but also plenty of vegetarian and less robust options.

Prices for a three-course dinner per person with a half-bottle of house wine:

£ = under £20
££ = £20–£30
£££ = £30–£45
££££ = more than £45

Pubs and Bars

Many of Oxford's finest pubs are close to water. The **Angel & Greyhound** (30 St Clement's Street) is a busy and friendly place, serving good Young's beer and specialising in traditional pub games. The nearby **Half Moon** (18 St Clement's) is probably Oxford's most authentic Irish pub, with a great reputation for folk music, poetry readings and local craic. On Osney Island, a characterful enclave of terraced houses, the **Waterman's Arms** (South Street, Osney Island) stands out as a traditional local, where the menu features simple home cooking in large portions alongside well-kept real ales: **The Perch** (Binsey Village), with decent pub food, attracts large crowds of Sunday walkers, especially in fine weather when even its large garden can become overcrowded. **The Trout Inn** (195 Godstow Road, Lower Wolvercote), much restored over the centuries, now contains a spacious and atmospheric bar and restaurant areas with good food and open fires. Just before Iffley Lock is the **Isis Tavern**, watering hole for many a rower and home to much boating regalia.

RIGHT: the Trout Inn, seen in TV's *Inspector Morse*.

OXFORD'S OUTSKIRTS

Beyond Oxford's suburbs, which include Cowley, the birthplace of Morris Motors, there are some stunning views of the "City of Dreaming Spires"

Large houses line the complex of narrow lanes that lead to **Boars Hill ❶**, and such was the pressure of development that the Oxford Preservation Trust purchased the remaining land in 1928 to ensure that the views would not be destroyed.

One Boars Hill resident, Sir Arthur Evans, famous for his archaeological discoveries at Knossos, worked with the trust to build an artificial mound at the summit of the hill. Evans' intention was partly to provide work for the local unemployed during a period of economic depression, and partly to create a vantage point from which to admire Oxford's dreaming spires.

The tumulus that Evans built, known as **Jarn Mound ❷**, rises to 50ft (15 metres), and the summit is 530ft (162 metres) above sea level. It was completed in 1931 and the surrounding area planted with trees to create a wild garden.

Now it is overgrown with bracken and scrub, and the topograph on the summit has gone, the column on which it stood broken. Even so, the views are unchanged: to the northeast the ancient buildings of Oxford appear, framed between ancient trees that seem deliberately planted to hide

the modern suburbs – go at dusk and the setting sun adds its own rich colouring to the scene. Turn round and you see another extensive view, stretching southwest over the Vale of the White Horse to the Berkshire Downs.

Happy Valley

Heading clockwise around the ring road, Chilswell Valley, better known as **Happy Valley ❸**, is reached by turning off the southern bypass (A34) at a well-signposted garden centre and following a footpath to

LEFT: the view of Oxford from Boars Hill.
RIGHT: you don't have to go too far from Oxford to really feel you are in the country.

Chilswell Farm. The view from this southern hillside is almost as perfect a picture of the celebrated dreaming spires as you will find, remarkably unobstructed by power lines and other modern-day eyesores. What is striking is how small Oxford seems from this vantage-point, its towers and steeples encircled by hills.

From the same exit from the ring road you can also visit the **Hinksey Heights Golf and Nature Park**, where the view is, if anything, even more beautiful. Here the golf club welcomes visitors (as long as they keep off the golf course itself) and you can use the bar and restaurant.

A well-marked trail takes you through woods and over streams until you come to a fishing lake, stocked with six types of coarse fish (day angling permits available for £5 from the golf club). The surrounding countryside is inhabited not just by golfers, but also by foxes, badgers and deer as well as a wide range of birdlife.

ABOVE: Iffley Lock.

Iffley and Cowley

From this point, it is 2 miles (3km) by the thundering ring road to **Iffley** ❹, a village on the southern edge of the city worth seeking out simply for its **parish church of St Mary the Virgin**. In the whole of England there is scarcely a more complete example of the late 12th-century Romanesque style. The rose window of the west end is later (inserted in 1856), but most of the remaining doorways, windows and arches – covered in sawtooth ornament and carved with beakheads, the signs of the zodiac, fighting horse-

Oxford's Outskirts

[Map of Oxford's Outskirts]

men and symbols of the Evangelists – date from around 1180.

After Iffley comes the extensive suburb of **Cowley** ❺, dubbed "Motopolis" by John Betjeman who hated this industrial town on the doorstep of his beloved Oxford because it was devoted to producing the motor car that "roars down the lanes with its cargo of cads, poisons the air, deafens the ears and deadens the senses".

Cowley was responsible for a massive 43 percent rise in the population of Oxford between 1921 and 1939, as the success of the Morris motor attracted labourers from the depression-hit Midlands and South Wales. They were accommodated in what John Betjeman called "strips of shoddy houses... indistinguishable from Swindon, Neasden or Tooting Bec".

St Bartholomew's Chapel

A small, historical gem is to be found hidden on **Cowley Road**, away from the suburban grime. Up a small pathway opposite the former bingo hall is **St Bartholomew's Chapel** ❻, flanked by a row of almshouses. Built in the early 14th century, the chapel was connected to a leprosy hospital, situated at a suitable distance from the medieval city. The buildings are still there in a special conservation area, a world away from the main road just a few hundred yards distant. There's a stillness about it, making it, believers say, a good place to pray.

This main artery is the epicentre of alternative and multicultural Oxford as well as a popular area for students to live. It contains countless ethnic restaurants and grocery stores as well as a good range of independent retailers.

In Cowley itself, the car plant, the successor to the Morris Motor Works and now owned by Germany's BMW, lies either side of the eastern bypass, with the woodland of Shotover Country Park rising behind. The car factory can be visited by appointment (*see margin on opposite page*).

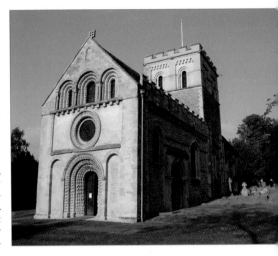

Shotover Country Park

The eastern and southern perimeter of the city, delineated by the busy ring road, offers some spectacular views of Oxford from surrounding hills as well as some interesting nature walks.

To reach **Shotover Country Park** ❼ by car, it is best to drive along Old Road from Headington, cross the ring road and climb up through a wooded residential area. The park itself comprises 250 acres (100 hectares) of mixed natural habitat, including grassland, heath, wetland and woodland. Recognised by English Nature as a Site of Special Scientific Interest, it has good views over the eastern part of Oxford.

Walks are clearly laid out and the area is a favourite with dog owners and mountain-bike enthusiasts. Some conspicuous hollows in the ground are what is left of what used to be a yellow ochre mining works. The area was also once the haunt of highwaymen, as the old London road passed over the hill, and carriages containing the well-to-do were an irresistible temptation for Oxford's equivalents of Dick Turpin.

ABOVE: beakhead carvings at the entrance to the church of St Mary the Virgin, Iffley.
BELOW: the stone footbridge at Iffley Lock.

Headington

Headington ❽ consists of several distinct "villages". **Headington Quarry** ❾, as its name suggests, originally supplied the limestone and roof tiles from which much of medieval Oxford was built. The current suburb developed around the quarrymen's cottages, some of which still remain, dating from the 17th and 18th centuries. This village is home to a well-known team of Morris dancers, the Quarrymen.

Old Headington lies on the opposite side of the London Road, and was once the resort of undergraduates seeking illicit pleasures in alehouses, beyond the jurisdiction of the proctors or bulldogs. In the 18th and 19th centuries, wealthy tradesmen built large houses on the leafy hillside. One of them, Bury Knowle House, is the Headington Library and occupies attractively landscaped grounds. Just to the north, restored 17th-century cottages surround St Andrew's Church, which has a Norman chancel arch and 15th-century chancel roof.

Headington Hill ❿, which plunges steeply into central Oxford,

was built up mainly in the 19th century. Oxford United used to have its football ground here until the club moved in the 1990s to a purpose-built stadium beyond Blackbird Leys, leaving the ground to be redeveloped as hospital facilities. Further down is Headington Hill Hall, once part of Robert Maxwell's publishing empire, Pergamon Press, but now owned by Oxford Brookes University. Opposite is the modern Gipsy Lane campus of Brookes *(see page 67)*, the growth of which has resulted in several blocks of student facilities and accommodation in and around Headington.

South Park

At the bottom of Headington Hill is the lower part of **South Park** ⓫, a large expanse of green stretching sharply upwards. There is usually a bonfire and fireworks in November. From the top of the park, where there are playing fields and a children's playground, you can look down on to the surprisingly compact city centre, picking out the major landmarks such as Magdalen Tower and Tom Tower. The view is particularly lovely at dawn or sunset. ❏

BELOW:
the controversial shark at Headington.

Shark!

One morning in August 1986 the residents of New High Street in Headington awoke to find a 25ft (8-metre) fibreglass shark plunging through the roof of one of its houses. Its owner, US-born entrepreneur and radio presenter Bill Heine, said the shark, the work of local architect John Buckley, symbolised the arbitrary horror of the nuclear age. The council said it infringed planning regulations, but eventually the shark's aesthetic merits were recognised with an award from the Southern Arts Council. You can see its tail from the London Road, but it's worth taking a detour down New High Street to get a better view.

BEST RESTAURANTS, PUBS AND BARS

Restaurants

The Aziz

228–30 Cowley Road. Tel: 01865-794 945. Open: daily. £

Perhaps the best of Cowley Road's many Indian restaurants, the Aziz is a welcome escape from flock wallpaper and predictable menus. With its spacious and tasteful atmosphere, it is the ideal place to sample the subtle variations within Asian cuisine at a very reasonable price. "Specials" change regularly and there is plenty of scope for vegetarians.

Brookes Restaurant

Gipsy Lane, Headington. Tel: 01865-483 803. Mon–Fri (except Mon out of term) L; last orders taken 1.30pm. £

Excellent value 3-course lunches as well as single dishes are on the menu at what is essentially a training school for chefs and other hospitality workers. The food is often better than that on offer from the professionals and is very reasonably priced. The cookery school also runs one-day classes for the public.

Prices for a three-course dinner per person with a half-bottle of house wine:

£ = under £20
££ = £20–£30
£££ = £30–£45
££££ = more than £45

Door 74

74 Cowley Road. Tel: 01865-203 374. Open: Tue–Sun L & D. ££

One of Cowley Road's new breed of stylish restaurant, this venue serves locally sourced, often organic, food in a fusion of British and Mediterranean influences. The desserts are particularly good, and there is a popular weekend brunch.

The Hi-Lo Jamaican Eating House

70 Cowley Road. Tel: 01865-725 984. Open: daily. £

A distinctive taste of the Caribbean in East Oxford, this eccentric institution allegedly charges customers what it thinks they can afford. True or not, the food includes classic Jamaican staples like rice 'n' peas, ackees and saltfish and curried goat. Service may be slow, but that is part of the experience, enhanced by Red Stripe lager and Jamaican rum. Guest rooms.

Kazbar

25–7 Cowley Road. Tel: 01865-202 920. Open: Mon–Fri D only, Sat–Sun L & D. £

Probably Oxford's premier tapas bar, Kazbar has lots of Moorish atmosphere, with ochre walls, benches and cushions and suitably attired staff. The generous portions of Andalucian-inspired food, including fish and delicious tortilla, are matched by a good selection of Spanish beers and house wines.

Pubs and Bars

The **Fox Inn** (Fox Lane, Boars Hill) is a welcoming place all year round, with a pretty garden in summer and real fires in winter. Good food is the order of the day and an unusually extensive wine list.

Iffley boasts the riverside **Isis**, with a lovely garden and good lunchtime menu, as well as the **Prince of Wales** (73 Church Way), a busy and friendly establishment on the village's pretty main street. **The Tree Hotel** (63 Church Way) contains the Annora restaurant/bar, serving a mix of British, Indian and Thai dishes. **The Bullingdon** (162 Cowley Road) is a lively student-oriented pub with a good-value menu and a large back room used for folk and jazz evenings and other musical events. The **City Arms** (288 Cowley Road) provides very good food at reasonable prices in a welcoming, student-dominated atmosphere. Across the road, **Baby** (213 Cowley Road) is the closest the street comes to chic, with retro decor, cocktails and a young crowd. Many move from there to the O2 Academy (formerly known as the **Zodiac**, 190 Cowley Road), where the atmosphere is less chic and more down-to-earth. Its range of music is unmatched in Oxford.

There are several good cafés on Cowley Road, not least **Café Coco** (23 Cowley Road), a bright and cheerful place offering good pizzas, salads and cocktails all day, vegetarian- and vegan-friendly. **Joe's** (21 Cowley Road), a great choice for burgers and/or cocktails, and **Café Baba** (240 Cowley Road), a North African-themed bar/café specialising in tapas. Of Headington's many pubs, the **Royal Standard** (78 London Road) stands out as a friendly single-bar establishment with an extensive menu of home-cooked lunches and good beer. The 17th-century **Black Boy** (91 Old High Street) is in Headington's picturesque old district and despite its politically incorrect name attracts a mixed crowd of students and regulars with its traditional pub atmosphere and good food.

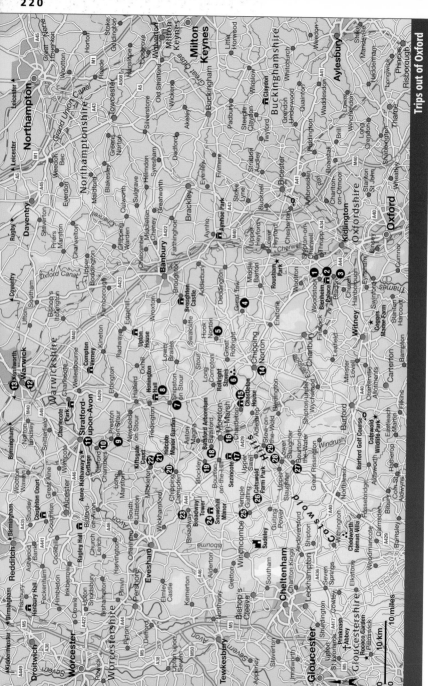

TRIPS OUT OF OXFORD

Within easy reach of Oxford are the lovely Cotswolds, alluring riverside towns, Stratford-upon-Avon's Shakespeariana, Warwick's popular castle, and celebrated stately homes such as Blenheim

Drive for just a few miles out of Oxford and you will be immersed in countryside that you didn't realise was so close to the busy city. To help you explore its beauties, the following chapters are divided into routes, beginning with the road to Stratford-upon-Avon. First on this route is Woodstock, famous for splendid Blenheim Palace and its associations with Winston Churchill, and a charming market town. The road on from Woodstock leads to the pretty villages of Great Tew and Hook Norton before reaching the ancient Rollright Stones. The final stretch to Stratford offers some more delightful villages with names like Compton Wynyates and Clifford Chambers.

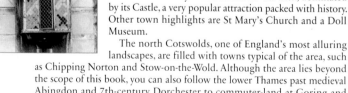

Stratford-upon-Avon is a shrine to the playwright William Shakespeare, and visitors from all over the world come to see what all the fuss is about. The tour around the town takes in all the important sights, such as his birthplace, his home at New Place, his school, the Guildhall, and his place of burial, Holy Trinity Church. It's even possible to take in one of the Bard's plays at the Shakespeare Memorial Theatre. There are other sights as well, such as the Garrick Inn and Harvard House, both 16th-century, the canal and beautiful Bancroft Gardens.

From Stratford you can detour to Warwick, dominated by its Castle, a very popular attraction packed with history. Other town highlights are St Mary's Church and a Doll Museum.

The north Cotswolds, one of England's most alluring landscapes, are filled with towns typical of the area, such as Chipping Norton and Stow-on-the-Wold. Although the area lies beyond the scope of this book, you can also follow the lower Thames past medieval Abingdon and 7th-century Dorchester to commuter-land at Goring and Streatley, the regatta-centre of Henley-on-Thames, and back to Oxford via the famous houses of Cliveden and Hughenden Manor. ❑

PRECEDING PAGES: view over the fields surrounding St James' Church, Chipping Campden.
ABOVE LEFT: Tudor window at Shakespeare's birthplace.
ABOVE RIGHT: Warwick Castle reflected.

THE ROAD TO STRATFORD

It would be a shame to rush to Stratford-upon-Avon along the busy main highways, missing out the memorable sights along the route

Stratford-
upon-Avon
Oxford
London

Stratford-upon-Avon lies about 60 miles (100km) northwest of Oxford and exerts a magnetic attraction, having acquired international status as the most important literary shrine in England. Its environs are fascinating, too.

Woodstock and Blenheim

Leaving Oxford on the A44, it is only a matter of minutes before you reach the handsome market town of **Woodstock ❶**. The main street (Park Street) lies off the main road and is flanked by fine Georgian-fronted houses, some now occupied by pubs, cafés and boutiques. One particularly fine building is occupied by The Bear Hotel, built on the site of a 13th-century coaching inn, and now as good a base as any if you wish to stay overnight in Woodstock.

The town derived much of its former prosperity from glove-making, and while all the factories in Woodstock itself are now closed, gloves are still made in surrounding villages and sold at the Woodstock Glove Shop, next to the town hall.

Also in Park Street, the Oxfordshire County Museum in Fletcher's House provides an overview of the region's archaeology, agriculture and domestic life, and the gardens to the rear are used to display contemporary sculpture. Opposite, the church of St Mary Magdalene was lavishly restored in 1878, but the best part is the 18th-century tower, carved with swags of flowers around the clock and parapet.

Blenheim Palace ❷

Tel: 08700-602 080
Opening Hrs: house and gardens mid-Feb–Oct daily, Nov–mid-Dec Wed–Sun 10.30am–5.30pm; park, daily all year 9am–4.45pm
Entrance Fee: Charge

LEFT: cottages in Woodstock.

At the far end of Park Street, a triumphal arch announces the entrance to **Blenheim Palace**. There is still half a mile (1km) to go before you reach this monumental building, for it lies at the heart of a vast estate, covering 2,700 acres (1,100 hectares) – the palace alone occupies an area of 7 acres (2.8 hectares). Not for nothing is it called a palace, rather than a mere manor, although that is what it was originally.

Royal blood

Woodstock was, as far back as records go, a royal manor, frequented by a succession of monarchs for deer hunting when the land was still part of the great forest of Wychwood. Henry II installed his mistress, "fair Rosamund" Clifford, at Woodstock, until Queen Eleanor discovered her hunting lodge hideaway. By the 16th century the original royal palace had decayed, and the last remaining buildings were demolished after the Civil War.

In 1705, Queen Anne gave both the manor and the funds to build the palace to John Churchill, 1st Duke of Marlborough and forefather of Winston Churchill. This was his reward for defeating the French army at Blenheim, on the Danube, the previous year, a major victory that temporarily thwarted Louis XIV's desire to dominate Europe.

The queen made it quite clear that the palace was to be no mere private house, but a national monument, a symbol of Britain's supremacy – by implication, a building to outshine even Louis XIV's own splendid palace at Versailles. Consequently, the best architects of the day were consulted. Christopher Wren was the obvious candidate, and many of his masons, men who had worked on St Paul's, were to be employed on the project. But Wren was rejected in favour of John Vanbrugh, whose designs for Castle Howard were greatly admired by Churchill. Vanbrugh is there-

ABOVE:
Blenheim Palace.
BELOW: the
Marlborough armorial
bearing, as seen on the
palace's east gate.

ABOVE: Japanese tourists visit Churchill's grave.

BELOW: Churchill leaves the first War Cabinet meeting, 1939.

Horace Walpole called it "execrable" and Alexander Pope, ever with an eye to practicalities, quipped "'tis very fine; but where d'ye sleep and where d'ye dine?"

Yet now Blenheim excites the imagination and invites superlatives. The skyline, with its bizarre chimneys, its pinnacles resembling stacks of cannon balls and its ducal coronets, creates a wonderful silhouette, viewed across the lakes and avenues of the park, landscaped by "Capability" Brown.

Symbols of soldiery

Everywhere you look there are symbols of military prowess – over the main entrance, Britannia stands supreme in armour above the Marlborough coat of arms. Chained slaves writhe on the upper pediment, and the gates to the side wings have carvings of the cock of France being savaged by the British lion.

Inside, the gilded state rooms are rich in furniture and portraits of the Marlboroughs. Tapestries, woven in Brussels, celebrate the 1st duke's victories. In the magnificent

fore credited as the architect of this Baroque masterpiece, but his assistant, Nicholas Hawksmoor, ought to share the credit – for it was he who supervised much of the work.

A true folly

In the event, it is remarkable that the building was completed at all, let alone on such a heroic scale. Parliament quibbled about the cost, funds ran out, and the Duchess of Marlborough constantly opposed the grandiose scheme, declaring "I mortally hate all gardens and architecture", and insisting that all she wanted was "a clean, sweet house and garden, be it ever so small".

The duke ended up bearing a great deal of the cost himself, and such was the enmity between architect and client that Vanbrugh never saw the finished building; when he tried to visit in 1725, the duchess refused him entrance.

Even when completed, Blenheim continued to be controversial:

Sir Winston Churchill

Winston Churchill was born on 30 November 1874 in a simple room to the west of Blenheim's Great Hall. Once used by the 1st duke's domestic chaplain, Dean Jones, the room now forms the core of a permanent exhibition of Churchilliana, including manuscripts, paintings and personal belongings. Visitors can also see letters written by Sir Winston, mostly to his father, Lord Randolph Churchill, as well as a piece of shrapnel that narrowly missed him in World War I.

It was at Blenheim that Churchill proposed to his future wife, Clementine, in the Temple of Diana. The house acted as inspiration for several of his paintings, some now on show.

saloon, life-size *trompe l'oeil* figures, representing the peoples of the four continents and painted by Louis Laguerre in 1719–20, lean over balconies as spectators to the state banquets that still are, on occasion, held in this huge, unheated room (for the sake of symmetry, there are no fireplaces).

Despite its scale and discomforts, Blenheim also serves as a home, and the small room where Sir Winston Churchill was born in 1874 attracts as much attention as the state apartments. Like his ancestor, the 1st duke, Sir Winston is remembered as a great war leader. Unlike the 1st duke, who is commemorated by a monument of exaggerated proportions in the palace chapel, Sir Winston is buried in a simple grave in the parish church of **Bladon** ❸, on the southern periphery of the estate.

Great Tew

Some 6 miles (10km) further north, the B4022 meets the A44, just outside Enstone, and the right turn leads to the picturesque village of **Great Tew** ❹. Dubbed "the place where time stood still", this estate village contains scarcely a modern building, simply because the late landlord permitted no new development; indeed, as the number of labourers employed on the estate steadily declined, the stone and thatch cottages were simply left to rot. One visitor, in 1972, described the derelict houses surrounding the green as "one of the most depressing sights in the whole country".

Now, thanks to new ownership, the cottages have been fully restored to their appearance in the early 19th century, when, as part of a model farm, the village was carefully landscaped. Quite a number of the cottages were given Gothic embellishments at the time, though many date to the 16th century. Set back behind colourful gardens, they present the kind of picture that calendar and chocolate-box manufacturers find irresistible.

The church of St Michael lies south of the village, just within the grounds of the park, and the churchyard is entered through a 17th-century stone gateway. Inside

ABOVE: traditional hostelries have been restored in villages such as Great Tew.
BELOW: Great Tew, where time stood still.

May Day festivities in Hook Norton and other Cotswold villages include Morris dancing. Often derided as folkloric kitsch, this strenuous dance may date back about 800 years and celebrates the coming of spring. The colourful costume includes dozens of bells attached to the legs and the dancers wield sticks or handkerchiefs.

ABOVE RIGHT: a new dray for the Hook Brewery.
BELOW: morris dancers at the Hook Norton festival of fine ales.

is a noteworthy monument to Mary Anne Boulton (died 1829) by Francis Chantrey. The Boultons, descendants of Matthew Boulton, the Birmingham engineer who made his fortune manufacturing steam engines as a partner of James Watt, acquired the estate in 1815 and gave the 17th-century house its current neo-Gothic appearance.

Hook Norton

The B4022 continues north for just over a mile (2km) to the A361. If you turn left, and then right via Swerford, a pretty village on the River Swere, you will reach **Hook Norton ❺**. Real-ale lovers will know this as the source of "Hooky", a beer made by traditional methods in the red-brick Victorian brewery at the west end of the village. This prominent building is surrounded by cottages built of the local orange-coloured ironstone – as is the church of St Peter, commanding the hilltop at the centre of the village. The Norman font inside is carved with a charmingly rustic Adam, with his hammer and spade, and a flirtatious Eve, holding her apple, as well as signs of the zodiac.

The Rollright Stones

Three miles (5km) west of Hook Norton, through the village of **Great Rollright** and across the A3400, you will find the remains of a prehistoric stone circle.

Standing on the high ridge of the northern Cotswolds, the **Rollright Stones ❻** form a henge 100ft (30 metres) in diameter. They date to around 3500 BC. The stones of the circle itself are known as the King's Men, while the solitary stone on the opposite side of the road is the King and the five further east, once the burial chamber of a long barrow, are the Whispering Knights.

The names refer to a legend, first recorded in 1586, that the stones represent petrified men who will one day wake to rule the land. They were tricked, according to the story, by a local witch who promised their leader that he would be king of England if he could see Long Compton, the village in the valley below, from this spot. This simple task proved impossible – some

say that the witch conjured up a mist – and so she transformed them with the words: *Thou and thy men hoar stones shall be/And I myself an elder tree.*

Other legends about the stones abound – to their detriment, since they have often been chipped away by visitors (including Civil War soldiers on their way to battle) believing in their magical properties.

The Rollright Stones are too close to the busy A3400 to make a good resting spot, but an ideal place for a peaceful picnic is along the unclassified road back to the main road, across and left towards the Sibfords. This high road, with fine views all round, drops, after 4 miles (7km), into the Stour Valley at **Traitor's Ford.** Nobody seems to remember now

who the traitor was, but the ford, with its clear stream and woodland either side, makes a perfect spot for relaxing on a hot summer's day.

From the ford, an ancient track, **Ditchedge Lane,** leads directly to

ABOVE: the Rollright Stones.
BELOW: Mrs Brown's Tea Room, Shipston on Stour.

ABOVE: Compton Wynyates House.
BELOW: dream cottage, Shipston on Stour.

Compton Wynyates, accessible only to walkers – motorists have to take the longer route through Sibford Gower. Compton Wynyates, a romantic Tudor mansion of rose-coloured brick, is no longer open to the public, but you can glimpse it, nestling into the wooded hillside, from the road to the west.

Windmill Hill, rising beyond to the north, is crowned by a stone tower mill, complete with its sails, while on **Compton Pike**, to the south, is a pyramidal structure, dating to the 16th century, built to be lit in the event of an invasion.

Some 5 miles (8km) west is **Shipston on Stour ⑦**. The name (originally Sheepston) is a reminder that the town was once host to one of England's largest sheep markets. It is home to many handsome former coaching inns.

Honington Hall ⑧

Tel: 01608-661 434
Opening Hrs: June–Aug Wed and Bank Holiday Mondays 2.30–5pm
Entrance Fee: Charge

Two miles (3km) north, **Honington Hall** is a 17th-century brick house that could pass for the ordinary domestic manor of some country squire, but for a series of busts all around the facades, depicting 12 Caesars. Even more extraordinary is

the sumptuous plasterwork inside.

The house was built in 1685 by Sir Henry Parker who, having made a fortune as a London merchant, had the village church remodelled in the style of Wren's elegant City of London churches. The monument to Parker and his son Hugh is the best of several splendid pieces of carving, in both marble and stone, inside.

Stylish church

From Honington, continue up the A3400 to Newbold-on-Stour and then, if you want to avoid the main road, take the minor road left that runs parallel to the pretty, winding River Stour.

At **Preston on Stour** ❾ you will find another stylish 18th-century church, this time in the Gothic style, and an east window made up of 17th-century glass from diverse sources, all illustrating the theme of death. The village has several ornate 16th- and 17th-century timber-framed houses; and even the red-brick Alscot housing estate of 1852, an early example of its kind, has a certain undeniable charm.

At **Clifford Chambers** ❿ attractive cottages line the single street that leads to the manor house, restored – or rather rebuilt – by Sir Edwin Lutyens in 1919. Here, too, is the first of many buildings associated with Shakespeare, for the 16th-century timber-framed rectory was the home of one John Shakespeare during the 1570s. Since William's father was called John, biographers have speculated whether this might possibly have been his childhood home.

From Clifford Chambers continue on the B4632 and A3400 to reach **Stratford-upon-Avon** ⓫. ❑

ABOVE LEFT: Honington village church.
ABOVE: Honington Hall.
BELOW LEFT: Shipston on Stour's High Street.
BELOW: the churchyard in Honington.

STRATFORD-UPON-AVON

Basking in Shakespeare's enduring fame, Stratford remains one of England's most crowded tourist destinations. To go or not to go? That is the question

The Shakespeare industry dates to the mid-19th century, when a pub called the Swan and Maidenhead, in Henley Street, came on the market. This had long been considered Shakespeare's birthplace, and in 1847 a public appeal was launched to buy the building as a national monument. A trust was formed and, between 1857 and 1864, the property was restored to its "original" appearance, a process that involved virtually rebuilding the house that is seen today.

You can, however, learn much more about Shakespeare at the **Shakespeare Centre B** just along the street (times as above). Here is an excellent exhibition entitled "William Shakespeare – Life, Love and Legacy", which gives a concise and visually appealing account of the context of the playwright's life in Stratford, then London, and finally Stratford again. There are displays on the town of Stratford itself and on the countryside that inspired so much of Shakespeare's imagery.

Shakespeare's Birthplace A

Tel: 01789-204 016
Opening Hrs: daily Apr–Oct 9am–5pm, Nov–Mar 10am–4pm
Entrance Fee: Charge

The best starting point for a tour of Stratford is **Shakespeare's Birthplace**. The rooms are furnished as far as possible in late 16th-century style, as well as having small-scale displays on aspects of family history and William's work. The room in which Shakespeare is supposed to have been born, on 23 April 1564, is lit by a window inscribed with the signatures of illustrious guests such as Sir Walter Scott, Thomas Carlyle and Isaac Watts.

LEFT: the Royal Shakespeare Theatre.
RIGHT: Shakespeare's Birthplace.

Who was Shakespeare?

Part of the lure of Shakespeare's birthplace is that so few details of the playwright's life can be authenticated. It is known that his father, John, was a successful glove-maker and wool merchant, and that his mother, Mary Arden, was the daughter of a well-to-do farmer. William went to school in Stratford. Having got a Shottery girl, Anne Hathaway, pregnant, he married her in 1582, when he was 18 and she 26; they had three children. Most of his professional career in the theatre, however, was centred in London, though he spent the last five years of his life in Stratford, where he died in 1616. The rest is largely speculation.

ABOVE:
Holy Trinity Church, where Shakespeare's tomb is to be found.
BELOW: where the Bard was born.

As well as original documents and copies of such items as his marriage licence bond, there are portraits, furniture, a wonderful model of the Globe Theatre in London, and a reconstruction of "Shakespeare's Study", the kind of room he may well have worked in.

Beyond the Shakespeare Centre, the pretty garden has been planted with many of the trees, shrubs and flowers mentioned in his plays.

Nearby is the broad expanse of Rother Street, where the town's market meets on Friday. The **American Fountain** was given to Stratford for

Queen Victoria's 1887 Jubilee by the Philadelphia newspaperman George C. Childs.

Wood Street, to the left, leads to the town centre and has a sprinkling of those heavily timbered properties that we associate with the ancient heart of England, when the extensive Forest of Arden, which once covered the country north of Stratford, provided a ready supply of materials.

The **High Street** has some of the town's most ornate buildings, many now stripped of 18th-century brick and stucco facades to reveal the original timber framing.

Harvard House

Tel: 01789-204 507
Opening Hrs: daily May–Sept 10am–4pm
Entrance Fee: Charge

Overlooking the little paved open space at the first crossroads, the **Garrick Inn** and **Harvard House** make an eccentric and flamboyant pair of buildings. Both date to about 1596, built just after a fire destroyed much of the town. Harvard House is elaborately carved with flowers and grotesque heads, and was the home of Katherine Rogers. She married Robert Harvard of Southwark, and their son, John Harvard, died in Massachusetts in 1638, a year after he emigrated to the New World. He bequeathed much of his estate to Harvard College, which now owns this house and uses it to display material relating to the Harvard family. The house also contains the Neish Collection of pewter, with pieces ranging from Roman times to the 19th century.

Originally called the Reindeer, the Garrick Inn was renamed after the great 18th-century Shakespearian actor David Garrick. He was greatly influential in the revival of interest in Shakespeare's dramatic works and helped to organise the first festival in his honour, the Garrick Jubilee, in 1769. The festival was a great social

ABOVE: an Old Bank mosaic pays tribute to the town's most famous tourist attraction.
BELOW: the Garrick Inn.

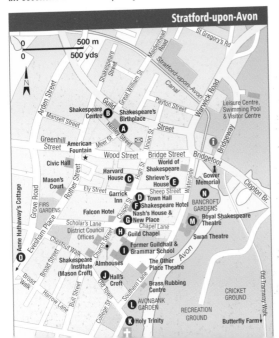

Stratford-upon-Avon

ABOVE:
the Knot Garden.

occasion, patronised by royalty – hence the bold slogan "God save the King" painted in the same year across the Chapel Street facade of the **Town Hall** , a solid neo-Palladian building marking the end of the High Street, completed in 1768. The statue of Shakespeare, on the Sheep Street frontage of the Town Hall, was presented by Garrick. Opposite the Town Hall, there is a mosaic portrait of the Bard over the doorway of the Victorian red-brick **Old Bank**.

Sheep and Chapel streets

On Sheep Street you will find numerous souvenir shops and restaurants not only flanking the street but also running up the alleys behind. The **Shrieve's House** (40 Sheep Street) is an interesting example of a 16th-century merchant's house, with a cart entrance and long, cobbled back yard, lined with buildings that would have been used as workshop and warehouse space – now converted to shops.

Chapel Street continues the timber-framed theme, first with the magnificent many-bayed and gabled

The town's name, "street ford", indicates that this was the point at which a Roman road crossed the River Avon. But Stratford's real history goes back only to Saxon times, when a monastery flourished here, probably located where the parish church now stands.

Shakespeare Hotel , and then, at the corner of Scholars Lane, the **Falcon Hotel**, the lower two storeys of which date from around 1500.

Nash's House and the Site of New Place

Tel: 01789-292 325
Opening Hrs: daily Apr–Oct 10am–5pm, Nov–Mar 11am–4pm
Entrance Fee: Charge

Opposite is another property of the Birthplace Trust, **Nash's House** and the **Site of New Place**. The former belonged to Thomas Nash, who married Shakespeare's granddaughter, Elizabeth Hall. It is now a museum of material relating to the history of Stratford. New Place was one of the town's largest houses, and Shakespeare was wealthy enough to purchase it in 1597. He later retired to the house and died there on his 52nd birthday, in 1616.

A later owner, Rev. Francis Gastrell, had little respect for the poet's memory. He was so annoyed by the constant stream of visitors wanting to see the mulberry tree in the garden, planted by Shakespeare, that he cut it down. In 1759 he demolished the house itself, rather than pay rates. Sensibly, no attempt has been made to reconstruct it. Instead, the foundations are exposed and paths thread through delightful gardens.

The **Knot Garden** is planted with flowers known to have been grown in the 16th century, and the Great Garden beyond, originally the orchard and kitchen garden to New Place, has box and yew hedges.

The **Guild Chapel**  opposite served as the chapel of the Guild of the Holy Cross, a body of local worthies who regulated trade in the town, fixing prices, collecting levies and allocating funds to charitable purposes. A wealthy member, Sir Hugh Clopton, later Lord Mayor of London, paid for the rebuilding of the nave in 1496. Just visible on the chancel wall is a *Last Judgement* painting.

The Guildhall

Adjoining the chapel is the 15th-century former **Guildhall** ❶, part of which was used as the town grammar school. It is conjectured, reasonably, that Shakespeare was a pupil here.

The delightfully named "Pedagogue's House" in the courtyard behind was probably the schoolmaster's dwelling. Beyond, 15th-century almshouses, still used as such, stretch for a distance of 50yds/metres, an impressive range with massive studs and a jettied-out upper storey.

Further down Church Street the character of the buildings begins to change, as timber gives way to the brick of elegant town houses. **Mason Croft**, an early 18th-century building, was the last home of Marie Corelli (1855–1924) – real name Mary Mackay – the prolific novelist who, despite critical derision, was as popular in her heyday as Shakespeare was in his. The house is now an international centre for Shakespearian research, owned by Birmingham University.

Hall's Croft ❶

Tel: 01789-292 107
Opening Hrs: daily Apr–Oct 10am–5pm, Nov–Mar 10am–4pm
Entrance Fee: Charge

Turning left, into the Old Town, you reach **Hall's Croft**. Of all the buildings associated with Shakespeare, this

ABOVE: statue of Lady Macbeth.
BELOW: an inn that catches Stratford's mood.

ABOVE: Stratford Canal.
BELOW RIGHT:
Shakespeare's place of burial.

ing Shakespeare's grave, is famously inscribed: *Good Frend For Jesus Sake Forbeare/To Digg the Dust Enclosed Heare:/ Blese Be Ye Man (that) Spares Thes Stones/And Curst Be He (that) Moves My Bones.* These words have often been interpreted as implying that the grave contains evidence of the "true" authorship of Shakespeare's works – for, despite substantial evidence to the contrary, many people still believe that Shakespeare was only a front for some other writer. All requests to investigate the tomb have been refused.

Burial places

Other Shakespeare family tombs are found nearby: namely, those of his wife Anne (*née* Hathaway), his daughter Susanna, and those of Thomas Nash and Dr John Hall. The misericords should not be missed: they date from around 1500 and provide an amusing commentary on contemporary domestic life.

Just north of Holy Trinity churchyard, back in the Old Town, a gate on the right leads to the **Avonbank Garden ℓ**, with its 19th-century summerhouse (now a brass-rubbing centre) and paths that follow the River Avon to the **Royal Shakespeare Theatre ⓜ** complex. The first part of the complex to come into view is the **Swan Theatre**, with a curved end and sweeping lead-covered roof, like some romantic mid-European castle. Partly used as a museum, displaying costumes, props and theatrical mementos, this incorporates all that remains of the original theatre, built in 1879 but damaged by fire in 1926.

is the least altered and most atmospheric. It dates to the late 16th century and was the home of Dr John Hall, husband of Shakespeare's daughter Susanna. One room is equipped as an apothecary's dispensary, and the walled garden has ancient mulberry trees and perennial borders.

Further down, an avenue of lime trees leads to **Holy Trinity Church ⓚ**, idyllically sited by the River Avon, and a fine example of a 13th-century church. You have to pay to visit the most interesting part of the church – the chancel – where Shakespeare's monument is the chief attraction.

The poet's son-in-law, Dr John Hall, took a wax impression of Shakespeare's face at his death, and this was used by the Dutch mason Gerard Jansenni, or Johnson, as the basis for the painted alabaster bust of Shakespeare. It is thus the best likeness we have of the poet; other portraits, based on this, have tried to make him look less self-satisfied.

The nearby tomb slab, cover-

The main theatre, completed in 1932, was a radical building in its time – shaped like a stack of bricks and almost windowless – but seemed somehow inadequate. Now it is being given a £100-million remodelling, due to be completed in 2011. Until then, the plays will be staged in The Courtyard, a 1,000-seat temporary theatre built in the former car park.

In front of the theatre, the **Bancroft Gardens**  surround a large canal basin, marking the point where the Stratford Canal joins the River Avon. The 1888 **Gower Memorial** has the alert figure of Shakespeare seated on a plinth, surrounded by statues of Hamlet, Prince Hal, Falstaff and Lady Macbeth. The **nine-arched bridge** was built in 1823 for the tramway whose horse-drawn carriages and goods wagons once rattled their way between Stratford and Shipston on Stour. It was converted to pedestrian use in 1918 and is a good place from which to get a grandstand prospect of activities on the river. Further north, the **Clopton Bridge** was built in the late 15th century.

The **Stratford Canal**, completed in 1816, runs north to the Grand Union. As an alternative to travelling by car, you can follow the canal towpath for 3 miles (5km) through the town and out, past a long flight of locks, to the hamlet of **Wilmcote**. Here, the Shakespeare Birthplace Trust has restored the 16th-century home of Mary Arden as a museum of country life in Tudor Warwickshire.

Anne Hathaway's Cottage

Tel: 01789-292 100
Opening Hrs: daily Apr–Oct 9am–5pm, Nov–Mar 10am–4pm
Entrance Fee: Charge

On the return journey you could visit **Anne Hathaway's Cottage** in the suburb of **Shottery**. This 15th-century thatched farmhouse was once the home of Shakespeare's wife, and stands in a delightful cottage garden. Furnished with Hathaway family heirlooms, pride of place is given to the famous bed that Shakespeare bequeathed to his wife – the only thing he left her in his will, fuelling speculation that their marriage might not have been happy. ❑

ABOVE: the Gower Memorial to Shakespeare.
BELOW: Anne Hathaway's Cottage.

WARWICK

The city of Warwick is best known for its magnificent castle but there are many other sights here including the glorious Beauchamp Chapel, built for earls but fit for kings

One of the most delightful old towns of the English Midlands with a wealth of late medieval and Georgian buildings, **Warwick** ⓬ is built on a rise above the Avon. From much of the surrounding countryside, the town, whose origins date from the 10th century, seems to be dominated by the majestic tower of St Mary's Church, but it is above all the great castle – often described as England's finest medieval stronghold – on its rocky bluff overlooking the river that draws visitors here.

The basic layout of the town is that of a cross, formed by the High Street, Church Street, Jury Street and Castle Street. Their meeting point is marked by substantial edifices all dating from the time of the town's rebuilding, including the **Court House** Ⓐ of 1725 whose ground floor is occupied by the Tourist Information Centre and which also houses the Town Museum and the Warwickshire Yeomanry Museum.

Lord Leycester's Hospital

Lined with dignified Georgian buildings, the High Street leads to the 12th-century **West Gate** with its massive archway partly cut into the rock. Above it is St James' Chapel and the beautiful timber-framed almshouses of **Lord Leycester's Hospital** Ⓑ (tel: 01926-491 422; Tue–Sun 10am–5pm, winter until 4.30pm; charge), founded in 1571 as a home for old soldiers. A highlight is a magnificent mid-15th-century **Guildhall**, and the atmospheric **St James' Chapel**, lit by a 15th-century candelabrum.

Modern life in Warwick centres on the area around the Market Place with its fine stone-built **Market Hall** Ⓒ of 1670. The building, its arches now blocked in with windows, houses the **Warwickshire Museum**

LEFT: Warwick Castle.

(due to reopen after refurbishment in spring 2010; tel: 01926-412 500; Tue–Sat 10am–5pm, Apr–Sept Sun only 11.30am–5pm; free). It has displays on local natural history as well as the striking mid-16th-century **Sheldon tapestry map** of Warwickshire.

St Mary's Church

The 174ft (53-metre) tower of **St Mary's Church ⓓ** rises above Church Street and can be climbed, the reward being superb views. Highlights include the Norman crypt with its massive columns, the Dean's Chapel with lovely fan vaulting, the 14th-century chancel, and the **Beauchamp Chapel**.

The gilded **brass effigy of Richard Beauchamp**, Earl of Warwick, was made 15 years after he died in 1439 and is rightly famous. The great magnate lies with his head resting on a helmet, his hands raised in supplication. At his feet are a bear and a griffin; around the tomb are figures of weeping people and angels.

Follow Church Street back to its junction with High Street and Jury Street. The latter leads to the charm-ing 15th-century **East Gate ⓔ** topped by a chapel dedicated to St Peter and now only used by pedestrians. Beyond is Smith Street, at the far end of which is **St John's ⓕ**, a fine early 17th-century stone building now part of the **Warwickshire Museum** (tel: 01926-412 132; Tue–Sat 10am–5pm, Apr–Sept Sun only 2.30–5pm; free) that includes reconstructions of a Victorian classroom and kitchen. The **Museum of the Royal Warwickshire Regiment** shares the building.

St Nicholas' Church ⓖ overlooks **Castle Bridge**. This handsome 100ft (30-metre) single-span structure was built in 1793 to replace the medieval bridge. Now a cul-de-sac, **Mill Street** completely escaped the effects of the Great Fire of Warwick (1694) and contains a fine array of timber-framed houses. From the **Mill Garden** at the far end is a fine view of the castle's Caesar's Tower high above.

The castle can be approached via its Stable Block at the foot of Castle Street. One of the prettiest of the town's streets, Castle Street also has one of the prettiest houses in

ABOVE: Warwick's Courthouse proclaims its authority.
BELOW LEFT: Lord Leycester's Hospital.
BELOW: Beauchamp Chapel in St Mary's Church.

Warwick: **Oken House** Ⓗ, a timber-framed early Elizabethan building named after its owner, Thomas Oken, a prosperous mercer and benefactor of the town. The building now houses traditional tearooms.

Warwick Castle Ⓘ

Tel: 0871-265 2000
Opening Hrs: daily Apr–Sept 10am–6pm, Oct–Mar 10am–5pm
Entrance Fee: Charge

Warwick Castle, which is owned by Madame Tussaud's, was once described as "the most perfect piece of castellated antiquity in the kingdom". The natural potential of the site – on a sandstone spur above the Avon – has been fully exploited by successive owners and builders and there are few views more emblematic of England's historic heritage than that of Warwick's walls and towers rising above luxuriant parkland and reflected in the river.

The castle's history stretches

over a period of more than 1,000 years, beginning with the fortification built by Ethelfleda. It was only two years after the Conquest, in 1068, that King William ordered the castle to be refounded, a standard Norman motte and bailey construction which was succeeded in the 12th and 13th centuries by a more permanent stone structure. Much of the fabric of this castle was replaced in the mid-14th century by Thomas Beauchamp, Earl of Warwick.

Eventually it became the property of the Greville family. The Grevilles, who became earls of Warwick in 1759, were responsible for the conversion of the medieval fortress into a princely palace. Walls and towers remain as reminders of medieval might, and basements, dungeons and undercroft preserve their ancient character, but the habitable part of the castle consists of a sumptuous series of state rooms of Jacobean and later date. In the 18th century, the grounds were

ABOVE: lying in state – a bedroom in Warwick Castle.
BELOW: old buildings in Mill Street.

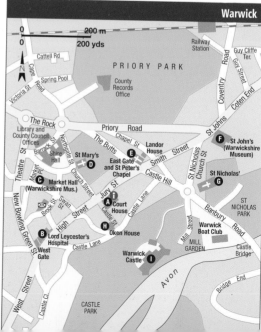

re-landscaped by "Capability" Brown and extended north.

From the **Stable Block** entrance, a curving pathway makes a dramatic approach to the **gatehouse and barbican** with **Guy's Tower** rising up splendidly on the right to a height of 128ft (40 metres).

Once within the great circuit of walls, the visitor has various choices. Beneath **Caesar's Tower** are the **Armoury**, **Torture Chamber** and **Dungeon**.

Further underground chambers and passageways of the medieval castle house an entertaining tableau, "Kingmaker". This is a convincing evocation of the preparations that preceded the Battle of Barnet in 1471. As well as armourers and others at work, there are children larking about, a horse giving off a powerful stable smell, and living costumed figures barely distinguishable from the waxworks.

A very different epoch is evoked in the tableaux of the **Royal Weekend Party of 1898**. Towards the end of the 19th century, Warwick had become a great social centre, largely because of the influence of the countess of Warwick, born Frances but universally known as Daisy. Among the guests populating some of the former private apartments are the young Winston Churchill, the future George V lighting a cigarette, and Edward prince of Wales, a frequent visitor and rumoured lover of Daisy.

The Chapel, Great Hall and State Rooms are reached by stairs. The early 17th-century **Chapel** has medieval stained glass and superbly carved wooden panels. The 18th-century Dining Room has splendidly framed royal portraits, including a famous study of Charles I on horseback. The **Great Hall** exudes the atmosphere of the Middle Ages with its displays of arms and armour. The **State Rooms** compete with each other in magnificence: the Red Drawing Room

has bold red lacquer panelling; the Cedar Drawing Room a superb plaster ceiling; the Green Drawing Room mementoes of the Civil War; the Queen Anne Bedroom a bed intended for that royal personage but never used; while the Blue Boudoir has a portrait after Holbein of Henry V.

Next to the so-called **Ghost Tower** the great **mound** rises to a surprising height. Topped by mock fortifications, it offers a magnificent prospect over the castle grounds, the river and the lush countryside.

Kenilworth ⑬

Tel: 01926-852 078
Opening Hrs: daily Mar–Oct 10am–5pm, Nov–Feb 10am–4pm
Entrance Fee: Charge

If Warwick is one of England's finest castles, then **Kenilworth**, barely 4 miles (6km) to the north of Warwick, must rank as one of its finest castle ruins. It was destroyed after the Civil War, but the original Norman keep still stands, as does the shell of the Great Hall. The castle's natural defences were strengthened by flooding the surrounding marshland. The lake is no longer there, but Kenilworth remains an evocative place. ❑

ABOVE:
Kenilworth Castle.
BELOW: costumed figure of Lady Sackville-West in the Ladies' Boudoir, Warwick Castle.

THE NORTH COTSWOLDS

The remarkable beauty of the Cotswolds, a prominent range of hills to the west of Oxford, owes much to the distinctive architecture of entire golden villages built of durable Cotswold stone

The soils of the Cotswolds are shallow, not easy to cultivate but ideal pasture for grazing sheep, and it was wool that kept the area's landowners affluent for centuries. This former wealth is visible everywhere in the landscape, characterised by opulent manor houses, cathedral-like barns and splendidly ornate parish churches.

Chipping Norton

Chipping Norton ⑭, 12 miles (20km) northwest of Oxford, is a prime example: a typical Cotswold town on the northwest limits of the limestone belt. Market Square was once the venue for an important sheep fair. Gabled almshouses – typical of Cotswold vernacular architecture, with their stone-mullioned windows and drip mouldings to channel rain away from the face of the buildings – line the path to St Mary's Church. To the north of the church are the extensive remains of a Norman motte and bailey castle.

Chipping Norton also has an imposing tweed mill, visible on the right as you leave the town on the A44 Evesham road. **Bliss Valley Mill,** with its domed tower, was designed in 1872 by the Lancashire mill architect George Woodhouse, to look like a country house – which is what it has ended up as, for after the mill closed in 1980 it was converted into luxury apartments.

Chastleton House ⑮

Tel: 01494-755 560 (info line); 01608-674 981 (booking line)
Opening Hrs: Apr–Sept Wed–Sat 1–5pm, Oct Wed–Sat 1–4pm; entrance by timed ticket, advance

ABOVE: Bliss Valley Mill, dating from 1872.
BELOW: Chastleton House.

booking recommended

Entrance Fee: Charge

Four miles (7km) on, a minor road leads left to **Chastleton House**, built around 1605 by another wool merchant, Walter Jones. Shortly afterwards, the family fortunes declined and the house escaped later improvements, surviving as an example of Jacobean domestic architecture. At the top of the house, a long gallery runs the length of the building. Originally intended for indoor games, such as bowls, like many of the rooms it is lavishly plastered with bold Flemish-style friezes and ceilings.

Moreton-in-Marsh ⑯ comes next, a busy town on the junction of the Roman Foss Way and the later Oxford to Worcester road. Numerous former coaching inns still do a brisk trade serving cream teas to passing motorists, but there is a cluster of characterful shops at the northern end of the High Street. Where the Oxford road joins the High Street stands a 16th-century curfew tower; the bell in the tower continued to be rung until 1860, reminding householders to "cover their fires" (the derivation

of "curfew") before retiring to lessen the risk of a blaze.

Two miles (3km) out of Moreton, the A44 climbs steeply up the Cotswold scarp, through the pretty but traffic-torn village of **Bourton-on-the-Hill**, and towards the summit a left turn leads to Sezincote.

Sezincote ⑰

Tel: no telephone number supplied; email enquiries@sezincote.co.uk
Opening Hrs: gardens Jan–Nov Thur, Fri and bank holidays 2–6pm; house May–Sept Thur, Fri and bank holidays 2.30–5.30pm; no children admitted to the house

Entrance Fee: Charge

Towards the summit a left turn leads to **Sezincote**. Here you will find one of the most curious and delightful houses ever built in the English countryside: an Indian palace made of golden limestone, tucked into the valley of the River Evenlode, which is channelled into a series of canals representing, in Moghul fashion, the rivers of life. Begun in 1805, Sezincote was built for Charles Cockerell who, on retiring from service with the East

India Company, wanted to create a rajah's palace, complete with onion domes and peacock-tail windows.

The Prince Regent, on seeing it in 1807, loved it so much that he ordered existing plans for Brighton Pavilion to be scrapped, and new ones drawn up "more like Sezincote". External appearances, though, are deceptive, for guided tours reveal that the interior is elegantly European in the classical tradition.

Batsford Arboretum ⑱

Tel: 01386-701 441
Opening Hrs: Feb–Nov daily 9am–6pm, Dec–Jan Thur–Tue 9am–4pm
Entrance Fee: Charge

Another expatriate returning home created **Batsford Arboretum**, on the opposite side of the A44. Lord Redesdale, a retired Tokyo diplomat, built his manor house in neo-Elizabethan style in 1888, but he planted the surrounding path with oriental species and decorated it with Japanese temples and statues of the Buddha. The arboretum is very colourful in spring, when the cherry trees blossom, and in autumn, when the Japanese maples turn a fiery crimson.

The village of **Blockley** ⑲, 2 miles (3km) west, brings us back to the traditional Cotswolds. Formerly an estate belonging to the bishops of Worcester, the surrounding hillsides once supported vast flocks of sheep, and flourishing villages round about were deliberately destroyed to create further grazing. But Blockley survived, and today's village consists of elegant town houses occupying the heights and smaller rows of cottages squeezed into narrow terraces all the way down the valley side. At the bottom only one mill (now a private house) survives of the six that produced silk to supply the ribbon makers of Coventry.

Blockley's church contains imposing Renaissance and Baroque monuments to the owners of **Northwick**

Park. This 17th-century mansion, now converted into apartments, lies just north of Blockley, and the road that skirts the western perimeter of the estate provides a splendid view of nearby **Chipping Campden** ⑳, whose oldest house (in the High Street, opposite Church Street) dates from around 1380.

Chipping Campden

Campden is the Cotswold's most beautiful market town. Certainly, it is the best preserved, thanks to the work of the Campden Trust, established in 1929 to restore and maintain town properties using traditional materials.

Early in the 20th century Campden was "invaded" by craftsmen from the Mile End Road in east London, where C. R. Ashbee, inspired by the example of William Morris, had founded his Guild of Handicrafts, devoted to reviving skills lost to industrial processes. Descendants of George Hart, one of the original 50 craftsmen who

ABOVE: Batsford Arboretum.
BELOW: Sezincote, a rajah's palace in the Cotswolds.

came with Ashbee in 1902, still make hand-crafted silverware in the Old Silk Mill in Sheep Street.

The village church is attributed to William Grevel, described on his memorial brass as "the flower of the wool merchants of all England". He left money for the church to be rebuilt and the work, completed some 100 years after his death, is a splendid example of the Perpendicular style at its best.

A mile (2km) northwest of Campden, over the summit of Dover's Hill, is a natural amphitheatre on the Cotswold scarp. Worth visiting for the panoramic views over the **Vale of Evesham**, this is also the venue for the "**Cotswold Olympicks**", held every year on the Friday after the Spring Bank Holiday, followed by the Scuttlebrook Wake Fair on the next day. The "Olympicks", which features shin-kicking and stick-fighting among its bizarre events, was founded by an eccentric local lawyer, Robert Dover, in 1612.

Two miles (3.5km) north of Campden are two of England's finest gardens, standing on opposite sides of the same road above **Mickleton**.

Hidcote Manor Garden ㉑

Tel: 01386-438 333
Opening Hrs: Jul–Aug daily, mid-Mar–June and Sept–Oct Mon–Wed, Sat–Sun 10am–6pm, Nov–mid-Mar Sat–Sun 11am–4pm
Entrance Fee: Charge

Hidcote Manor Garden, for all its maturity, was begun only in 1948. All that existed before were a few walls and 11 acres (4.5 hectares) of windswept Cotswold upland. Major Lawrence Johnson transformed this into one of the most influential gardens of our age, "a cottage garden on the most glorified scale", according to the writer Vita Sackville-West.

Its structure is relatively formal, based on the concept of a series of rooms, walled with yew and planted thematically – yet the underlying discipline is hardly evident as climbers tumble from one room to the next, and happy combinations of self-seeded flowers are left to do as they will. Visitors can also enjoy the fine views.

Kiftsgate Court ②

Tel: 01386-438 777
Opening Hrs: May–July daily noon–6pm, Aug daily 2–6pm, Apr and Sept Mon, Wed and Sun 2–6pm
Entrance Fee: Charge

Kiftsgate Court is equally renowned in gardening circles for its prolific rambling rose, *Rosa filipes* "Kiftsgate". Having colonised several trees, it must surely be England's largest climbing rose, and is delightful in early summer, cascading down in showers of white blooms. The rest of the garden is full of unusual plants, and the views from the swimming-pool terrace look over wooded slopes to the Vale of Evesham.

Broadway

From Mickleton, the B4632 southwest follows the Vale, with the steep-faced Cotswold scarp rising to the left, all the way into **Broadway** ㉓. Packed with tourists throughout the summer months, this town with its ancient golden houses nevertheless merits a visit.

Many of the ancient and wisteria-clad town houses in Broadway now serve as tea shops, boutiques or art galleries, and the renowned furniture maker Gordon Russell has his showroom and factory at the bottom end of the High Street.

To escape the crowds, you can follow the Cotswold Way long-distance footpath from the centre of the town, up the steep sides of **Broadway Hill**, to the **Tower** at the summit. This folly was built in 1800 and stands 65ft (20 metres) tall on top of a 1,024ft (412-metre) hill. Extensive views are to be had; on a clear day they stretch out to the cities of Worcester and Warwick. William Morris used the tower as a holiday retreat, and displays are contained within about his life and work, and

BELOW LEFT:
Hidcote Manor Garden.
BELOW: the gardens at Kiftsgate Court.

**ABOVE AND ABOVE
RIGHT:** the golden-
stone houses of
Broadway.
BELOW:
St James' Church,
Chipping Campden

about the Cotswold wool industry.

Less than a mile (about 1km) to the northeast, along the ridge of the hill, is another picturesque folly, built in the 18th century as a "gaze-about house", now part of the Fish Inn.

At the western end of Broadway, a narrow road signposted to Snowshill Manor passes the Norman **church of St Eadburga**, standing next door to the Court House, whose ancient topiary yews spill from the garden into the churchyard.

Snowshill Manor ㉔

Tel: 01386-852 410
Opening Hrs: mid-Mar–Oct Wed–Sun noon–5pm
Entrance Fee: Charge

Two miles (3km) on is **Snowshill Manor**, a popular National Trust property best avoided at busy weekends. It houses a magpie collection of extraordinary diversity: everything from bicycles to Samurai armour. The terraced garden brims with colourful flowers.

Cotswold heritage

From Snowshill, a high and narrow lane crosses the heights of the Cotswold uplands, attractive in summer, but bleak and chill in winter, through Taddington and into the beautiful wooded Windrush Valley. **Temple Guiting** ㉕ (pronounced *guyting*) was once a property of the crusading Knights Templar, and the Windrush, much diminished in size since the stream has been tapped to provide drinking water, used to drive the hammers of fulling mills, used in wool processing.

This industry continued into the 18th century: the tomb of John Mowse (died 1787) in St Mary's Church records that he was a wool dyer, who employed a great number of the poor of the parish in the various parts of his trade. He may also have contributed to the rebuilding of the church, with its fine wooden furnishings and George II coat of arms, unusually made out of plaster. Two miles (3km) southeast is **Cotswold Farm Park** ㉖ (*see panel*).

Six miles (10km) downstream, the River Windrush flows through the centre of **Bourton-on-the-Water** ㉗, crossed by a series of elegant 18th-century stone bridges. Bourton is a village to avoid if you do not like people, for the combination of the Model Village – a one-ninth scale replica of Bourton itself, made in 1937 – a Motor Museum, Model Railway and Birdland all make this a busy spot.

The Slaughters

This same fate has overtaken the nearby hamlets of **Lower** and **Upper Slaughter** ㉘, so named because of the sloughs, or marshes, that once bordered the River Eye flowing through the two villages. Simple clapper bridges, made of huge planks of limestone, cross the stream as it flows between carefully tended banks and in front of the much-photographed mill in Lower Slaughter.

Similar in character, but far more peaceful, is the little hamlet of **Upper Swell**, with its 18th-century bridge, watermill and mill pool fed by the

River Dikler. Occasionally in summer the **Abbotswood** estate, south of Swell, is open under the National Gardens Scheme. Well worth visiting, Abbotswood is one of the finest works of Sir Edwin Lutyens, who designed the garden, with its pools and water channels, as well as the striking house, in 1902.

ABOVE: tranquillity at Lower Slaughter.
BELOW: Cotswold Farm Park.

Stow-on-the-Wold

Stow-on-the-Wold ㉙, a mile (2km) east, sits on the summit of an 800ft (244-metre) hill and has the reputation for being a chilly place: "Stow-on-the-Wold, where the wind blows cold" is an ancient taunt.

The great Stow Horse Fair is now held at **Andoversford**, near Cheltenham. It was moved because of the nuisance often caused by gypsy horse breeders converging on the town. Stow these days prefers more genteel visitors and caters for them with numerous antique shops, tearooms and a museum of antique dolls in Sheep Street. ❑

Cotswold Farm Park

This is the headquarters of the Rare Breeds Survival Trust and home to a flock of the traditional breed of Cotswold sheep. It is upon this breed that the medieval prosperity of the region was based.

Nicknamed "Cotswold lions" because of their distinctive long, curly fleece, these big-limbed animals are descended from sheep introduced by the Romans. Another 40 or more rare breeds, such as Gloucester Old Spot pigs and Old Gloucester cows, are protected and displayed at the Farm Park, along with goats, rabbits, ponies and huge shire horses. Most are placid, so the park is suitable for children.

Cotswold Farm Park is open Apr–Oct, tel: 01451-850 307; charge.

INSIGHT GUIDES TRAVEL TIPS
OXFORD

TRANSPORT

GETTING THERE AND GETTING AROUND

GETTING THERE

By Air

London Heathrow Airport is situated to the west of London on the M25/M4, 45 miles (72km) southeast of Oxford. From Heathrow central bus terminus and Terminal 5, the Oxford Bus Company operates the X70 Oxford Espress coach service, which departs every 20 minutes during the day and every 2 hours overnight (80 mins journey time to Heathrow central bus terminus and 100 mins to Terminal 5). Reserve a seat by booking online at www.oxfordbus.co.uk, or call 01865-785 400.

London Gatwick is situated to the south of London on the M23, 85 miles (136km) southeast of Oxford. The X80 Oxford Espress coach from Gatwick (north and south terminals) runs hourly and every two hours overnight (journey time 2 hours).

Birmingham International Airport is 65 miles (104km) from Oxford; there are regular train connections, as well as six coach services a day operated by National Express (National Express bookings and enquiries tel: 08717-818 181).

Oxford airport is located at nearby Kidlington but operates only special charters. A twice-daily scheduled flight to Cambridge (a tedious commute by road) was launched in 2006 using eight-seater Piper Chieftains, but it failed after six weeks owing to lack of demand.

By Sea

Oxford is one of the UK's most inland towns. The nearest port offering a cross-Channel service is Portsmouth (80 miles/128km). A National Express *(see below)* bus service links Oxford to the south coast every hour daily.
Brittany Ferries, tel: 0871-244 0744, www.brittanyferries.co.uk
P&O European Ferries, tel: 08716-645 645, www.poferries.com
Stena Line, tel: 0870-5707 070, www.stenaline.co.uk

By Train

There is a regular train service between **London Paddington** station and Oxford. The journey takes about an hour, depending on the number of stops. Travellers can also use the fast services between London Paddington and Midlands destinations such as Worcester and Birmingham, which stop in Oxford. Trains from London depart regularly about twice an hour during the day. Oxford train station is a 5-minute walk from the centre of the city.

While any train can be boarded with a full-fare return ticket, with all other return tickets restrictions are applied to peak period departures (from Paddington between 4–7pm) on Great Western trains. Travellers should be given a leaflet advising on these restrictions when buying their ticket. Cheap Day Returns between Oxford and London are sold from 9.30am and are much cheaper than the normal return.

For fare enquiries and general information, telephone the **National Rail Enquiry Service** on 08457-48 49 50.

By Coach

Regular coach services run between Oxford and London. Stagecoach operates the **Oxford Tube**, and the Oxford Bus Company runs **Oxford Espress** services. With fares about half that of a Cheap Day Return train ticket, these services are very popular indeed.

From London, **Oxford Tube** coaches leave from Grosvenor Gardens (turn left out of the main Victoria British Rail and Underground stations). All coaches stop on request at Marble Arch (10 minutes after departing Victoria),

Notting Hill Gate (15 minutes) and the Kensington Hilton at Shepherd's Bush (20 minutes). The service runs every 10 minutes during rush hours, at 20-minute intervals for most of the day, and hourly between 12.15am and 5.10am. For travel information, see www.oxfordtube.com or call 01865-772 250.

The **Oxford Bus Company**'s **Oxford Express** coach services depart daily every 15–20 minutes from London's Victoria Coach Station (Gate 10) and also pick up at Marble Arch (on Park Lane) and Baker Street (on Gloucester Place). Most journeys take about 1 hour 40 minutes but during peak periods you should allow more time due to traffic congestion in London. For travel information, tel: 01865-785 400, www.oxfordbus.co.uk.

Both the above services arrive at and depart from Oxford's Gloucester Green Bus Station in the heart of the city. **National Express** offers a nationwide network of coach services from Oxford and has an office at Gloucester Green. For enquiries and credit card bookings, tel: 08717-818 181 or visit www.nationalexpress.co.uk.

The cheapest pre-booked fares are offered by **MegaBus**, who run Oxford coach services every 20–30 minutes from London (75 minutes journey time). See www.megabus.com or call 0900-160 0900.

By Car

From both London and the Midlands, Oxford is well served by the M40 motorway, which passes within 8 miles (13km) of the city. The journey from central London takes about 80 minutes, except during rush hour when it can take considerably longer to get out of the city along the A40. Drivers coming from London should exit at Junction 8, while those coming from the Midlands should turn off at Junction 9.

If you are coming from Gatwick or Heathrow airports, join the M40 via the London orbital motorway, the M25. Oxford is accessible from Southampton and Portsmouth by the M3 and A34 and from Bristol by the M4 and A34.

GETTING AROUND

Orientation

The busy city centre is pedestrianised and, as a result, access to motor vehicles is very limited. Cornmarket is closed to all traffic 10am–6pm, as is High Street 7.30am–6.30pm. The western end of Broad Street is closed all day and night, and Turl Street and Market Street are closed to all but delivery vehicles.

Buses in the city run along bus priority routes, closed to other traffic.

Public Transport

Oxford and the surrounding area are served by local buses, minibuses and the direct buses between the Park and Ride stations and the centre. The local services are covered by the Oxford Bus Company and Stagecoach. In addition, Stagecoach operates numerous services to outlying towns. Both bus companies offer special day-return tickets and family tickets, as well as travel cards with unlimited travel in the city. You purchase your ticket from the driver.

The Key pass allows unlimited travel on Oxford Bus Company services: depending on the scope of your pass prices start at £3.20 for 1 day or £12.50 for 7 days. Pick up a copy of the City Bus Guide at the Gloucester Green travel shop or see www.oxfordbus.co.uk, where you can check timetables and download bus route maps.

CYCLING

Cycling is popular in Oxford and, as well as many cycleways, there are clear signs to enable cyclists to avoid the main thoroughfares.

You can hire bicycles from several outlets. All kinds of bikes are available, and they are supplied with a lock. Lights, basket and helmet are optional extras.

Bikes can be hired from:
Bike Zone, 6 Lincoln House, Market Street, tel: 01865-728 877.
Cycle King, 128–30 Cowley Road, tel: 01865-728 262.
Cyclo-Analysts, 150 Cowley Road, tel: 01865-424 444.
Summertown Cycles, 202 Banbury Road, tel: 01865-316 885.
Warlands, 63 Botley Road, tel: 01865-723 100.
For cycle maps see:
www.cyclemaps.org.uk
www.sustrans.org.uk

BELOW: traffic streaks past Magdalen College.

TRANSPORT

ACCOMMODATION

ACTIVITIES

A – Z

CAR RENTAL

Conditions for car rental state that the driver must be over 21 (over 25 for some companies) and have held a full driving licence for more than a year. Most hire charges include insurance, unlimited mileage, road tax and a 24-hour breakdown service. Ask for special weekend deals. There are vans and minibuses available, too, and some of the companies offer one-way rentals at extra cost. Payment can usually be by cash, cheque or credit card.

Budget
Unit 1, Oxford Business Centre, Osney Lane
Tel: 01865-724 884
www.budget.co.uk

Enterprise Rent-A-Car
53 West Way, Botley
Tel: 01865-202 088
www.enterprise.co.uk

Europcar
Littlemead Business Park, Ferry Hinksey Road
Tel: 01865-246 373
www.europcar.co.uk

Taxis

The main taxi ranks are at Oxford railway station, Gloucester Green, St Giles, Broad Street and High Street. There are additional ranks at Carfax and Bonn Square in the evening only.

Due to the one-way traffic system there is no short route across the city to the railway station, so fares tend to be high. Some taxi meters start at £1.50, others might have a minimum charge of £2.

A.B.C Taxis, tel: 01865-770 077
Euro Taxis, tel: 01865-430 430
Oxford City Taxis, tel: 01865-794 000
Radio Taxis, tel: 01865-242 424
001 Cars, tel: 01865-240 000
24seven Taxis, tel: 01865-722 799

Driving

Rules of the Road

In Britain you should drive on the left-hand side of the road and observe speed limits. It is strictly illegal to drink and drive, and penalties for drink driving are severe. Drivers and passengers, in both front and back seats, must wear seat belts where fitted. Failure to do so can result in a fine. For further information on driving in Britain consult a copy of the *Highway Code*, sold in bookshops.

If you are bringing your own car into the UK you will need a valid driving licence or an International Driving Permit, plus insurance coverage, vehicle registration and a nationality sticker.

In Oxford there are many cyclists on the road: be extra careful to be bike aware.

Parking

Parking in central Oxford is very limited, and in residential areas you often need a resident's parking permit.

There is a multistorey car park at the Westgate Centre (pay on return to your car). There is an underground car park at Gloucester Green (entrance on Beaumont Street) and pay-and-display outdoor parking at St Clements and Worcester Street (enter from Park End Street). Finally, there is metered street parking on St Giles', Broad Street, Parks Road and Beaumont Street, but during the day it is hard to find a space. Payment applies per hour 8.30am–6.30pm from Monday to Saturday, after which there is a fixed charge payment until 10pm. On Sunday there is a fixed charge payment however long you stay.

Visitors should note that traffic wardens in Oxford are extremely vigilant. In the evening (after 6.30pm) city centre parking is much easier.

Park and Ride

Major areas of the city centre are traffic-free zones. If you want to avoid the problem of parking, take the reliable Park and Ride service offered by the Oxford Bus Company. You can park your car at the following sites on the Oxford ring road (colours refer to codings at bus stops):

Thornhill (yellow square) in the east of the city – for traffic coming in on the A40 from London.
Redbridge (red square) in the south – for those arriving by the A34 from Abingdon or the A4074 from Reading.
Seacourt (pale blue square) in the west – convenient for A420 or B4044 traffic.
Pear Tree (green square) in the northwest – for motorists coming in on the A40 from Cheltenham, the A44 from Chipping Norton, the A34, or the A4260.
Water Eaton (dark blue square) in the northeast – for traffic arriving by the A34 or A4260.

Parking is 60p (free at Thornhill and Water Eaton) and buses to the city centre leave every 10–15 minutes. Bus fares cost less than the city centre car parks and journeys take only 10–20 minutes. Don't forget to make a note of the colour symbol at your bus stop (eg yellow for Thornhill). For more details of locations and bus services see www.parkandride.net.

A special Freedom travel card allows you unlimited travel on the Cityline and Park and Ride network for a day. Services are frequent during the daytime but there are no services on Sunday evening for Redbridge, Pear Tree and Seacourt, and none at all on Sunday on the Water Eaton route.

Breakdown Services

The following motoring organisations operate 24-hour breakdown assistance. They have reciprocal arrangements with other national motoring clubs. All calls to these numbers are free.
AA: 0800-887 766
RAC: 0800-828 282
Green Flag: 0800-400 600
Britannia Rescue: 0800-591563

A CCOMMODATION

HOTELS, YOUTH HOSTELS, BED & BREAKFASTS

Choosing a Hotel

Accommodation in Oxford is not cheap, and while there are plenty of bed and breakfast places (B&Bs), there is only a limited number of hotels. Not all establishments take young children, so do check in advance.

Booking ahead is therefore essential, especially in summer, at weekends and during public holidays. For visitors arriving in the city without accommodation, the Oxford Tourist Information Centre (*see page 275*) offers a room-booking service for a modest fee. Also bear in mind that during the university vacations you can stay in college rooms through the University Rooms scheme (www. oxfordrooms.co.uk).

The following websites have accommodation-finders:
● www.visitoxford.org – if you require accommodation within the next seven days, call 01865-252 200.
● www.stayoxford.co.uk – the Oxford Association of Hotels and Guest Houses.
● www.oxfordcity.co.uk
● www.oxfinder.co.uk
● www.oxtowns.co.uk (for outside Oxford).
● www.abodesofoxford.com offer bed-and-breakfast accommodation and host-family stays.

The *Accessible Oxford Guide* (available from the Oxford Information Centre) lists places to stay that have good access for people with limited mobility.

Hostels and "Ys"

Ideal for the budget traveller are two hostels situated in the city centre close to the bus and railway stations. Both have internet access, a TV/games room and luggage storage (*see listings*).

The **Youth Hostel Association** also offers accommodation for all ages at their new purpose-built hostel just behind the train station with 2-, 4- and 6-bed rooms. Non-members can join on arrival.

A Place of Your Own

If you are planning to stay in the area for an extended period, it may be more economical to choose a short-term rental. For a good selection click on "Apartments & Self-Catering" at www.oxfordcity.co.uk. Among the agencies that offer this service is Oxford Shortlets, tel: 01865-318 591; www.oxfordshortlets.co.uk.

Camping

The Camping & Caravanning Club has a site just over a mile from the centre at 426 Abingdon Road, tel: 01865-244 088. You can join online at www.

campingandcaravanningclub.co.uk.
Cotswold View Caravan and Camping Site, Enstone Road, Charlbury, tel: 01608-810 314.
Heyford Leys Camping Park is a family-run park situated on old 17th-century farm premises: Camp Road, Bicester, tel: 01869-232 048; www.heyfordleyscamping park.co.uk.

For others, see www.visitoxford. org. *Camping Beside the River Thames* is a free leaflet giving details of campsites on or near the River Thames, available from Environment Agency Thames Information: tel: 0845-601 5336, www.visitthames.co.uk.

BELOW: Barceló Oxford Hotel.

CENTRAL AREA

HOTELS

Luxury

Barceló Oxford Hotel
Godstow Road
Tel: 01865-489 988
www.barcelo-hotels.co.uk
This recently revamped four-star hotel is 2 miles (3km) out of town on Woodstock Road. The modern rooms have cable TV and internet access, and leisure facilities include fitness suite, splash pool, steam room and squash courts. The bus into town stops around the corner in Mere Road.

Macdonald Randolph Hotel
Beaumont Street
Tel: 0844-879 9132
www.randolph-hotel.com
❶ p262, B3
Oxford's most famous hotel is situated in the city centre, opposite the Ashmolean Museum. There are two restaurants, two lounges, the Morse Bar and a spa with steam rooms, saunas, ice fountain and all manner of beauty treatments. Extensive conference facilities too.

Old Bank Hotel
92–4 High Street
Tel: 01865-799 599
www.oldbank-hotel.co.uk
❷ p263, D4
This stylish boutique hotel is housed in a former bank. Centrally located, it features a lively brasserie-restaurant, and even hosts jazz evenings.

Old Parsonage Hotel
1 Banbury Road
Tel: 01865-310 210
www.oldparsonage-hotel.co.uk
❸ p262, D1
This beautiful and well-located hotel in the renovated old parsonage next to St Giles' church offers 30 luxuriously appointed en suite bedrooms. The Parsonage Bar restaurant is open all day (including to non-residents) and serves excellent afternoon tea.

Expensive

Bath Place Hotel
4–5 Bath Place
Tel: 01865-791 812
www.bathplace.co.uk
❹ p263, D3
Charming family-run hotel occupying a group of restored 17th-century cottages in the heart of Oxford. Reputedly the scene of Richard Burton–Elizabeth Taylor trysts.

Cotswold Lodge Hotel
66a Banbury Road
Tel: 01865-512 121
www.cotswoldlodgehotel.co.uk
Four-star hotel set in a beautiful Victorian building just outside the city centre. The rooms – some named after colleges – are traditional in style and very comfortable. Bar and restaurant.

Holiday Inn Oxford
Pear Tree Roundabout
Tel: 0871-942 9086
www.ichotelsgroup.com
Chain hotel with an indoor pool and health centre on site, a short bus ride away from the centre of town.

Linton Lodge Hotel
Linton Road, off Banbury Road
Tel: 01865-553 461
www.bw-lintonlodgehotel.co.uk
Part of the Best Western chain, this hotel has extensive conference facilities and regularly organises dinner-dances for 150. Rooms have TV, radio, telephone and en suite bathrooms.

Mercure Eastgate Hotel
73 High Street
Tel: 01865-248 322
www.accorhotels.com
❺ p263, D4
A former 17th-century coaching inn, the traditional-style Eastgate is located adjacent to the site of Oxford's old East Gate and opposite the Examination Schools. Facilities include a restaurant and bar.

Moderate

The Galaxie Hotel
180 Banbury Road
Tel: 01865-515 688
www.galaxie.co.uk
This friendly, family-run hotel is located in the genteel Summertown residential district of Oxford.

Marlborough House Hotel
321 Woodstock Road
Tel: 01865-311 321
www.marlbhouse.co.uk

A small, luxurious hotel, situated in a residential area about 1½ miles (2½km) from the city centre, the Marlborough serves breakfast in guests' rooms – which are all en suite and have their own kitchenettes.

The Old Black Horse Hotel
102 St Clements
Tel: 01865-244 691
www.oldblackhorse.com
An attractive hotel in a 17th-century coaching inn located just across Magdalen Bridge, this friendly, family-run hotel offers en suite rooms, a restaurant and bar, and secure car parking. Airport and London coaches stop outside.

Parklands Hotel
100 Banbury Road
Tel: 01865-554 374
www.oxfordcity.co.uk/hotels/parklands
This privately run hotel was originally an Oxford dons' residence built in the Victorian era. It offers mainly bed and breakfast accommodation but will provide meals when required. Parking facilities.

The Tower House
15 Ship Street
Tel: 01865-246 828
www.towerhouseoxford.co.uk
🚇 p262, C3
Located in a central position just off Cornmarket, this friendly, family-run guesthouse dates to the 17th century. The seven bedrooms are furnished with antiques and decorated to a high standard.

Westgate Hotel
1 Botley Road
Tel: 01865-726 721
www.westgatehoteloxford.co.uk
Very convenient for both the city (5 minutes' walk) and the coach and railway stations, this family-run hotel also offers the benefits of a restaurant and bar.

Budget

Lakeside Guest House
118 Abingdon Road
Tel: 01865-244 725
www.oxfordcity.co.uk/accom/lakeside
This former Edwardian rectory overlooks Hinksey Park with its tennis courts and open-air heated swimming pool (for the summer). The family-run hotel is situated 15 minutes' walk from the city centre and is on a major bus route. Satellite TV in all en suite rooms.

River Hotel
17 Botley Road
Tel: 01865-243 475
www.riverhotel.co.uk
In an excellent riverside location on the Thames – as well as being situated near the bus and railway stations – this small hotel is certainly convenient, but it is also friendly and comfortable.

B&Bs

Burlington House
374 Banbury Road
Tel: 01865-513 513
www.burlington-house.co.uk
Top-rated guesthouse in an elegant, comfortable and impeccably maintained Victorian house in Summertown, North Oxford. The breakfasts are substantial and of excellent quality.

College Guest House
103–5 Woodstock Road
Tel: 01865-552 579
www.omshanti-group.com/college.htm
A good-value family-run guesthouse located in one of the huge red-brick Victorian houses that typify the Woodstock Road. Offers 12 modest but cosy rooms, some with en suite or private bathrooms.

Cotswold House
363 Banbury Road
Tel/fax: 01865-310 558
www.cotswoldhouse.co.uk
Highly commended B&B accommodation in a modern house in North Oxford. Non-smokers only.

Eurobar
48 George Street
Tel: 01865-725 087
🚇 p262, B3
These rooms above an all-day café-bar are located right in the centre of the city.

Head of the River
Folly Bridge
Tel: 01865-721 600
www.fullershotels.com
🔟 p264, C3
This large pub-restaurant on the Thames also offers 12 en suite bedrooms that overlook the river.

Newton House
82–4 Abingdon Road
Tel: 01865-240 561
www.oxfordcity.co.uk/accom/newton
The closest guesthouse to historic Christ Church, just half a mile (1km) from the city centre, this pair of handsome Victorian town houses retain many original features, with a high standard of decor and period furniture. Special diets are catered for.

Sportsview Guest House
106–10 Abingdon Road
Tel: 01865-244 268
www.oxfordcity.co.uk/accom/sportsview
This family-run Victorian guesthouse is located south of the city centre, overlooking Queens College sports ground and the Oxford University boathouse on the river. The owners are happy to cater for vegetarians and those with special dietary requirements.

Youth Hostels

Central Backpackers
13 Park End Street
Tel: 01865-242 288
www.centralbackpackers.co.uk
🔢 p262, A4
This friendly, smoke-free hostel near the train station offers female-only or mixed-sex dorms with 4 to 12 beds. Beds are £16–19, breakfast included. Passports are required on check-in. Facilities include a TV lounge, internet access, laundry service, kitchen for self-catering and lockers where non-guests can also store

luggage (£2 per day). Free tennis racquet hire for nearby tennis courts, and rugby balls, frisbies and footballs.

Oxford Backpackers Hostel
9a Hythe Brige Street
Tel/fax: 01865-721 761
Email: oxford@hostels.co.uk
www.hostels.co.uk
🔟 p262, A4
This hostel is ideally situated, at only two minutes' walk from train or bus stations. Facilities include a self-catering kitchen and a licensed bar with pool table. Prices are £12–19 per bed, though there is also a weekly rate starting from £70 per person. Passports are required on check-in.

YHA
2A Botley Road
Tel: 0845-371 9131
Email: oxford@yha.org.uk
www.yha.org.uk
Oxford's official youth hostel offers budget accommodation for all ages in a new purpose-built 4-star building with 2- to 6-bed dormitory rooms. Facilities include a restaurant, garden and games room, as well as internet access. It is conveniently located directly behind the railway station. Over 18s: £20.95; Under 18s: £15.95, includes breakfast. Non-members may join on arrival (£10 a year for adults).

PRICE CATEGORIES

An approximate guide to price categories for a double room:

Budget = under £70
Moderate = £70–95
Expensive = £95–150
Luxury = over £150

OUTSKIRTS OF OXFORD

HOTELS

Luxury

Oxford Thames Four-Pillars Hotel
Henley Road, Sandford-on-Thames
Tel: 01865-334 444
www.four-pillars.co.uk
Located 4 miles (7km) from the city centre, this luxury hotel incorporates medieval buildings yet offers all the benefits of the modern world, with a superb leisure centre and fine conference facilities.

Expensive

The Westwood Country Hotel
Hinksey Hill Top
Tel: 01865-735 408
www.westwoodhotel.co.uk
With more of the feeling of a country retreat, this comfortable hotel is set in gardens and woodland. The Oaks Restaurant offers smart dining.

Wheelchair users are welcome.

Moderate

Foxcombe Lodge Hotel
Fox Lane, Boars Hill
Tel: 01865-326 326
www.foxcombelodge.co.uk
Friendly hotel offering restaurant and conference facilities. All rooms are equipped with TV, radio, direct-dial telephone and computer with internet.

Hawkwell House Hotel
Church Way, Iffley
Tel: 01865-749 988
www.hawkwellhouse.co.uk
The country house experience at an affordable price. Set in its own grounds, the hotel also makes an attractive setting for weddings, conferences, etc.

The Tree Hotel
Church Way, Iffley Village
Tel: 01865-775 974
www.treehotel.co.uk
Situated in an attractive setting, just over a mile (2km) from the city

centre, the Tree Hotel incorporates the Annora International Restaurant and Bar serving Indian, Thai and English cuisine.

B&Bs

Broomhill Bed and Breakfast
Broomhill, Lincombe Lane, Boars Hill, Oxford
Tel: 01865-735 339
www.broomhill-oxford.co.uk
This beautiful house set in large gardens is a wonderful place to retreat to from the bustle of Oxford city centre. A self-contained flat is available for short-term lets – ideal for longer-term business visitors wanting a weekday base.

Conifers Guest House
116 The Slade, Headington
Tel: 01865-763 055
www.conifersguesthouse.co.uk
The rooms at this family-run B&B are all en suite and equipped with TV. Situated in a pleasant

suburb, the house also has a large garden.

Gables Guest House
6 Cumnor Hill
Tel: 01865-862 153
www.oxfordcity.co.uk/accom/gables
The owner of this establishment has won AA Landlady of the Year along with four red AA diamonds. Immaculately maintained, very comfortable and vegetarian-friendly.

Tilbury Lodge
5 Tilbury Lane, Botley
Tel: 01865-862 138
www.tilburylodge.com
This AA four-diamond award winner has excellent facilities, including internet access and a jacuzzi. A self-contained flat is also available.

OUTSIDE OXFORD

HOTELS

Luxury

Bay Tree Hotel
Sheep Street, Burford
Tel: 01993-822 791
www.cotswold-inns-hotels.co.uk
Once the home of Sir Lawrence Tanfield, Elizabeth I's lord chief baron of the exchequer, this 16th-century house has 23 en suite rooms, some oak-panelled and

with four-poster beds. There's also a walled garden and terraced lawns.

The Bear Hotel
Park Street, Woodstock
Tel: 0844 879 9143
www.macdonaldhotels.co.uk/bear
Occupying a gorgeous ivy-clad building – parts of which derive from a 13th-century coaching inn – right in the heart of Woodstock, this hotel is justly renowned for its luxurious accommodation and

magnificent cuisine. Modern refinements include WiFi and conference facilities.

Calcot Manor
Tetbury, Gloucestershire
Tel: 01666-890 391
www.calcotmanor.co.uk
Calcot Manor, with its 17th-century farm buildings, has been converted into a complex combining one of the area's most popular restaurants, the Gumstool Inn, and a separate hotel with a range of rooms.

Choose between four-posters and antiques, or family rooms with bunk beds for the kids and playroom. Calcot Spa has excellent health and beauty facilities.

The Feathers Hotel
Market Street, Woodstock
Tel: 01993-812 291
www.feathers.co.uk
This 17th-century hotel in the centre of this quaint market town near Blenheim Palace has 20 cosy traditionally furnished rooms, one with its own steam room. The hotel restaurant is celebrated for its fine modern English food.

Lords of the Manor Hotel
Upper Slaughter, Gloucestershire
Tel: 01451-820 243
www.lordsofthemanor.com
This much-extended 17th-century rectory is the stuff of film locations. Honey-coloured stone buildings nestle in extensive gardens and parkland, through which the trout-filled River Eye meanders. The restaurant is Michelin-starred. All facilities for both the business traveller and the weekend visitor.

Lower Slaughter Manor
Lower Slaughter, Gloucestershire
Tel: 01451-820 456
www.lowerslaughter.co.uk
This 17th-century manor, on the edge of one of the Cotswolds' prettiest villages, offers tennis courts, a croquet lawn and putting green, plus indoor pool and sauna.

The Oxford Belfry
Milton Common, near junction 7 off M40
Tel: 01844-279 381
www.qhotels.co.uk
This hotel caters especially to business visitors and the conference trade. Its 60 bedrooms are all en suite with satellite TV, and the leisure club has a swimming pool.

Expensive

The Bell at Charlbury
Charlbury
Tel: 01608-810 278
www.bellhotel-charlbury.co.uk
This quintessentially Cotswolds hotel occupies an 18th-century building, with all the character to match. It's also situated in ideal gliding, fishing and horse riding country and the hotel is happy to help arrange these activities for you.

Burford House Hotel
High Street, Burford
Tel: 01993-823 151
www.burford-house.co.uk
Set in a mellow Tudor building full of beams and maze-like corridors. The decor is beautiful, the rooms cosy and there's no lack of personal touches – ideal for a relaxing stay.

The Swan Hotel
Bibury, Gloucestershire
Tel: 01285-740 695
www.cotswold-inns-hotels.co.uk
This idyllic 17th-century former coaching inn is situated on the banks of the River Coln in what William Morris called "the most beautiful village in England". A meal in the award-winning restaurant caps off a very comfortable experience.

Weston Manor
Weston-on-the-Green
Tel: 01869-350 621
www.westonmanor.co.uk
This impressive 17th-century manor house is set in 12 acres (5 hectares) of beautiful gardens and has a croquet lawn and an outdoor heated pool. Excellent cuisine is served in the Baronial Hall and there is also a cosy lounge for afternoon tea.

Moderate

Bibury Court
Bibury, Gloucestershire
Tel: 01285-740 337
www.biburycourt.com
This glorious Jacobean house fulfils everyone's idea of the perfect Cotswold manor: an ivy-clad house coupled with glorious gardens. Rarely does such a sense of history come at such a reasonable price.

Otmoor Lodge
Horton Hill, Horton-Cum-Studley
Tel: 01865-351 235
www.otmoorlodge.co.uk
Otmoor Lodge is an 18th-century inn with contemporary-style rooms, for peace and tranquillity on Oxford's doorstep. The up-market restaurant serves international dishes.

Budget

The Coach and Horses Inn
Watlington Road, Chislehampton
Tel: 01865-890 255
www.coachhorsesinn.co.uk
Comfortable inn on the B480, 7 miles (11km) from Oxford, 5 miles (8km) from junction 7 on the M40, and adjacent to farmland. The oak-beamed restaurant and bar, coupled with well appointed rooms, make for a very pleasant place to stay.

The Maytime Inn
Asthall, between Burford and Witney
Tel: 01993-822 068
www.themaytime.com
Comfortable accommodation, all on the ground floor, with private bathroom, shower, TV, radio and tea- and coffee-making facilities. The restaurant offers a very reasonably priced seasonal menu.

Tavern House
Willesley, Tetbury, Gloucestershire
Tel: 01666-880 444
www.tavernhouse.co.uk
Occupying a former coaching inn near the beautiful Westonbirt Arboretum, this up-market B&B represents a good base for exploring the surrounding area.

B&Bs

The Bungalow
Cherwell Farm, Mill Lane, Old Marston
Tel: 01865-557 171
www.cherwellfarm-oxford-accom.co.uk
As you might expect, a quiet, modern bungalow, and set in 5 acres (2 hectares) of open countryside. It's located within 3 miles (5km) of Oxford city centre – though not on the bus route, unfortunately.

Lewis Lodge
2 Lewis Close, Headington
Tel: 01865-762 285
www.lewislodgeoxford.com
Comprises modern and immaculate hotel-standard en suite rooms in a brick house near The Kilns, C.S. Lewis's former home in Risinghurst. Good value for money.

Mulberry Guest House
265 London Road, Headington
Tel: 01865-767 114

PRICE CATEGORIES
An approximate guide to price categories for a double room:
Budget = under £70
Moderate = £70–95
Expensive = £95–150
Luxury = over £150

www.mulberryguesthouse.co.uk
Smart rooms, all with en suite bathrooms, spread over two detached suburban houses. Internet access is also available.
Oak Tree Copse
Woodfarm, Worminghall
Tel: 01865-358 751
www.oxfordfarmhouses.co.uk
This country farmhouse B&B, 10 miles (16km) from Oxford on the

Buckinghamshire border, has pleasant rooms and very reasonable rates.
Riversdale Bed & Breakfast
The Walk, Islip
Tel: 01865-373 376
www.islipbandb.co.uk
Five miles (8km) from Oxford this 18th-century family home in the centre of Islip village offers en suite double

rooms and a beautiful secluded garden.

YOUTH HOSTELS

Stow-On-The-Wold Youth Hostel
The Square, Stow-On-The-Wold
Tel: 0845-371 9540
www.yha.org.uk
Not many youth hostels

occupy a listed 16th-century townhouse in the centre of a historic market town. Wonderfully situated for visiting the picturesque villages thereabouts, the Rollright Stones, and more. Restaurant, kitchen for self-catering, laundry, cycle shed; families especially welcome. Adult £15.95, under 18s £11.95.

IN AND AROUND STRATFORD-UPON-AVON

HOTELS

Luxury

Alveston Manor
Clopton Bridge,
Stratford-upon-Avon
Tel: 0844-879 9138
www.macdonaldhotels.co.uk/alvestonmanor
Large, partly 16th-century, half-timbered hotel on the far bank of the River Avon from the Royal Shakespeare Theatre, believed to be the site of the first performance of *A Midsummer Night's Dream*. Notable assets include four-poster beds, spa and health club, and indoor swimming pool.
Welcombe Hotel and Golf Club
Warwick Road,
Stratford-upon-Avon
Tel: 01789-295 252
www.menzies-hotels.co.uk
This grandiose, 19th-century, Jacobean-style mansion is set in its own spacious parkland and offers every amenity including its own golf course and gourmet restaurant.

Expensive

Best Western Salford Hall Hotel
Abbots Salford,
Stratford-upon-Avon
Tel: 01386-871 300
www.bestwestern.co.uk
This romantic Tudor manor offers log fires, four-posters and an award-winning restaurant. Sauna, solarium, tennis court.
The Stratford
Arden Street,
Stratford-upon-Avon
Tel: 01789-271 000
www.qhotels.co.uk
This modern 4-star hotel built in Victorian style is within walking distance of many attractions. Gym, spa, and an award-winning restaurant.

Moderate

White Swan
Rother Street,
Stratford-upon-Avon
Tel: 01789-297 022
www.pebblehotels.com
A prime example of Stratford's heritage of half-timbered buildings, the Swan dates from the 16th century and has a wall-painting of that era in its impressive Oak

Room. Bedrooms mostly in later extensions.

Budget

Emsley Guest House
4 Arden Street,
Stratford-upon-Avon
Tel: 01789-299 557
www.theemsley.co.uk
This smart Victorian town house in the town centre (5-minute walk to the train station) benefits from attentive staff and excellent breakfasts.

B&Bs

Brook Lodge
192 Alcester Road,
Stratford-upon-Avon
Tel: 01789-295 988.
www.brook-lodge.co.uk
Immaculately run guesthouse with en suite rooms, close to Anne Hathaway's Cottage and to open country.
Firs Cottage
Dorsington
Tel: 07969-052 575
www.firscottage.co.uk
A wonderful opportunity to stay in a 400-year-old thatched cottage, in a quiet village on the Heart of England Way.

Heron Lodge
260 Alcester Road,
Stratford-upon-Avon
Tel: 01789-299 169
www.heronlodge.com
A mile (2km) from Stratford town centre, this friendly four-diamond rated B&B is known for its good food. Their ground floor en suite room is very well-suited to those with limited mobility.

YOUTH HOSTELS

Youth Hostel
Hemmingford House, Alveston,
Stratford-upon-Avon
Tel: 0845-371 9661
www.yha.org.uk
Splendid Georgian mansion house set in its own grounds in a quiet village 2 miles (3km) from Stratford-upon-Avon. Has family rooms.

ACTIVITIES

FESTIVALS, THE ARTS, NIGHTLIFE, SHOPPING, TOURS AND SPORTS

CALENDAR OF EVENTS

Festivals and Holidays

The Oxford Tourist Information Centre *(see page 275)* will be able to give visitors precise dates and times of events. **Degree Days** (days on which degrees are conferred by the university) are listed in the university diary.

February

Torpids
Traditional college rowing races on the Isis. Usually held in the 6th week of Hilary Term. One of the great rowing events in the university calendar. In February or early March a competition is held to introduce freshmen (first-year undergraduates) to the university rowing course between Iffley Lock and Folly Bridge.

May

May Morning
1 May.
At 6am, the Magdalen College choir sings from Magdalen Tower. Morris dancing in Radcliffe Square and Broad Street – a not-to-be-missed event. Take up position half-way across Magdalen Bridge at about 5.30am, and after the chorus wander into town for a boozy

breakfast and to watch the revellers making merry in all manner of fancy or formal dress.

Lord Mayor's Parade
On Spring Bank Holiday Monday. A parade of decorated floats starts at St Giles and finishes at South Parks.

Eights Week
Held in late May or early June, this is a series of inter-collegiate rowing races. College crews move up and down a league table depending on each day's racing. The race is in a single line and each crew attempts to "bump" or touch the boat in front. Once this has been achieved the race is won.

Beating the Bounds
Ascension Day.
Starts at the Church of St Michael at the Northgate at 10.30am.

Artweeks
Artists and crafts-people of all ages open their workshops and

WHAT'S ON IN OXFORD

Pick up a copy of *In Oxford*, the free monthly guide to what's on. See also www.in oxfordmag.co.uk, www.ticketsoxford. com and www.dailyinfo.co.uk.

homes so that the public can meet them and discover their methods and motivations. From mid-May to beginning of June. See www.artweeks.org.

Whitsun
The Headington Quarry Morris Dancers occupy a unique position in Oxford's history and in the story of Morris dancing. A chance meeting between the folk song collector Cecil Sharp and William Kimber's Headington Quarry Morris Dancers, on Boxing Day 1899, led eventually to the national revival of interest in Morris dancing. William Kimber was to lead the Headington Morris to world fame. He inherited his skills from his father, who in turn had learned his Morris from an earlier generation of Quarry dancers. The tradition continues to this day.

June

Encaenia
The ceremony takes place at noon on the first Wednesday in the week following full Trinity term. Honorary degrees are conferred by the university at the Sheldonian Theatre.

July

Sheriff's Races
Held on Wolvercote Common.

Amateur horse races, side shows and stalls.

August

Oxford Regatta

Details from the City of Oxford Rowing Club, tel: 01865-242 576.

September

St Giles' Fair

Held on the first Monday and Tuesday in September.
A once-famous annual enjoyment for town, gown and surrounding country folk. It can still be fun, but some see it as an expensive, tacky fair with a dubious safety record and ankle-deep litter.

October

Oxford Round Table Firework Display

Britain's firework displays traditionally take place on Guy Fawkes' Night (5 November). This one is held in late October in South Parks, and is a worthwhile spectacle.

November

Christ Church Regatta

Generally held the 7th week of Michaelmas term.
All enquiries to the Boat Captain, Christ Church, St Aldate's, Oxford.

New College

End November.
Advent Carol Service. See www.newcollegechoir.co.uk.

December

Lord Mayor's Carols

Held in the Town Hall.
Date announced in autumn.

Christmas Music

At Christmas the chapel choirs of Christ Church, Magdalen and New College combine their regular liturgical duties with carol concerts that sometimes feature major orchestras and famous soloists. Advance tickets available.

Christ Church

23 December.
Nine Lessons and Carols. Apply to the Chapter Secretary for tickets no later than 16 November, enclosing a stamped, addressed envelope.

Magdalen College

Mid-December.
Carols by Candlelight (tickets in advance from the College Office).

New College

Early December.
Carol Service (tickets in advance from the Precentor).

The Headington Quarry Morris Dancers' Mummers Play and Sword Dance

Boxing Day.

THE ARTS

Museums and Galleries

Oxford has Britain's oldest public museum, the Ashmolean Museum of Arts and Archaeology (see page 165). Britain's oldest purpose-built museum building is also here, housing the Museum of the History of Science. Its reputation continues with plans for the new Science Oxford building in the West End of the city.

Other notable institutions include Modern Art Oxford, the Pitt Rivers Museum and the Oxford University Museum of Natural History – home to the Oxford Dodo and winner of the Guardian's Family Friendly Museum 2005 award. For more museum information visit www.ox.ac.uk/museums and www.oxfordcity.co.uk.

Some museums are closed on Monday (the Ashmolean, Modern Art Oxford, Museum of the History of Science, Museum of Oxford). Others are open daily (the University Museum, Pitt Rivers Museum).

Art Galleries

Apart from the permanent and changing exhibitions in Oxford's museums, there are several private art galleries, and the art colleges at the university hold regular exhibitions.

The best time to explore the art scene is during Artweeks, in May and June, when local artists open up their studios to the public.

From May to September local artists display their work along the railings of University Parks, Parks Road (Sunday 2–6pm).

Here are a few venues exhibiting art:

Christ Church Picture Gallery

Oriel Square
www.chch.ox.ac.uk
An important collection of Old Master paintings and drawings, with rotating selection.

Modern Art Oxford

30 Pembroke Street
Tel: 01865-722 733
www.modernartoxford.org.uk
One of the leading modern art spaces in Britain, with a changing programme of exhibitions. Café and shop.

O3 Gallery

Oxford Castle
www.ovada.org.uk
A new gallery at Oxford Castle presenting exhibitions of contemporary visual and applied arts by local artists. The work is for sale.

Wiseman Gallery

40–41 South Parade
www.wisegal.com
Commercial gallery showing contemporary art.

University of Oxford Shop

106 High Street
www.oushop.com
Watercolours and commissions.

There are also regular exhibitions on the walls at both **Freud Café** (119 Walton Street) and the **Jericho Café** (112 Walton Street).

Oxford Colleges

The majority of colleges are open to visitors in the afternoon only, usually from 1 or 2pm to 4 or 5pm. Some colleges do open longer, however: Christ Church Mon–Sat 9–5pm, Sun 2–5pm; Magdalen daily 1–6pm; New College daily 11am–5pm; Trinity College Mon–Fri and weekends out of term 10.30am–noon and 2–5pm.

These colleges charge a fee, with Christ Church being the most expensive; admission to all the other colleges is free, including to St Edmund Hall, which is open daily, morning and afternoon.

The Queen's College is only usually open to visitors on a tour booked at the Oxford Information Centre with the Oxford Guild of Guides. University College, Oriel College and Templeton-Green College are generally closed to the public, though it is still worth enquiring at the porter's lodge.

Visitors should note that the above times can only be used as a guide, particularly during exam times. Colleges have a habit of closing as a result of building works or simply at the whim of the all-powerful porter.

Theatre and Opera

New Theatre Oxford
George Street,
Oxford OX1 2AG
Tel: 0844-847 1585
www.newtheatreoxford.org.uk
A varied programme of

commercial theatre for all ages, including opera and ballet, plays, musicals, pop and classical concerts, comedy, pantomime, and shows for young theatre-goers.

**OFS Studio
(Old Fire Station)**
George Street
Tel: 01865-297 170
www.ofsstudio.org.uk
Contains a fully-equipped (if small) studio theatre and rehearsal space in a complex of bars, restaurants and galleries. Student productions often staged here.

Oxford Playhouse
11–12 Beaumont Street
Tel: 01865-305 305
www.oxfordplayhouse.com
A recently renovated premises with a diverse range of productions, including a traditional Christmas pantomime and experimental theatre and dance.

Burton Taylor Studio Theatre
Behind the Oxford Playhouse,
Gloucester Street
Tel: 01865-793 797
www.oxfordplayhouse.com/BurtonTaylor
Built in 1973 after a generous donation to the university by Richard Burton and Elizabeth Taylor, and recently refurbished with a new foyer and dressing rooms. Specialises in student and fringe productions with new plays and Edinburgh Festival comedies all year round.

Newman Rooms
Rose Place, St Aldate's
Tel: 01865-722 651
The venue for a variety of plays and musicals at reasonable prices.

The Theatre At Headington
Headington School,
Oxford
Tel: 01865-759 138
www.headington.org
A wide-ranging programme of theatre, comedy, music and dance.

Creation Theatre
Tel: 01865-766 266
www.creationtheatre.co.uk
Creation puts on site-specific theatre in atmospheric locations, including Headington Hill Park and Oxford Castle.

Pegasus Theatre
Magdalen Road,
off Iffley Road
Tel: 01865-722 851
www.pegasustheatre.org.uk
Youth theatre and dance activities. The company is currently touring while their old home theatre building is being replaced with a new one (due to reopen at the end of 2010).

Cinemas

Odeon George Street and **Odeon Magdalen Street**
Tel: 0871-224 4007
www.odeon.co.uk
For mainstream film fare in the city centre.

Phoenix Picture House
57–8 Walton Street
Tel: 0871-704 2062
www.picturehouses.co.uk
Shows some mainstream movies but concentrates on modern cult films, classics and a variety of international productions.

Ultimate Picture Palace
Jeune Street
Tel: 01865-245 288
www.ultimatepicturepalace.co.uk
An atmospheric venue for classic flicks. They also have Wednesday screenings of films exclusively for parents with babies under one year old.

BELOW: final bow at the Oxford Playhouse.

Ozone Multiplex Cinema
Ozone Leisure & Entertainment
Park, Grenoble Road
Tel: 0870-444 3030
www.ozonemultiplex.com
Further out from the centre (bus
Nos 5, 5A, 5B, 5C, 106).

Classical Music

Holywell Music Room
Holywell Street
Tickets available through the
Playhouse box office, tel: 01865-
305 305
www.ticketsoxford.com
The oldest music room in Europe;
many famous musicians,
including Haydn, have played
here since it opened in 1748.
Excellent acoustics. Chamber
music concerts are held here
most Sundays at 11.15am (www.
coffeeconcerts.com).

Jacqueline du Pré Music Building
St Hilda's College
Tel: 01865-305 305
www.sthildas.ox.ac.uk/jdp
This hall was created in the
memory of the great cellist
Jacqueline du Pré and is one of
the best modern music venues in
the city. A variety of musical
styles are performed, as well as
music examinations taken.

Sheldonian Theatre
Broad Street
Tel: 01865-305 305
www.ticketsoxford.com
Designed and built by
Christopher Wren in the style of a
Roman theatre, the famous
Sheldonian is used for concerts,
university ceremonies and other
events. Be aware, however, that
the seats are mainly wooden with
no back rests.
Music At Oxford puts on
classical concerts at various
locations; see www.musicatoxford.com.

Church Music

The world-famous New College
Choir performs at New College
Chapel. You can find latest
concert dates and buy CDs at
www.newcollegechoir.co.uk.

For Christmas carol concerts
*see Calendar of Events, page
261.*

Rock and Pop Concerts

The main venues for rock and
pop concerts are the 02
Academy, the New Theatre,
Aylesbury Civic Centre and the
Cellar. There are also many more
pubs, cafés and restaurants
with live music. For details of
venues and gigs, *see Live Music,
below.*

NIGHTLIFE

Oxford has many traditional
pubs and some trendy bars too.
The Jericho area is up-market,
gown and trendy, with an
arthouse cinema and lots of
cool bars and restaurants. East,
over Magdalen Bridge, Cowley
Road is also lively, trendy and
studenty but with a less
up-market vibe.
Oxford has quite a few
nightclubs for a small city but
they are largely geared to the
young and there is a lot of
"cheese" (kitsch) and R'n'B
about.

Nightclubs

Lava & Ignite
Park End Street
Tel: 01865-250 181
www.parkend.co.uk
Top dog of Oxford clubs. Two
dance floors. Long queues are
the norm.

The Bridge
6–9 Hythe Bridge Street
Tel: 01865-242 526
www.bridgeoxford.co.uk
Up-market alternative to Park
End. The pre-club Anuba bar
inside is one way to avoid the
queue.

The Cellar
Frewin Court,
Cornmarket Street
Tel: 01865-244 761
www.cellarmusic.co.uk
The cognoscenti's choice,
offering a range of specialist
nights.

Po-Na-Na
13–15 Magdalen Street (at the
bottom of St Giles')
Tel: 01865-249 171
http://old.eclecticbars.co.uk/
oxfordponana
Intimate Moroccan-style decor
and cocktails. Alternative, laid-
back and catering to fans of
funk, soul or anything not
cheesy.

BELOW: there is a variety of clubs.

The 02 Academy
190 Cowley Road
Tel: 01865-420 042
www.o2academyoxford.co.uk
Considered by many to be
Oxford's best club. Formerly
known as the Zodiac. A variety of
regular and special club nights.
Large, dark and popular.

The Coven II
Oxpens Road
Tel: 01865-242 770
Much more town than gown, with
regular drum 'n' bass, trance and
hard house nights.

Escape
9A High St
(1 Market Avenue)
Tel: 01865-246 766
www.escape-oxford.co.uk
Restaurant, bar and dance area
on first floor with chill-out lounge
above. Mon–Sat 5pm–late.

Jongleurs Comedy Club
3–5 Hythe Bridge Street
tel: 0844-499 4071
www.jongleurs.com
Comedy/live acts, food and DJs.

Live Music

Having spawned a number of
great rock bands, including
Radiohead and Supergrass,
Oxford is well known for its live
music scene. For major Rock/
Pop concert venues see above.

The 02 Academy (see above)
Probably Oxford's leading live
music venue, with a busy diary of
live acts.

The Cellar (see above)
Establishing itself as one of the
centres of musical life in Oxford.
Good sound system.

Exeter Hall
1 Oxford Road
Tel: 01865-776 431
Large friendly pub with very good
value live music. On bus routes 1
and 5 towards Cowley.

Jericho Tavern
56 Walton Street
Tel: 01865-311 775
www.thejerichotavern.co.uk
Birthplace of Radiohead and
Supergrass. Gigs on Tuesday,
Wednesday (jazz) and Saturday.
Gourmet pub food noon–11pm.

The Bullingdon
162 Cowley Road
Tel: 01865-244 516
Music or DJs every night (blues on
Monday, jazz on Tuesday).

Wheatsheaf
129 High Street
Tel: 01865-721 156.

Gay Scene

Bars

Paradise Street has **The Castle**
(No. 24) and **The Jolly Farmers**
(No. 20), one of the oldest pubs
in Oxford. Nearby is the **Brewery
Gate** on St Thomas' Street,
which is less male-dominated.
On Cowley Road there is **Baby
Bar and Restaurant** (No. 213)
and the **Brickworks Café Bar**
(No. 182). Other gay-friendly
bars include the **Angel &
Greyhound**, 30 St Clements
Street, and the **Kings Arms**, 40
Holywell Street.

Clubnights

Flirt
Monday at the **Old Fire Station**,
George Street
Tel: 01865-297 170.

Pop-tarts
Tuesday in Baby-Love bar, 3 King
Edward Street.

Loveshack
Friday at The Coven II (see facing
page).

CLOUD 9
Saturday at The Studio Lounge
34–5 The Westgate Centre
Tel: 01865-245 136.

SHOPPING

Oxford offers an intriguing
mixture of traditional and modern
shops, catering for every taste
and pocket. The main shopping
area is compact and easy to
explore on foot. There are two
modern indoor shopping arcades
in the centre: the Westgate
Centre and the Clarendon Centre.
If it is raining, sheltered shopping
can also be had in the Covered

Market or one of the department
stores – Marks & Spencer, Bhs
(both on Queen Street) or
Debenhams (at the junction of
George Street and Cornmarket
Street).

Most of the shops in the city
centre are open Monday to
Saturday 9am–5.30pm,
although some (increasing all the
time) open on Sunday as well,
10am–4pm. There is late-night
shopping every Thursday, when
many shops remain open until
8.30pm.

Shopping Areas

Oxford's central crossroads is
known as **Carfax**, where
Cornmarket, High Street, Queen
Street and St Aldates meet.

Cornmarket leads north, and
is closed to all traffic (including
buses) 10am–6pm. Along
Cornmarket are many of Britain's
high street chains, including W.H.
Smith, Boots, Gap, Miss Selfridge
and HMV.

Just off Cornmarket, near the
Carfax end, is the historic **Golden
Cross Inn Arcade**, which leads to
the Covered Market (see
Markets, page 267). This small
courtyard contains a Puccino's
café, a Pizza Express, and a
variety of gifts and goods from
souvenirs and jewellery to health
foods.

The **Clarendon Centre**, which
you can enter either from
Cornmarket, Queen Street or New
Inn Hall Street, is a modern
arcade with shoe shops, fashion
boutiques, sports shops,
electrical goods and computer
shops. Gap, at the Cornmarket
entrance, has a Gap Kids on the
first floor.

Broad Street, running east
from the northern end of
Cornmarket, is Oxford's book
street, with no fewer than six
bookshops, including Blackwell.
At No. 17 is the first ever Oxfam
shop. Professional and amateur
artists will be interested in the
excellent art and craft shop
Broad Canvas at No. 20, while

TRANSPORT
ACCOMMODATION
ACTIVITIES
A – Z

Blackwell's Art and Poster shop at No. 27 has a great range of posters, prints and books.

West from Carfax runs **Queen Street**, also a pedestrian area but open to buses. It includes a large Marks & Spencer store, Bhs, Next and Gap, as well as many smaller shops. At the end of Queen Street is the fully enclosed **Westgate Centre** with numerous stores including Sainsbury's, Claire's Accessories and a Next Clearance store. The fine public Central Library, with a large local history section and a periodicals reading room, is at the entrance to the Westgate Centre. The Westgate is also easily accessible from the multi-storey car park to which it is linked. An ambitious new Westgate centre is slated for development, commencing in 2010. Opposite the library is New Inn Hall Street with Argos, Culpeper and Scribbler (which sells smart stationery).

The **High Street** strikes east from Carfax, curving down to Magdalen Bridge. The college buildings which line it are interspersed with small traditional businesses, including antique and print dealers, as well as trendy modern shops. Near

the Oxford University Press Bookshop, Shepherd & Woodward at Nos 109–14 sells traditional menswear (including Barbour jackets), while Sanders of Oxford at No. 104 sells rare prints and maps. In Wheatsheaf Yard behind No. 128 is Gill & Co, Britain's oldest ironmongers (although this is not the original site). Established in 1530, they stock over 7,000 lines.

There are several modern designer fashion boutiques. Particularly interesting is Sahara at 46 High Street, which donates 50 percent of the profit from its sales to endangered forest conservation projects and to the support of indigenous people's rights. Other interesting fashion boutiques are Narda Fashion Studio at No. 67–8 and Agnès B fashion at No. 56. And should you need a new pen, Pens Plus at No. 70 is the right place to go. They buy, sell and repair old pens.

High Street is connected to Broad Street by **Turl Street**, where there are a number of traditional shops, including Walters & Co. at No. 10, selling high-class menswear, and Scriptum at No. 3, an old-fashioned shop crammed with pens, quills and leather-bound

notebooks. Ducker & Son at No. 6 sells high-quality handmade shoes. Next door at No. 7 is the Whisky Shop.

The fourth arm of Carfax is **St Aldate's**, which leads south. At 107 St Aldate's is Touchwoods, a sports and outdoor gear shop. A little further down is the main Post Office at No. 102, with a philatelic counter and the post shop, selling a selection of stationery. At No. 83, opposite Christ Church, is Alice's Shop, the little 15th-century "Sheep Shop" said in Lewis Carroll's *Through the Looking Glass* to be "full of all manner of curious things". The real-life Alice, daughter of the dean of Christ Church, to whom Lewis Carroll told his tales, used to buy her barley sugar sweets here. Carroll wove the shop into his story, transforming the old lady who kept it into a sheep who sat at the counter knitting with a multitude of needles. It now sells the largest selection of "Alice" memorabilia in the country, together with Oxford gifts and souvenirs, Oxford University T-shirts and sweatshirts in the university colours.

George Street, with a variety of shops and restaurants, links

BELOW: a tempting display in the Covered Market.

Cornmarket to **Gloucester Green** (not a green but a square) where the city's open markets are held. The gallery of shops surrounding the square houses a wide range of shops. Worth a look is Once a Tree at No. 99, with a surprising array of high-quality wooden items, functional and decorative, small and large, from sustainable sources around the world.

Beyond Gloucester Green, **Walton Street**, at the heart of trendy Jericho, has some interesting shops, particularly of the crafts and design variety. There is a print and picture shop and plenty of second-hand books at Jericho Books and Mind. It is quieter than the city centre streets and the numerous cafés and bars allow for a pleasant stroll.

Little Clarendon Street, which cuts through to St Giles', also mixes interesting shops with plenty of places to take a break. There are designer women's clothes at Hobbs and independent boutiques, plus Uncle Sam's vintage clothes store. For a caffeine-free lift, try the Juice café at the Walton Street end. Emerging onto St Giles', there is Taylor's gourmet delicatessen – a great place to buy provisions and a bottle of traditional lemonade if planning a post-shopping picnic, or just for coffee and snacks on the hoof.

Markets

Built in 1774 to provide a permanent home for the many stallholders who had earlier cluttered the city streets, the **Covered Market** is located between High Street and Market Street. There are several entrances from both, plus access through Golden Cross Arcade off Cornmarket Street. It still has fresh and cooked meat, game, cheese, fruit, vegetables and flowers but now there are also many boutiques

LEISURE CENTRES AND HEALTH CLUBS

Bourton Mill Health & Leisure Club
6 High Street
Tel: 01865-251 261
www.bourtonmill.net
Aerobics studio, resistance training machines and free weights. Personal trainers and various fitness classes. Jacuzzi, sauna, sunbeds, treatments and therapies. Central location.

Ferry Sports Centre
Diamond Place,
Summertown
Tel: 01865-467 060
www.oxford.gov.uk
Off the Banbury Road. Swimming, fitness suite, racket sports and classes.

Peers Sports Centre
Sandy Lane West,
Littlemore
Tel: 01865-467 095
www.oxford.gov.uk
Facilities include swimming pool, fitness centre, gym, badminton, basketball, tennis and table tennis.

Temple Cowley Pools
Temple Road, Cowley
Tel: 01865-749 449
www.oxford.gov.uk
The fitness room offers a wide range of modern exercise machines and cardio-vascular equipment. Before using the equipment an induction and basic health check are required. Call for details of fitness classes.

Blackbird Leys Leisure Centre and Pool
Blackbird Leys
Tel: 01865-467 020
(pool: 01865-467 040)
www.oxford.gov.uk
Approximately 5 miles (8km) southeast of the city centre. Sports hall with badminton and tennis courts, pitches for basketball, volleyball, football and netball, a snooker room and a fitness suite, plus a café, licensed bar and crèche. Fitness classes and coaching sessions are offered. Booking ahead is essential. Times for general swimming are imited.

and shops. These are either traditional or foodie, craft- or gift-related, including: traditional shoe shops and a barber, a tea and coffee merchant, a hat shop, and shops selling leather goods and art prints. Running almost the length of the market, Nothing has a selection of hand-knitted sweaters, jewellery and cards along it's endless, segmented counter. Opposite is Next-To-Nothing with an interesting selection of eccentric t-shirts, some genuinely amusing. Within the market and around its entrances. There is also a wide choice of cafés.

The city's **open market** is held every Wednesday in **Gloucester Green** next to the bus station. Stalls sell food and a wide range of other goods. On Thursday morning there is an antique and crafts market here.

Bookshops

Oxford is the home of bookshops and Broad Street is where most of the bookshops are located, almost monopolised by the name of Blackwell. Blackwell have always operated a policy of allowing shoppers to browse freely, and this is nowhere more enjoyable than at the main Blackwell bookshop at No. 48–51, where there is a café on the first floor.

The main competition to Blackwell is provided by Waterstone's on the corner of Cornmarket and Broad Street which also has a café inside. W.H. Smith is at No. 22 Cornmarket and in Templar's Square, Cowley.

Those interested in second-hand and rare books might want to browse in: Arcadia Booksellers at 4 St Michael's Street; Classics

Bookshop upstairs at 3 Turl Street; Oxfam bookshop on St Giles; or Jericho Books on Walton Street.

Everything published by Oxford University Press can be bought at their outlet at No. 116 High Street, while St Andrew's Christian Book Shop at No. 57c St Clement's sells religious books. Books on the mind, body, spirit and health can be found at The Inner Bookshop, 111 Magdalen Road.

Down St Aldate's you will find St Philip's Books, at No. 82, and Reservoir Books (No. 84) with philosophy, literature, theology, history, anthropology, fine art and architecture collections.

TOURS

Open-top Bus

City Sightseeing Oxford
Railway Station
Tel: 01865-790 522
www.citysightseeingoxford.com
Operates open-top sightseeing tours daily, year-round. The complete tour lasts approximately one hour, but your ticket is valid all day and you can get off and on the buses at your leisure at any of the 20 marked bus stops in the city. Departures every 10–15 minutes 9.30am–5pm; ticket price £11.50.

Coach Tours

Cotswold Roaming organises half-day and full-day tours from Oxford to Blenheim Palace, the Cotswolds, Stratford and Warwick Castle, Bath, Stonehenge and Avebury. You can book at the Tourist Information Centre (see page 275) or tel: 01865-308 300; www.oxfordcity.co.uk/cotswold-roaming.

Walking Tours

Walking tours of the City and Colleges, led by qualified members of the **Oxford Guild of Guides** (Blue Badge guides), leave the Oxford Information Centre daily at 11am and 2pm, with additional tours at busy times. There are also walking tours from Carfax Tower on Friday, Saturday and Sunday at 1.45pm.

The Oxford Information Centre also organises special interest tours such as C.S. Lewis and Lewis Carroll tours, Inspector Morse Walking Tours, Spooky Ghost Tours, Pub Tours and Family Tours. Do-it-yourself MP3-guided walking tours are also now available for exploring at your own pace. For further information, call 01865-726 871 or see website: www.visit oxford.org.

Further walking tours, taking in sites of literary and historical interest, are organised by **Blackwell's Literary Walking Tours**; they start from Blackwell bookshop at 53 Broad Street (Apr–Oct Tue 2pm, Thur 11am, Sat noon; tel: 01865-333 606).

Boat Tours

No visit to Oxford is complete without a trip on the water. Punts, canoes, rowing boats and private cruisers can be hired for use on the Thames, Cherwell or the Oxford Canal. *For punting and rowing boats see page 269.* For those who like to take it easy, excursions on the Thames are arranged by:
Salters Bros
Folly Bridge
Tel: 01865-243 421
www.salterssteamers.co.uk
From May to September there are 40-minute cruises on the Thames and a regular Oxford–Iffley–Sandford–Abingdon service (2 hours duration).
Oxford River Cruises
7 Rogers Street (over Folly Bridge)
Tel: 08452-269 396
www.oxfordrivercruises.com
Trips, picnic trips, and charters in Edwardian-style craft.

College Cruisers Narrowboat Hire
Combe Road Wharf, Oxford
Tel: 01865-554 343
www.collegecruisers.com
Two-to-12-berth canal boats for short breaks or longer holidays.

Cycle Tours

Gentle Cycle Tours
Tel: 01296-631 671
www.capital-sport.co.uk/gentle-cycling
Sunday guided tours of Oxford and surrounding countryside run from May throughout the summer. Tours leave at 10am and last around 3 hours. Cycle hire is included in the price of £25. You need to book a place by 5pm Friday, by phone, email or online.

SPORT AND LEISURE

Participant Sports

Golf

Oxford and its surrounding area is well supplied with golf courses. For more golf clubs consult www.oxford.gov.uk (click on Leisure).

Burford Golf Club
Swindon Road, Burford
(19 miles/30km from Oxford, 1 mile/1½km off the A361)
Tel: 01993-822 583
www.burfordgolfclub.co.uk
A fine course, developed in the 1930s.
Frilford Heath Golf Club
Frilford Heath, near Abingdon
(7 miles/11km from Oxford on the A338)
Tel: 01865-390 864
www.frilfordheath.co.uk
Three full-length golf courses.
Hinksey Heights Golf and Nature Park
South Hinksey
(just off the A34 southwest of Oxford)
Tel: 01865-327 775

www.oxford-golf.co.uk
Fairly new course to the west of
the city with stunning views of
Oxford's spires. Membership or
pay as you play. Lessons available. Also nature park and trail
and licensed bar.
North Oxford Golf Club
Banbury Road,
Oxford
Tel: 01865-554 924
www.nogc.co.uk
A short course only 3 miles (5km)
from the city centre.
Southfield Golf Club
Southfield, Hill Top Road,
Oxford
Tel: 01865-242 158
www.southfieldgolf.com
Beautiful course with views back
to the spires of Oxford, about 3
miles (5km) away.

Swimming
Hinksey Open Air Pools
Lake Street or Abingdon Road
Tel: 01865-247 737
www.oxford.gov.uk/leisure
Mixed swimming in a range of
renovated open-air pools. Open
from end May to early
September.
    There are indoor pools at
Blackbird Leys, Ferry, Peers, and
Temple Cowley sports centres
(see box page 267).

Ice Skating
Oxford Ice Rink
Oxpens Road
Tel: 01865-467 000
www.oxford.gov.uk
Not far from the railway station.
Facilities include a 185 by 52ft
(56- by 16-metre) rink, fully
licensed bar and fast food
cafeteria, professional
instructors, ice shows and
special events, and a fully
stocked skate shop.

Bowling
Bowlplex
Ozone Leisure & Entertainment
Park, Grenoble Road (bus Nos 5,
5A, 5B, 5C, 106)
Tel: 01865-714 100
www.bowlplexuk.com
With 24 lanes, pool tables, video

games and a late licence. Open
10am–midnight, 2am at
weekends.

Go-Karting
Children and adults alike will
enjoy buzzing around the race
track at **Karting Oxford**. Located
to the south of the city just off
the B480 Watlington Road, near
to the BMW Mini car factory
(Oxford Stadium, Sandy Lane,
Cowley; tel: 01865-717 134;
www.kartingoxford.co.uk). Children's
only sessions are held on Monday, and restrictions apply at
other times (check the website
for details).

Punting and Boating
For messing about on the river in
punts, rowing boats or canoes,
the following operate Easter to
October.
Cherwell Boathouse
At the bottom of Bardwell Road
Tel: 01865-515 978
www.cherwellboathouse.co.uk
Punts, rowing boats and canoes,
£12–14 an hour (£60 deposit or
credit card weekdays, £70
deposit weekends). Also a fine
restaurant.
C. Howard & Son
Magdalen Bridge
Tel: 01865-202 643
www.oxfordpunting.co.uk
Punts and rowing boats. £14 an
hour weekdays, £30 cash
deposit. Also chauffeured punts
£25 per half hour (with free bottle
of wine).
**Salter's Steamers Boat Hire
Station**
Folly Bridge
Tel: 01865-243 421
www.salterssteamers.co.uk
Punts, skiffs and canoes: £20 an
hour, £25 deposit, or £45 per
hour for chauffeured punts.

Spectator Sports

Athletics
Regular meetings are held at the
Iffley Road running ground and at
the city-owned track at Horspath

Road Sports Ground. www.
oxfordcityathleticclub.com.

Cricket
Oxford University plays first-class
games against county sides in
the University Parks, Parks Road;
tel: 01865-241 335; www.cricket
intheparks.org.uk.
Banbury Cricket Club, Bodicote,
Banbury; tel: 01295-264 368;
www.banburycricketclub.co.uk.

Football
Oxford United FC (Coca-Cola
Football League 2) plays at The
Kassam Stadium, Grenoble
Road; tel: 01865-337 500; www.
oufc.co.uk.
Oxford City FC (Spartan South
Midlands League) plays at Court
Place Farm, Marston; tel: 01865-
744 493; www.oxfordcityfc.co.uk.

Ice Hockey
The Oxford City Stars play home
matches on Sunday Sept–Apr at
the Oxford Ice Rink, Oxpens
Road; tel: 01865-467 002; www.
oxfordstars.com.

Rugby
Oxford University Rugby Club
plays at Iffley Road; tel: 01865-
432 000. The Oxford Rugby
Football Club plays at the
Southern Bypass; tel: 01865-243
984; www.oxfordrfc.co.uk.

ACTIVITIES FOR CHILDREN

Indoor Activities
The **New Theatre** (see page 263)
often has entertaining productions
for children. **Bowlplex**, Ozone
Leisure & Entertainment Park (see
Bowling, above), is also a good
place to go with kids; as well as
bowling it has a video game
arcade and American pool. Ozone
also has a multiscreen cinema
(see Cinemas, page 263).

Museums
An ideal place for a rainy day is
Hands-On, Science Oxford, 1–5

London Place, tel: 01865-728 000; www.scienceoxfordlive.com; open Saturday (daily during school holidays) 10am–5pm. A hands-on science gallery with exciting interactive experiments and a changing menu of themed activities. Recommended age 5–12 years. Best to book a 2-hour session in advance (starting at 10am, noon or 2pm).

Children will be particularly fascinated by the **Pitt Rivers Museum** *(see page 184)* where they can ask the attendant to show them the giant toad or even the witch in a bottle. Adjacent is the **Oxford University Natural History Museum**, which won the *Guardian's Family Friendly Museum* 2005 award.

As well as the dinosaurs, the **University Museum** *(see page 182)* also has the portrait of the same Dodo that features in Lewis Carroll's *Alice's Adventures in Wonderland*.

Young visitors to the **Ashmolean Museum** *(see page 165)* will be enthralled by its large collection of Egyptian mummies as well as Powhattan's Mantle (Powhattan being the father of Pocahontas).

Displays in the **Museum of Oxford** *(see page 154)* include some interesting finds from prehistoric times, as well as a large placard with a simplified version of the Legend of St Frideswide, the city's patron saint.

Outdoor Activities

For kids who prefer to be outdoors, there are plenty of attractions within easy reach of the city.

Shotover Country Park, beyond Headington *(see page 215)*, is a delight for all those who like playing hide and seek and climbing trees; there is also a "natural" sandpit.

At **Port Meadow** *(see page 210)* children will enjoy patting the horses and also feeding the

ducks, geese and swans at the bridge over the Thames.

To the north of the city, beyond the ring road, **Cutteslowe Park** has an aviary, ornamental carp pond and a refreshment kiosk plus a fine playground, tennis and orienteering (call Park Services, tel: 01235-770 836; www.oxford. gov.uk/leisure). On Sunday the City of Oxford Society of Model Engineers operates the miniature train circuit. A bridge links the park to nearby Sunnymead Recreation Ground which includes a new skate park.

Closer to the centre are the **University Parks** *(see page 185)* – 70 acres (30 hectares) of parkland, sports and landscaped areas on the west bank of the River Cherwell, www. parks.ox.ac.uk.

Outside Oxford

The environs of Oxford also have much to offer children.

Cotswold Wildlife Park near Burford, (tel: 01993-823 006, www.cotswoldwildlifepark.co.uk; open daily 10am–6pm or dusk if earlier), is a half-hour drive from the city (towards Cheltenham on

the A40). Even before seeing the wide variety of animals and birds or visiting the Children's Farmyard *(see page 249)*, children will probably demand a session in the adventure playground as well as a ride on the narrow gauge railway (Apr–Oct only). Penguin feeding takes place at 11am and 4pm. Gift shop and restaurant.

Blenheim Park (tel: 0800-849 6500, www.blenheimpalace.com; *see page 222)*, at Woodstock, 8 miles (13km) down the A44 towards Evesham, also has an adventure playground and railway.

At **Cogges Manor Farm Museum** in Witney (tel: 01993-772 602; www.cogges.org; Tue–Fri 10.30am–5pm, Sat–Sun 11am–5pm), most children will be fascinated by the hand-milking and butter-making, as well as the crafts demonstrations held in the barn.

Young steam buffs should be taken to the **Didcot Railway Centre**, Didcot (tel: 01235-817 200, www.didcotrailwaycentre.org.uk; Sat–Sun 10.30am–5pm, consult website for other days of opening). Call beforehand to enquire when the steam trains will be put through their paces.

Below: a Science Day at University Museum captures young imaginations.

A – Z

ACCOMMODATION

A HANDY SUMMARY OF PRACTICAL INFORMATION, ARRANGED ALPHABETICALLY

ACTIVITIES

A dmission Charges

Most colleges do not charge for entrance. Of those that do, Christ Church is the most expensive at £6 per adult (£12 for a family ticket). Similarly, admission at most museums is free of charge – including the Ashmolean, the University Museum and the Pitt Rivers. If, however, you are visiting sights in the countryside around Oxford, expect to pay to get in; all stately homes and most wildlife and country parks will charge entrance.

B udgeting for your Trip

A beer or a glass of house wine will set you back around £3.50. A main course at a budget restaurant runs to around £8, at

a moderate one £12, and at an expensive one, towards £20. Budget, moderate and luxury accommodation costs under £50, between £50 and £100, and over £100 respectively per room per night. Hostels, however, cost much less (below £20 per person per night), and at the very top end, hotels can cost over £250 per night. A taxi from the railway station to the centre of town should be relatively inexpensive (between £5 and £10) despite the one-way circuit. Finally, a ticket for a local bus will cost from around £2 to £3.

C hildren

Children are well catered for in Oxford, especially in recreation centres. During holiday periods,

special programmes are designed by theatres, museums and sporting associations – the Tourist Information Centre *(see page 275)* has full details. *(See also Activities for Children page 269).*

Oxford for the Under-Eights, which is published by the New Parent Network, is available in bookshops, and contains a wealth of useful tips for parents with young children. Pick up a free copy of the bi-monthly *Families in Oxfordshire* from the Tourist Information Centre.

Nappy-changing facilities are usually available in department stores (such as Marks & Spencer on Queen Street); there are also limited facilities at Gloucester Green bus station.

A – Z

Climate

In addition to the general vagaries of English weather, Oxford is famous for its damp climate, enhanced by its position in the Thames Valley.

Even if the sun is shining in the vicinity, there may well be a pall of mist hanging over the city itself, particularly during the winter months. January is usually the coldest month – the average temperature is 3.6°C (38°F), with a mean minimum of 1.2°C (34°F) and a mean maximum on 6.6°C (44°F). Most of the summer is cool enough for a jacket. The hottest month is usually July, when, historically, the average maximum mean temperature has been 21.4°C (70°F; though the record overall high was 35.1°C/95°F, recorded in 1932).

Expect rain at any time of the year, though October is the wettest month. Average annual rainfall is 642mm.

For recorded weather forecasts (Berks, Bucks and Oxon) call Weathercall 09068-500 406.

Consulates

Most countries have diplomatic representation in London – a selection is given below. For others telephone a directory enquiries service (eg 118 247, or 118 888) or see www.yell.com or www.192.com.

Australia
Australia House,
Strand, London
WC2 4LA
Tel: 020-7379 4334

Canada
1, Grosvenor Square,
London
WIX OAA
Tel: 020-7258 6600

New Zealand
80 Haymarket,
London
SW1Y 4TQ
Tel: 020-7930 8422

United States
24 Grosvenor Square,
London
W1A 1AF
Tel: 020-7499 9000

Crime and Safety

Crime exists in Oxford, as anywhere else. Take special care in car parks. Don't leave any valuables in the car and secure the vehicle properly. For bicycles, ensure you have a good quality lock, and, if possible, secure it to a railing or bicycle stand.

D isabled Access

The Oxford City Council publishes the booklet, *The Accessible Oxford Guide*, for people using a wheelchair. This, and a list of premises which are accessible to wheelchairs, is available at the Tourist Information Centre (*see page 275*). Another useful leaflet is *Oxford city centre parking for people with disabilities*, which shows all Blue Badge parking spaces.

Free wheelchairs or scooters can be borrowed from **Oxford Shopmobility**, a scheme funded by the city council. Booking is required, tel: 01865-248 737. People using wheelchairs are welcome to join any of the guided tours. Stagecoach runs modern easy-access buses on most of the city's bus routes.

The County Disability Information Centre, **DIALability**, can help you find out what's available in Oxfordshire for disabled people. Their information and advice line is 01865-763 600; www.dialability.org.uk.

Another useful website is www.oxfordcity.co.uk/info/disability.

E lectricity

240 volts is standard; plugs have three square pins. Hotels will usually have dual 110/240-volt sockets for razors with two-pin plugs (round pins).

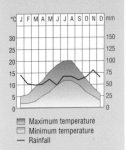
Emergency Numbers

Emergency services (fire, police, ambulance) dial **999**.
Thames Valley Police, tel: 0845-850 5505 (burglaries, stolen bicycles and lost property).
Citizens' Advice Bureau, 95–6 St Aldate's, tel: 0844-573 0608.
Samaritans, tel: 01865-722 122 or 08457-909 090. Assistance available 24-hours.
Oxford Rape Crisis Line, tel: 01865-726 295. Operates Mon and Thur 6.30–9pm, Wed 3.30–6pm, and Sun 6–8.30pm. Answerphone at other times.

G ay and Lesbian

Oxford has an active gay scene. For details contact: **Oxford Friend**, Gay and Lesbian Helpline for counselling, advice and help, 111 Magdalen Road (open till 2am, 4am weekends), tel: 01865-726 893 (Tue, Wed and Fri 7–9pm), www.oxfordfriend.co.uk.

Oxford Lesbian and Gay Community Centre, Northgate Hall, St Michael's Street, tel: 01865-200 249.

For gay nightlife see page 265. For Oxford's annual Gay Pride event see www.oxfordpride.org.uk.

TRANSPORT
ACCOMMODATION
ACTIVITIES
A – Z

H ealth and Medical Care

If you are a national of the EU you are entitled to free medical treatment for illnesses arising while in the UK. Many other countries also have reciprocal arrangements for free treatment. However, most visitors have to pay for medical and dental treatment and should ensure they have adequate health insurance.
NHS Helpline, tel: 0845-4647.

Medical Emergencies

In a medical emergency, either call an ambulance (dial 999) or make your way to the nearest Accident and Emergency department (John Radcliffe Hospital, Headington, *see below*).

Hospitals

John Radcliffe Hospital (with accident and maternity units)
Headley Way, Headington, Oxford
Tel: 01865-741 166
Churchill Hospital
Old Road, Headington, Oxford
Tel: 01865-741 841
Children's Hospital and West Wing
Headley Way, Headington, Oxford
Tel: 01865-741 166
Abingdon Hospital
Abingdon Tel: 01235-205 700

Dental Treatment

Oxfordshire Primary Care Trust Dental Helpline
Tel: 01865-337 267
They will give you information on emergency dental services as well as general information.
NHS Emergency Dental Treatment Helpline
Tel: 0845-345 8995

Pharmacies

There are several chemists all over Oxford open during regular business hours. As well as selling over-the-counter medicines, they make up

prescriptions. The Ten O'Clock Pharmacy, 59 Woodstock Road, Tel: 01865-515 226 is open daily 9am–7.30pm. The pharmacy counter in Sainsburys, Heyford Hill, is open till 11pm.

I nternet

There are very few internet cafés in the centre of Oxford. The city's public library at the entrance to the Westgate Shopping Centre provides some facilities. Other options include:
Budget Internet Café
196 Banbury Road
Tel: 01865-515 955
IT Café
76 Cowley Road
Tel: 01865-200 211

L ost Property

Enquiries should be made, or lost property handed in, at the Central Police Station, St Aldate's (Mon–Thur 8.45am–4.30pm and Fri 8.45am–4.15pm, tel: 01865-266 214). It is important to inform the police if you recover any property previously reported lost.

M aps

The *Oxford A to Z* is an invaluable map covering the whole city. The Ordnance Survey Landranger Map (scale 1:50,000) provides a good overview of Oxford and the surrounding area. It is an ideal aid to planning walks and drives in the vicinity of the city.

Media

Local Newspapers

The *Oxford Mail* is the city's leading evening newspaper. The *Oxford Times*, published on Friday, carries the week's news and the biggest coverage of property for sale. *The Star* and the *Courier Journal* are free weekly papers delivered locally.

Foreign Newspapers

Wendy News, 4 Broad Street, and W.H. Smith, 22 Cornmarket, usually have a reasonable selection of foreign newspapers.

Local Radio

BBC Radio Oxford
95.2 FM
www.bbc.co.uk/oxford
Tel: 08459-311 444
Local news and talk programmes. When there are no local programmes, the channel reverts to BBC Radio 2.
Heart Radio FM
102.6 FM
www.heartoxfordshire.co.uk
Tel: 01865-871 000
An Oxfordshire commercial station with music and chat programmes. On air 24 hours a day.
Oxide 87.9 FM
www.oxideradio.co.uk
Oxford's very own student radio, which produces more speech-based radio than any other student station in the country.
Passion 107.9 FM
www.passion1079.com
Local pop station.

Local Television

ITV Meridian
www.itv.com/meridian
Tel: 0844-881 2000
Broadcasts local television news as well as other programmes in the central and southern area of England.

Money

Some city centre banks offer bureau de change facilities on weekdays and Saturday morning, as do some travel agents.
The majority of branches have automatic cash machines (ATMs) where cashpoint or international credit cards can be used, with a personal identification number (PIN), to withdraw cash.
International credit cards are accepted in most shops, hotels

and restaurants. However, there are exceptions in some shops.

When it comes to charges for service in hotels and restaurants, most places automatically add 10–15 percent to your bill. You are not expected to tip in pubs, cinemas, theatres or lifts, but it is customary to tip hairdressers, sightseeing guides, railway porters and taxi drivers about 10 percent.

Opening Hours

Most of the shops in the city centre are open Mon–Sat 9am–5.30pm, although many now also open on Sunday 10am–4pm. There is late-night shopping every Thursday, when many shops remain open until 8.30pm.

Supermarkets on the outskirts of Oxford tend to be open Mon–Sat 8.30am–8pm and on Sunday 10am–4pm, although some are now beginning to open 24 hours from Monday to Saturday.

Offices usually operate Mon–Fri 9am–5.30pm.

British pubs are now permitted flexible opening hours, with the potential for up to 24-hour opening, seven days a week. Typically, most still open 11am–11pm. People over 18 years may buy alcohol in a bar; children under 14 must be accompanied by an adult.

Postal Services

The main post office at 102–4 St Aldate's is open Mon–Sat 9am–5.30pm. A currency exchange service and a shop selling a wide range of stationery is also available there. The last collection for nationwide next-day delivery is at 7pm, or midnight for local mail. Most post offices close at 5.30pm but those in shops may close for lunch and on Tuesday or Wednesday afternoon. For help or advice on all counter

services call the Customer Help Line, tel: 08457-223 344. For enquiries about parcels, try Parcel Force, tel: 0844-800 4466.

Public Holidays

New Year's Day (1 January)
Easter Monday
May Day (first Monday in May)
Spring Bank Holiday (last Monday in May)
Summer Bank Holiday (last Monday in August)
Christmas Day (25 December)
Boxing Day (26 December).
If 25 or 26 December or 1 January fall on a weekend the following Monday is a Bank Holiday.

For festivals and holidays, see page 261, Calendar of Events.

Religious Services

Public services are held at Christ Church Cathedral on Sunday at 8am, 10am and 6pm, and on weekdays at 7.35am and 6pm throughout the year. There are also services generally open to the public in the college chapels of Magdalen, New College, Mansfield (United Reformed) and Manchester (Unitarian) colleges during the three university terms (Michaelmas: 1 October to 17 December; Hilary: 7 January to 25 March or the Saturday before Palm Sunday. whichever is earlier; and Trinity: 20 April or the Wednesday after Easter, whichever is later, until 6 July).

Anglican Churches

St Aldate's Church,
St Aldate's.
St Andrew's,
Linton Road.
St Barnabas,
Cardigan Street, Jericho.
St Mary-the-Virgin,
High Street (University Church). Includes a Taizé service (only during term-time) and a Lutheran service every fortnight.

St Michael-at-the-Northgate,
Ship Street (City Church).
St Ebbe's,
Pennyfarthing Place.
St Giles',
St Giles'.
St Mary Magdalen,
Magdalen Street.
St Peter and St Paul's,
Elms Parade, Botley.

Roman Catholic

St Aloysius Gonzaga,
25 Woodstock Road. The Catholic parish church for the centre of Oxford and where Tolkien went to Sunday Mass. Some masses in Latin.
Catholic Chaplaincy,
Rose Place (off St Aldate's).
Blackfriars Priory,
62–4 St Giles. Includes a Spanish Mass on Sunday.

Baptist

Baptist Church,
Bonn Square, opposite the Westgate Centre.
South Oxford Baptist Church,
Wytham Street. Asian Christian services are also held here.

Other Churches

First Church of Christ Scientist,
36 St Giles'.
Orthodox Church of the Holy Trinity and the Annunciation,
1 Canterbury Road. Used by Greek and Russian Orthodox communities.
Quaker Meetings,
Friends' Meeting House,
43 St Giles'.
Salvation Army Citadel,
Albion Square.
St Columba United Reformed Church,
Alfred Street (off High Street).
Wesley Memorial Church
(Methodist) New Inn Hall Street.

Buddhist

Thrangu House, 42 Magdalen Road, tel: 01865-241 555. Oxford's Buddhist centre.

Jewish

Oxford Synagogue,
21 Richmond Road.

Muslim

Central Oxford Mosque and Islamic Education Centre, Manzil Way, Cowley.

Student Travellers

Students should always travel with a valid student ID card. This will gain them discounts on coach fares, museum admission charges and even tickets at some cinemas. For travellers on a tight budget, Oxford offers some good accommodation in the lower price ranges, including an excellent range of hostels.

Telephone

Almost all of the modern phone boxes still accept coins (taking 10p, 20p, 50p and £1 coins) as well as phonecards (sold by newsagents and post offices in denominations of £2, £5 and £10). The minimum call charge is 30p. Numbers starting with 0800 are free, 0870 and 0845 are charged at local rate and 0990 at national rate.

Directory enquiries (local and national calls): 118 321 or 118 554 (premium rate charges). Websites: www.yell.com (businesses) and www.192.com (residential).

International directory enquiries: 118 190 and 181 505 offer among the less expensive rates per minute.

Operator (local and national calls): 100.

Toilets

Public toilets are becoming increasingly rare in Britain, and those still in operation tend to be somewhat neglected. Better to use the conveniences provided by department stores or museums. For baby-changing facilities, *see Children, page 271*.

Tourist Information

Oxford Tourist Information Centre
15–16 Broad Street,
Oxford OX1 3AS
Tel: 01865-252 200
Email: tic@oxford.gov.uk
www.visitoxford.org
Provides information on accommodation, attractions, local events and guided walking tours and bus tours. A hotel and guesthouse booking service is also available. Open Mon–Sat 9.30am–5pm, Sun (during summer months) and public holidays 10am–4pm.

Limited visitor information is available from a kiosk in Oxford train station.

Websites

General

www.visitoxford.org – website of the tourist information centre.
www.oxfordcity.co.uk – local and tourist information.
www.oxfordshire.gov.uk – for the wider Oxfordshire area.
www.thisisoxfordshire.co.uk – including local news, movie listings, pubs and restaurants.
http://oxford.openguides.org – a "wiki" (ie edited by users).
www.chem.ox.ac.uk/oxfordtour – offers a virtual tour of Oxford with interactive maps.

Accommodation

www.oxfinder.co.uk – including camping
www.stayoxford.co.uk – the Oxford Association of Hotels and Guest Houses.
www.oxtowns.co.uk – for outside Oxford.

Leisure and Sport

www.oxford.gov.uk/leisure
www.inoxfordmag.co.uk

Transport

www.oxfordbus.co.uk – for London and local services and the Zone Freedom Pass.
www.citysightseeingoxford.com
www.parkandride.net
www.cyclemaps.org.uk

University

www.ox.ac.uk – information on the University of Oxford's colleges and their departments, as well as its museums.

Other

www.tolkiensoxford.com – with links to the Oxford Tolkien Society.
www.ivu.org/oxveg – Oxford vegetarians website.

What to Wear

In youthful, cosmopolitan Oxford, you can wear just about anything and not be considered out of place. Students wear very casual clothes – often jeans and sweaters of doubtful age and condition, or the fashions of the day. Older people tend to wear a range from everyday casual wear to smart outfits, depending on the situation. As weather is unpredictable at all times, it is advisable to bring along clothes for both rain and shine.

Even in summer, the weather is variable, so you will need some warm clothing as well as comfortable footwear for the notably uneven flagstones of some streets. Formal dress is encouraged in some hotels and restaurants and for evening entertainment, particularly in university circles.

University dress code: During Encaenia, the main honorary degree ceremony in June, the chancellor of the University leads a procession of dignitaries and dons along Broad Street. The magnificent scarlet and pink robes they wear are a reminder of the days up until the Reformation when all members of the university were in holy orders.

This applied to students, too, and their successors today are still required to wear their black and white "sub fusc" garments while sitting exams and receiving degrees.

FURTHER READING

General

Hugh Casson's Oxford, by Sir Hugh Casson (Phaidon Press). An illustrated guide to Oxford with watercolour drawings and pen and ink sketches by the author.

Oxford, by Jan Morris (Oxford Paperbacks). A brilliant account of the character, history, mores, buildings and much else by a top travel writer.

Oxford: an Architectural Guide, by Geoffrey Tyack (Oxford University Press). A detailed description of buildings and features characteristic of Oxford's architecture.

The Oxford Book of Oxford, by Jan Morris (Oxford Paperbacks). An entertaining, lively anthology, tracing Oxford's history back to its origins.

Oxford in Verse, edited by Glyn Pursglove and Alistair Ricketts (Perpetua Press). An anthology of poetry on the city of dreaming spires.

The Story of Alice, by Mavis Batey (Macmillan). By using diaries, newspapers and university records, this book tells the story behind Lewis Carroll's Alice.

Fiction

Alice's Adventures in Wonderland, by Lewis Carroll (Puffin Classics). First published in 1865. The famous fantastical adventures of Alice.

Brideshead Revisited, by Evelyn Waugh (Penguin Classics). First published in 1945. Young aristocrats in Oxford living a sybaritic life of eternal summers.

His Dark Materials, by Philip Pullman (Scholastic). This epic trilogy in the fantasy genre, which focuses on the adventures of orphan girl Lyra and deals with complex issues from parallel worlds to theology, has achieved near-cult status among both children and adults.

Inspector Morse Mysteries, by Colin Dexter (Macmillan and Pan). A series of crime novels set in Oxford, which achieved worldwide fame in their television adaption.

Through the Looking-Glass, by Lewis Carroll (Puffin Classics). First published in 1872. The sequel to *Alice's Adventures in Wonderland*; both books were inspired by Oxford, its people and sights.

Zuleika Dobson, by Max Beerbohm (Modern Library). First published in 1911, this is a satirical story of the devastating effect of a beautiful adventuress on Oxford students.

Oxford Guides

An Encyclopedia of Oxford Pubs, Inns and Taverns, by Derek Honey (Oakwood Press). A concise, alphabetical reference book of Oxford's pubs.

Our Canal in Oxford, by Mark Davies and Catherine Robinson (Towpath Press). A guided walking tour along the towpath from Wolvercote to the city centre, with lots of keen historical details.

Oxford for Under-Eights, edited by Vicki Cullen and Dave Dalton (New Parent Network). Extremely useful information for parents with young children in Oxford.

Pubwalks in Oxfordshire, by Nick Channer (Countryside Books). Thirty circular walks around Oxfordshire inns.

Other Insight Guides

More than 180 **Insight Guides** and **Insight City Guides** cover every continent, providing information on culture and all the top sights, as well as superb photography and detailed maps. In addition, a companion series of **Insight Guides Great Breaks** provides a selection of clearly timed walks and tours within UK locations. Titles which highlight destinations in this region include:
Insight Guide: England
Insight Guide: Great Britain
Great Breaks: Oxford

OXFORD STREET ATLAS

The key map shows the area of Oxford covered by the atlas
section. An index of street names and places of interest
shown on the maps can be found on the following pages.
For each entry there is a page number and grid reference

Map Legend

Motorway with Junction	✈ Airport	Motorway
Motorway (under construction)	✝ Church (ruins)	Dual Carriageway
Dual Carriageway	✝ Monastery	Main Roads
Main Road	Castle (ruins)	
Secondary Road	∴ Archaeological Site	Minor Roads
Minor Road	∩ Cave	
Track	★ Place of Interest	Footpath
International Boundary	Mansion/Stately Home	Railway
County Boundary	☀ Viewpoint	Pedestrian Area
National Park/Reserve	⌐ Golf	Important Building

🚌 Bus Station	
❶ Tourist Information	
✉ Post Office	
✝ Cathedral/Church	
☾ Mosque	
✡ Synagogue	
🏛 Statue/Monument	
Tower	

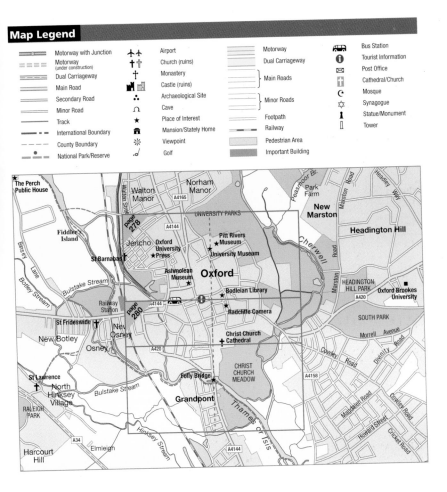

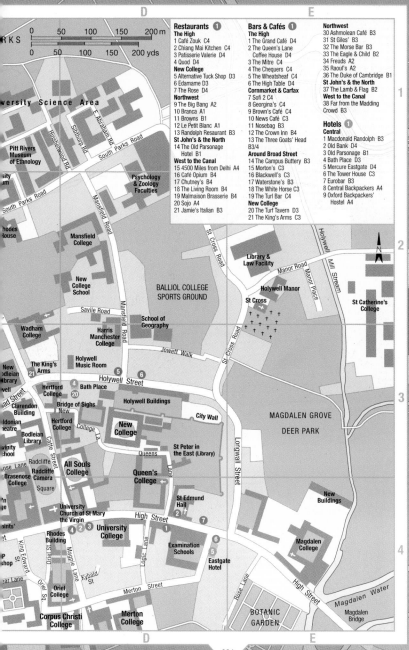

Restaurants ❶
The High
1 Café Zouk C4
2 Chiang Mai Kitchen C4
3 Patisserie Valerie D4
4 Quod D4
New College
5 Alternative Tuck Shop D3
6 Edamame D3
7 The Rose D4
Northwest
9 The Big Bang A2
10 Branca A1
11 Browns B1
12 Le Petit Blanc A1
13 Randolph Resaurant B3
St John's & the North
14 The Old Parsonage
Hotel B1
West to the Canal
15 4500 Miles from Delhi A4
16 Café Opium B4
17 Chutney's B4
18 The Living Room B4
19 Malmaison Brasserie B4
20 Sojo A4
21 Jamie's Italian B3

Bars & Cafés ❶
The High
1 The Grand Café D4
2 The Queen's Lane
Coffee House D4
3 The Mitre C4
4 The Chequers C4
5 The Wheatsheaf C4
6 The High Table C4
Cornmarket & Carfax
7 Sofi 2 C4
8 Georgina's C4
9 Brown's Café C4
10 News Café C3
11 Nosebag B3
12 The Crown Inn B4
13 The Three Goats' Head
B3/4
Around Broad Street
14 The Campus Buttery B3
15 Morton's C3
16 Blackwell's C3
17 Waterstone's B3
18 The White Horse C3
19 The Turl Bar C4
New College
20 The Turl Tavern D3
21 The King's Arms C3

Northwest
30 Ashmolean Café B3
31 St Giles' B3
32 The Morse Bar B3
33 The Eagle & Child B2
34 Freuds A2
35 Raoul's A2
36 The Duke of Cambridge B1
St John's & the North
37 The Lamb & Flag B2
West to the Canal
38 Far from the Madding
Crowd B3

Hotels ❶
Central
1 Macdonald Randolph B3
2 Old Bank D4
3 Old Parsonage B1
4 Bath Place D3
5 Mercure Eastgate D4
6 The Tower House C3
7 Eurobar B3
8 Central Backpackers A4
9 Oxford Backpackers'
Hostel A4

A   B

Royal Oxford Hotel

Park End Street

Nuffield College

St Peter's College

Frewin Hall

Frewin Court

Market St

Covered Market

Clarendon Centre

Bulwarks Lane

New Road

New Inn Hall St

Shoe La.

Cornmarket St

Carfax Tower

Kem

Town Hall

Muse of Oxfo

Hollybush Row

St Thomas Street

Tidmarsh Lane

Castle (remains)

St George's Tower

Castle St

Queen Street

Library

27

Blue

Woodbine Pl.

Malmaison Hotel

County Hall

Westgate Shopping Centre

Modern Art Oxford (MAO)

23

28

Osney Lane

Paradise Street

Oxford Castle Unlocked

Castle Street

St Ebbe's

St Ebbe's Street

Pembroke Street

St Aldate's

St Aldate

24

1

St Ebbe's

ST EBBE'S

Beef Lane

Paradise Square

Pembroke College

Pembroke Sq.

Oxpens Road

Norfolk Street

Old Greyhars

Turn Again La.

Littlegate St.

Brewer Street

Campion Hall

Rose Place

St Aldate's

College of Further Education

Pike Terrace

Fauvier Street

Albion Place

22

25

8

Coach Station

Oxford Ice Rink

Trinity Street

Blackfriars Rd.

Preachers La.

Speedwell Street

Thames Street

Butter-Wyke Pl.

Cromwell Street

2

Castle Mill Stream

Dale Close

Friars Wharf

Thames Street

29

Thames

3

Marlborough Road

Ingham Street

Brook St

Western Road

GRANDPONT

Whitehouse Road

Salter Ct.

Whitehouse Ro

Chisel Road

Kineto

4

N

0   50   100   150   200 m

0   50   100   150   200 yds

A   B

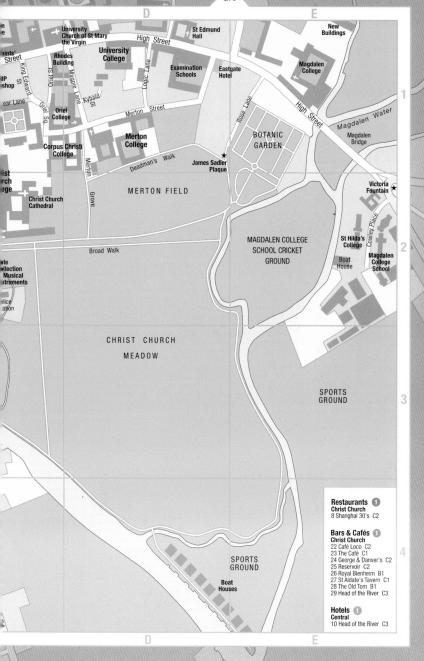

Restaurants ❶
Christ Church
8 Shanghai 30's C2

Bars & Cafés ❶
Christ Church
22 Café Loco C2
23 The Café C1
24 George & Danver's C2
25 Reservoir C2
26 Royal Blenheim B1
27 St Aldate's Tavern C1
28 The Old Tom B1
29 Head of the River C3

Hotels ❶
Central
10 Head of the River C3

STREET INDEX

ART AND PHOTO CREDITS

Map Production: original cartography Phoenix Mapping

©2010 Apa Publications GmbH & Co. Verlag KG, Singapore Branch

Production: Linton Donaldson

GENERAL INDEX

Page references in *italics* refer to pictures

INSIGHT GUIDE
OXFORD

Project Editor
Alexia Georgiou
Art Director
Ian Spick
Picture Manager
Steven Lawrence
Series Manager
Rachel Fox
Series Editor
Rachel Lawrence

Distribution

UK & Ireland
GeoCenter International Ltd
Meridian House, Churchill Way West
Basingstoke, Hampshire RG21 6YR
sales@geocenter.co.uk

United States
Langenscheidt Publishers, Inc.
36–36 33rd Street 4th Floor
Long Island City, NY 11106
orders@langenscheidt.com

Australia
Universal Publishers
1 Waterloo Rd
Macquarie Park, NSW 2113
sales@universalpublishers.com.au

New Zealand
Hema Maps New Zealand Ltd (HNZ)
Unit 2, 10 Cryers Road
East Tamaki, Auckland 2013
Tel: (64) 9 273 6459
sales.hema@clear.net.nz

Worldwide
Apa Publications GmbH & Co.
Verlag KG (Singapore branch)
38 Joo Koon Road, Singapore 628990
Tel: (65) 6865-1600
apasin@singnet.com.sg

Printing

Insight Print Services (Pte) Ltd
38 Joo Koon Road, Singapore 628990
Tel: (65) 6865-1600
apasin@singnet.com.sg

ABOUT THIS BOOK

What makes an Insight Guide different? Since our first book pioneered the use of creative full-colour photography in travel guides in 1970, we have aimed to provide not only reliable information but also the key to a real understanding of a destination and its people.

Now, when the internet can supply inexhaustible (but not always reliable) facts, our books marry text and pictures to provide that more elusive quality: knowledge. To achieve this, they rely on the authority of locally based writers and photographers.

This new edition of *City Guide Oxford* was commissioned by series editor **Rachel Lawrence** and edited by **Alexia Georgiou**. The book was thoroughly updated by arts and travel writer **Michael Macaroon**, a graduate of Merton College and former resident of Oxford. Another Oxford resident, **Tony Halliday**, a senior managing editor with Insight Guides, was consultant on the guide.

The chapter on Warwick in the excursions section was written by **Michael Ivory**, and the feature on architecture by **David Horan**. The Travel Tips listings were compiled by **Richard Carmichael**.

This edition has retained much of the work of the original contributors, including **Christopher Catling**, who wrote many of the Places chapters; **Roland Collins** and Helen **Turner**, who wrote the history section; **Ray Hutton**, who traced Oxford's history as a car-manufacturing centre; **Mark Davies**, who lived on a canalboat and wrote the feature Canal Life; **David Leake**, a gardener at Corpus Christi College who wrote about the city's elusive gardens; and **Yvonne Newman**, a Headington resident who wrote several of the one-page information panels.

The principal photographers were **Glyn Genin**, **Tony Halliday** and **Frank Noon**. Out-of-house designer **Andy Hunter** worked on the layout.

Thanks also go to **Pam Barrett** who proofread the guide and to **Isobel McLean** who brought the index up-to-date.

SEND US YOUR THOUGHTS

We do our best to ensure the information in our books is as accurate and up-to-date as possible. The books are updated on a regular basis using local contacts, who painstakingly add, amend, and correct as required. However, some details (such as telephone numbers and opening times) are liable to change, and we are ultimately reliant on our readers to put us in the picture.

We welcome your feedback, especially your experience of using the book "on the road". Maybe we recommended a hotel that you liked (or another that you didn't), or you came across a great bar or new attraction that we missed.

We will acknowledge all contributions, and we'll offer an Insight Guide to the best letters received.

Please write to us at:
Insight Guides
PO Box 7910, London SE1 1WE
Or email us at:
insight@apaguide.co.uk

Greater Oxford

0   1 km
0   1 mile

RIVERS, MEADOWS AND ABBEYS (RIVER CHERWELL)
map on page 205

RIVERS, MEADOWS AND ABBEYS (RIVER THAMES)
map on page 203